E. M.

Plato's (

Literally translated, with an introductory essay, containing a summary of the

argument

E. M. Cope

Plato's Gorgias
Literally translated, with an introductory essay, containing a summary of the argument

ISBN/EAN: 9783742864857

Manufactured in Europe, USA, Canada, Australia, Japa

Cover: Foto ©Thomas Meinert / pixelio.de

Manufactured and distributed by brebook publishing software
(www.brebook.com)

E. M. Cope

Plato's Gorgias

image
not
available

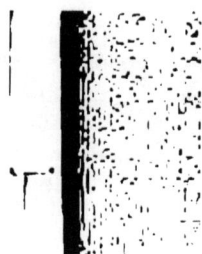

PLATO'S GORGIAS.

Cambridge:
PRINTED BY C. J. CLAY, M.A.
AT THE UNIVERSITY PRESS.

PLATO'S GORGIAS,

LITERALLY TRANSLATED,

WITH AN INTRODUCTORY ESSAY, CONTAINING
A SUMMARY OF THE ARGUMENT.

BY

E. M. COPE,

FELLOW OF TRINITY COLLEGE.

CAMBRIDGE:

DEIGHTON, BELL, AND CO.

LONDON: BELL AND DALDY.

1864.

PREFACE.

THE object aimed at in this Translation is, as the title-page sets forth, to render Plato's text as nearly as possible word for word into English, and it is therefore *not* intended specially for English readers. On the contrary, it is intended principally for students and scholars, for those who are learning or have learnt to compare the structure and resources of the Greek and the English language, and the several modes of expression which the habits of thought prevailing in times and places so far removed from one another have stamped upon their respective idioms. Those who have done so are the only fair judges of such an attempt, and will be the first to make the requisite allowance for the defects and shortcomings which will most assuredly be found in this translation. My *endeavour* has been not only to convey the spirit and freedom, which of course must be the aim of every translator, but also as far as possible to preserve the form of the original language; and I have done my best to hold a middle course between the pedantic and servile adherence to the letter by

which grace ease and English grammar are alike
sacrificed, and the looseness of a paraphrase, which
may indeed faithfully reproduce the thoughts of the
writer, but must needs fail to give any idea of the
dress in which those thoughts are clothed. It seems
to me that the true spirit of an author can be conveyed only in his own words, that is, in a literal
translation; and this view is I think supported by
the fact that all those translations which are generally recognised as the best are literal; I need go no
further than our English version of the Bible for an
instance in support of this assertion. Of the great,
perhaps insuperable, difficulties that stand in the way
of any such attempt none can be better aware than
myself: still this union of the letter with the spirit is
and must be, the ideal of a perfect translation, and
as such should always be kept in view by any one
who attempts faithfully to represent *any* work of
literature in the idiom of a foreign language; but still
more when the interest of that work depends, as in
most of the Platonic dialogues, in no slight degree
upon the external form and graces of style. The
difficulty of the task of translating is of course in-
creased in proportion to the distance of the age and
country in which the work was composed from those
in which it is invested with its new dress. The
circumstances and associations amongst which the
Greeks lived, and which impressed their distinctive
character upon their modes of thought and expres-

sion, are so entirely remote from those which prevail in this England of the nineteenth century that a modern translator cannot fail to be constantly at a loss for an exact equivalent in his own language for the technical terms, for example, the metaphor, the proverb, the allusion, the distinctions, the turns of phrase, which were current and familiar two thousand years ago. Hardest of all is the task of doing justice to the language of a subtle as well as imaginative writer like Plato; of rendering adequately the graceful flow of his natural and easy dialogue; of expressing in simple and yet appropriate terms the nice distinctions, the rigorous and systematic, often abstruse, trains of reasoning which yet are made to follow the turns of a lively conversation, and never except in his later dialogues take a formal and didactic shape; of worthily representing the playful humour, the happy and ingenious phrase, the brilliant metaphor, the sly stroke of satire, the burst of eloquence, the sally of passion, the indignant invective, or the lofty flight of poetical imagery: and yet all these have to be in their turn encountered by one who undertakes to translate Plato.

One of the most marked characteristics of Plato's earlier and more dramatic dialogues, and one that I have been *most* anxious to preserve, is the perfect simplicity ease and familiarity with which the ideas are expressed and the conversation carried on: here there are no laboured antitheses, no balanced clauses, no artificially constructed periods[1], no pompous phrases, no technical terms of science or philosophy; all the grace is unstudied and the harmony natural. It seems to me that this unartificial character has been occasionally in some degree overlooked in more than one of the most approved, and otherwise most excellent, of the recent English versions of Plato. Translators in turning their phrases and rounding their periods are constantly liable to lose sight of the unstudied and simple graces which charm us in the original, and to convey to their version a certain appearance of stifness and constraint altogether alien from the unrestrained freedom of the Platonic style. It is quite possible to translate Plato too neatly. In endeavouring to avoid this error I have myself as far as possible eschewed the use of all long and technical words, formal and set phrases, and elaborately turned periods, and have been content, as far as I could manage it, to let Plato speak in his own manner, as well as in his own language. With this view likewise I have sometimes preserved even the anacolutha, and always as far as I could retained the same order of the words as that in which Plato wrote them.

One of the most prominent and striking difficulties which a translator of this author has to overcome

[1] Plato's style in respect of the structure of his sentences—they are hardly to be called regular periods—is well described by Dissen, in the Essay *De Structura Periodorum*, prefixed to his edition of Demosth. *de Coron.* pp. lxx—lxxv.

in the attempt to impart simplicity and freedom to
his version lies in the treatment of the Greek particles. These, singly and in endless combinations,
are so numerous, the shades of meaning conveyed
by them are so fine and delicate, often by their sub-
tlety escaping detection, always difficult to render;
they have so few equivalents in our own language,
and many of these awkward and cumbrous words,
which· thrust themselves forward and force themselves unduly upon our notice—whereas ·in the
Greek those which most frequently occur are little
creatures of no more than two or three, or at the
most four, letters[1], occupy little space and attract
little attention to themselves—that they throw an
endless series of traps and stumblingblocks in the
way of a translator who is bent upon expressing
them, as perplexing and provoking as they are un-
avoidable. The simplest and most usual mode of
dealing with these particles is to omit them altogether. Here however I must make a special exception in the case of Schleiermacher, who carrying
the literal and rigorous exactness by which his work
is characterised down to these minute particulars
conscientiously translates them all: though how far
the German substitutes actually correspond to the
Greek originals no foreigner probably is competent

---

[1] μέν δέ γε γάρ που ποι πως τοι δή αὖ ἄρα οὖν μήν ἀλλά ποτε with their
various combinations make up pretty nearly the entire list of the particles in common use in a Greek dialogue.

to decide. If I might venture to express my own
opinion upon the point, I should say that in this as
in other respects his version is rather over dry and
formal. But in omitting these particles we sacrifice
in a great measure the expression, so to call it, of
the dialogue. It is by these in a great degree that
the irony the insinuation the sneer, modesty delicacy
reserve hesitation diffidence vehemence resolution
positive assertion contempt indignation derision, and
numberless other shades and refinements of thought
feeling and character are conveyed, or at any rate
aided and heightened; they give point to an observation and connection to an argument: they are the
light shades and delicate touches of the picture—
like the play of features in the actor—hard to catch,
easy to overlook or misapprehend, but essential no
less to the harmony and finish, the expression and
character of the performance. I have therefore never
designedly omitted any one of them, except in the
few cases where it seemed that such omission would
more faithfully represent the original than their in-
sertion[1]; and in so doing have often I fear run the
risk of encumbering and impeding Plato's lively narrative, smart cut and thrust dialectics, or easy
conversation, with a number of disproportionately
lengthy words—or more commonly phrases, for long

---

[1] The case of the particle γάρ, when it occurs as introductory to a
narrative, is one of these. Schleiermacher always renders this by näm-
lich 'that is to say, as follows': but I doubt if we have in our language
anything exactly corresponding either to the one or the other.

words I have always done my best to avoid—which often must be employed in default of any others in our own language capable of adequately expressing the same meaning with greater conciseness.

Another error to be carefully avoided by a translator who desires to adhere faithfully to the simplicity and freedom of the Platonic style is the use of technical terms to convey the doctrines and conceptions of philosophy. One of the most striking peculiarities of Plato's philosophical writings which distinguishes them in a very marked manner from those of his successors is the almost entire absence of any scientific terminology: with the exception of one or two peculiar terms such as εἶδος or ἰδέα and διαλεκτική, and the special appropriation of διάνοια and θυμοειδές in the Republic, and possibly one or two others, Plato's philosophy is absolutely devoid of any technical phraseology. This is no doubt in a great measure due, and especially in the earlier dialogues such as Gorgias, to the conversational and dramatic form into which he has chosen to throw the greater part of his writings, and also to the fact that in the departments of mental and moral philosophy which he especially cultivated there was no terminology sufficiently established and popular to be suited to his purpose; and partly also I should suppose from what he says in the Phædrus and elsewhere to a dislike and suspicion of technical as well as all other pompous phrases, as unable to 'give an account of themselves,'

and without a detailed explanation and modification
according to circumstances likely only to mislead and
confuse, to pass off fallacies under cover of wisdom.
That this may be, and indeed often is, actually the
effect of them, will hardly I believe be denied by any
one who has ever read even a few pages of any
modern German philosophical work: nor do I think
that the harsh and ill-sounding terminology of the
Stoics, or even, may I say? of Aristotle, contributes
in any degree to render their systems more intelli-
gible. But whatever the reason may be, the fact at
all events is that the stock of words and phrases by
which Plato carries on his arguments, and arrives at
his philosophical conclusions is borrowed almost
entirely from the commonest language of common
life, and the translator is therefore bound on his
part to abstain as far as possible from all technical terms, though they may seem perchance to
express the same ideas more neatly and compactly,
however authority may have sanctioned and subsequent usage familiarised us with them.

I may here just notice two other classes of expression which offer some difficulty—trifling compared
with the preceding—in a literal translation of Plato,
namely the complimentary formulas and the oaths;
these though of comparatively slight importance will
still often be found somewhat troublesome and im-
practicable. In regard of the former, which in
Plato's text are constantly making their appearance

where they seem least wanted, our English stock of current and familiar expressions of this kind—titles always excepted—is at the present day very low indeed, and greatly reduced from what it was in the more ceremonious days of our forefathers. Even 'fair Sir' has no longer a familiar sound in our ordinary speech, and 'dear Sir' 'good Sir' 'worthy Sir' 'my dear fellow', or the same adjectives with 'friend', and perhaps one or two more, fill up the list of those which would nowadays be admitted on any terms into a friendly conversation; and even these are by no means adequate representations of the ὦ γενναῖε, ὦ κάλλιστε, ὦ ἄριστε, ὦ μακάριε, ὦ βέλτιστε, ὦ δαιμόνιε, ὦ θαυμάσιε, ὦ φίλτατε and the rest, which occur with such provoking frequency in Socrates' courteous addresses. As however these phrases so seldom present themselves in an English dialogue, as they are quite isolated, and affect as little as possible the general meaning or spirit of the passage in which they are found, the motives for retaining and making the best of them are by no means so strong as they have been shown to be in the case of the particles, indeed it may be said that the omission of them is justifiable or perhaps even advisable, when by their introduction the translation would assume an antiquated or unfamiliar aspect.

Our modern stock of oaths recognised nowadays as admissible in polite conversation is happily still more limited than that of complimentary expressions. If

*

we still believed in saints sufficiently to swear by them,
Our Lady or St George or St Sophia might perhaps
be allowed to take the place of Ἥρα or Ἄρης or Ἀθηνᾶ
in the Greek adjurations; the chaste Ἄρτεμις might
be represented by one of the virgin martyrs; and St
Sebastian with his juvenile and faultless figure might
do duty for the beardless Apollo—unless indeed the
somewhat important difference between the two, that
the one was a discharger the other a mere recipient of
arrows, the one an archer the other only a mark, were
thought to disqualify him for sustaining such a part:
but in these Protestant times such a resource is no
longer available. As to the commoner forms of
adjuration which are of such constant occurrence, νὴ
Δία, μὰ Δία, νὴ τοὺς Θεούς, πρὸς Διός, the rendering that
first suggests itself is to be sure appropriate and expressive enough, but shocking to modern ears; what
was harmless in a Greek and a heathen becomes
profane in a Christian and an Englishman: and
though your Italian would think no harm of translating νὴ Δία by the plain per Dio, which he habitually
employs in his own ordinary conversation, and even
Schleiermacher sometimes blurts out an undisguised
'bei Gott', the reverence with which we are accus-
tomed to surround the sacred name of the Deity will
not allow us to have recourse to the same mode of
representation, and we are obliged therefore to fall
back upon the somewhat poor and tame substitutes
of 'by heaven' 'upon my word' 'by my faith' 'upon

my honour' 'egad' 'in heaven's name', which fall
short indeed of the expressive force of the original,
but are the strongest forms which propriety permits
us to employ.

As this professes before all things to be a literal
translation, it may be well perhaps in order to avoid
the possible charge of carelessness or ignorance from
such scholars—if indeed there be any such—who
would in all cases sacrifice the English idiom to
the preservation of the Greek, to notice a few points
in which I have not always rigorously adhered to
certain rules of translation which have been inculcated
in us from our earliest years by lessons addressed
alike to the reason and the feelings, and enforced at
the same time by a priori authority and by a poste-
riori application. My *rule* however has been to pay
due attention to such niceties, and I have only neglected them when the exigencies of translation seemed
to me to require the sacrifice in order to avoid stifness and awkwardness in the English expression.
Some of these points are : the distinction of the
Greek aorist and perfect, the uniform observance of
which has been by some scholars so peremptorily
insisted on. The fact however is that the idiom of
our own language differs in this particular so far
from the Greek that we are *obliged* very frequently
to express the Greek aorist by the English perfect.
For instance in the common phrase ἤδη εἶδον, in which
the verb is rendered 'I have seen', the adverb which

is supposed to account in this particular case for the
perfect sense of the aorist has really nothing whatever to do with it[1]. Where the Greeks said 'I once
saw', we say 'I have seen'. Again; who would think
of rendering the exulting song of the initiated, ἔφυγον
κακόν, εὗρον ἄμεινον, by anything but the English perfect? There is a similar difference between the French
and German idioms and our own in the use of these
tenses; that is, in sometimes expressing our aorist
by a perfect and vice versâ, as waren sie? 'have you
been?'; j'ai été... 'I was...'

Again a Greek not unfrequently writes γίγνεσθαι
where an Englishman says simply 'to be'; and
though I hold that the distinction between the two
verbs is so philosophically important that it should
always be maintained when it is possible so to do—
and it will be seen that I have sometimes gone a
little out of my way to maintain it—yet the neglect
of it is sometimes (not often I believe) not only justifiable but absolutely required.

Of minor importance is the occasional omission
of the article in rendering οἱ ἄλλοι, and perhaps other
similar phrases; the non-observance of the *position*
of the article with substantive and adjective, in which

---

[1] I cannot agree with Mr Shilleto, crit. not. on Demosth. de F. L.
§ 228, in thinking that the addition of temporal particles such as ἄρτι,
πολλάκις, οὐ πώποτε, can make any difference whatsoever in the "nature"
or sense of the tense: the translation of the Greek aorist by our perfect
in such cases is a mere matter of idiom. The text was written before I
had seen Mr Shilleto's note, and without any reference to it.

the Greek form of expression likewise not unfrequently differs from familiar and idiomatic English ;
the substitution of the indefinite for the Greek definite article when the latter denotes a class. On this
subject see Buttmann's Greek Grammar, § 124.
Obs. 2 (Engl. Transl.). It is explained quite unconsciously and accidentally by Aristotle, Rhet. II. 4. 31.
τὸ δὲ μῖσος καὶ πρὸς τὰ γένη· τὸν γὰρ κλέπτην μισεῖ
κ. τ. λ. See also Schneider's note on Plato de Rep.
VIII. 564 A.

Passing over other idiomatic differences of a similar character, there remains one point which is
important enough to be treated at greater length ;
more especially as the question is still unsettled, and
a writer of high authority has pronounced a very
uncompromising opinion upon it entirely opposed to
what I believe to be the truth. I refer to the translation of οὐ πάνυ, and I will take this opportunity to
enter in detail upon the consideration of the whole
question ; but as the note promises to be a somewhat
long one, it may perhaps find a fitter place in the
Appendix[1].

As to the aids of which I have availed myself
in the translation, besides the notes of the Commen-
tators, I have constantly had before me Schleiermacher's version and the Master of Trinity's Platonic
Dialogues for English Readers ; with the exception

---

[1] See note C, in the Appendix.

ḫ

of Cousin's translation, which I looked through
many years ago, I have seen no other. Schleiermacher's version of this as of the other dialogues
is so literal and so exact that it serves the purpose
of a commentary of no mean order: as far as my
observation extends, he *very* seldom misses the
precise meaning of the original, and his extreme
acuteness and thorough knowledge of his author
render his assistance always valuable. Cousin's for
any such purpose is absolutely worthless. The former
however is, if I may venture to say so, too flat and
lifeless—at least to an English reader—to furnish
much assistance in turning a phrase or suggesting
an expression. Of Dr Whewell's work perhaps not
much more than a third of this particular dialogue is
a direct translation. To this I have to acknowledge a
few obligations, for here and there a vigorous phrase
or a happy turn of expression. But such direct
obligations amount I believe scarcely to half a dozen;
any other coincidences that may be found between
our versions are accidental.

It only remains to say that the text I have
followed is that of the Zurich Editors, except in
a few rare instances which I have been careful to
point out.

INTRODUCTION.

Self-reverence, self-knowledge, self-control,
These three alone lead life to sovereign power.
Yet not for power (power of herself
Would come uncalled for), but to live by law,
Acting the law we live by without fear;
And, because right is right, to follow right
Were wisdom in the scorn of consequence.

TENNYSON, *Œnone.*

THE course of the argument of this dialogue is somewhat intricate and at first sight desultory, and the subjects treated in it are so multifarious, that the most various and diverse opinions have been entertained as to the leading purpose and intention of Plato in its composition. A good deal of the complexity and consequent difficulty vanishes upon closer inspection; but enough remains to render the main scope and design in some degree doubtful; and accordingly the most recent writers upon the subject are by no means in agreement with one another upon the point. A fair summary of their views is given by Stallbaum, Introduction, pp. 31—35, and I need not therefore repeat them here. Amongst these, a treatise by Bonitz, published in the transactions of the Viennese Academy of Sciences (to which my references are made) and also separately in Part I. of his Platonische Studien, deserves especial mention. It contains a careful analysis of the argument together with an inquiry into the leading idea of the dialogue, and a criticism of the views of two of his predecessors, Steinhart[1] and Susemihl, upon the same subject.

---

[1] This name, that of the author of Introductions prefixed to Hieronymus Müller's translation of the Platonic dialogues, has been systematically converted

This essay is distinguished throughout by clearness moderation and good sense.

The Greek title of the dialogue is Γοργίας, ἢ περὶ ῥητορικῆς, ἀνατρεπτικός, Diog. Laert. Vit. Plat. § 59. These second titles, though it is generally agreed that they do not proceed from Plato himself, and have therefore no final and decisive authority in determining the true subject of his dialogues, yet as representing the earliest opinion as to the nature of their contents of native and probably well informed Platonists, should not I think be entirely set aside; and in this particular instance, as it seems to me, Rhetoric, the subject assigned by the title as the leading one, may when properly understood fairly put in its claim with the rest to be that which was uppermost in the author's mind in writing the Gorgias.

The term ἀνατρεπτικός, subversive, destructive, opposed to κατασκευαστικός, constructive, denotes that the Gorgias, like the Theætetus and Meno for example with which Schleiermacher places it in immediate connection, belongs to the class of polemical or dialectical dialogues; in which the object is not so much to establish a doctrine or build up a system, as to clear the ground for either of these by the removal of popular errors and fallacies and the refutation of antagonist speculations and theories. Of this class of the Platonic dialogues, to which Schleiermacher assigns the middle division in his arrangement, between the elementary and the constructive, placing the Gorgias at their head, he says, Introd. to Gorg.[1] p. 4, that "they no longer treat as the first (the elementary) did of the Method of Philosophy, but of its object, with a view to attain a complete conception and a right distinction of it; nor yet at the same time do they seek

---

by Stallbaum into Reinhart, under which form it invariably appears in his Introduction, to the possible perplexity of many of his readers.

[1] In citing Schleiermacher's Introductions I refer always to the original Introductions prefixed to his translation of the dialogues, not to Mr Dobson's English version.

like the latter properly speaking to *represent* the two real sciences, Physics (in its widest sense including Cosmology and Ontology or Metaphysics) and Ethics, but only in a preparatory and progressive way to determine what they are; and, whether considered singly or in their mutual connection, they are distinguished by a construction, less uniform than in the first division, but particularly artificial and almost difficult." Compare general Introd. pp. 49, 50. Accordingly this dialogue occupies pretty nearly the same position in Ethical, as the Theætetus in Intellectual, Philosophy: as there the various existing theories of knowledge, and especially the ultra Sceptical, and, as we may call it from its originator and supporters, Sophistical theory of Protagoras are examined and refuted; so here the same course is pursued with the current notions and doctrines about justice virtue and the rule of life; and amongst them, the Sophistical paradoxes that might is the only right and justice nothing but a convention of society, and that pleasure is the only good, are most prominently brought forward and most signally refuted. The solution of all these great questions, and the true views of Knowledge and Science, of Justice and the Good, are to be sought for in the Constructive or Demonstrative Dialogues, the Philebus and Republic. In the Gorgias, as in the Theætetus, the process is indirect or dialectical, and the result in some sense negative—negative that is for *philosophical* purposes and as regards the construction of a system, the conclusions being all of a practical character and bearing solely upon the regulation of life and conduct. This will appear from the summary of them p. 527 B, C. Compare the remarks of Bonitz u. s. p. 272.

But before we proceed to inquire into the claims of Rhetoric to be regarded as the principal subject in this dialogue, we must first consider the sense in which this Rhetoric is to be interpreted, and what is the light in which Plato here regards it.

The modern and narrower sense of Rhetoric as the art of

speaking, and even the ancient definitions of it, as 'the art of
persuasion,' the original definition, or Aristotle's correction of
this, 'the faculty of discerning the possible means of persuasion in a given subject,' or any of the various definitions
enumerated by Quintilian in the 15th Chapter of his second
book, would give us a most inadequate notion of the real extent and bearings of this new art as it was understood and
practised by its Sophistical originators and Professors in the
time of Socrates; and would leave entirely unexplained the
character ascribed to it in this dialogue, and the connection
in which it there stands with the multifarious discussions
upon virtue and politics which are made to arise out of the
consideration of its nature and true meaning. The functions
which it assumed in the hands of its earliest Professors, and
the prominent part that it consequently plays in the Gorgias,
will be best understood from the account that they are made
to give of themselves by Plato, and similar notices of their
profession and practice which are to be found in other
writers.

In Protag. 318 E, Protagoras in describing his own professional occupation says, "The instruction that I give is
good counsel with a view to the best management of a man's
private affairs and the administration of his own household,
and with regard to affairs of state, to qualify him most effi-
ciently to act and speak in public life," that is, practical
economics and politics. To which Socrates replies, "I understand you to mean the art political, and that what you
profess is to make men good citizens." "That is," answers
Protagoras, "precisely the profession that I make." This was
in fact the usual profession of the early Sophists, and was
implied in their undertaking to teach virtue.

The same is ascribed to them by Meno, the pupil of
Gorgias, in the dialogue of that name p. 91 A. "He
(Meno)," says Socrates, "has been telling me ever so long
that the kind of wisdom and virtue that he covets is that
which enables men to administer well their houses and na-

tive cities, and to pay due respect to their parents, and to know how to entertain and dismiss citizens and strangers in a manner worthy of a good man. To acquire these accomplishments a youth must be sent to those famous men who profess to be teachers of virtue, and place themselves at the disposal of any Greek who desires to learn it, for which they have fixed and exact a certain fee." "And who do you mean by these, Socrates?" inquires Anytus. "Why you surely must know yourself that these are they whom men call Sophists," is the reply.

To the same effect it is said, Rep. x. 600 c, that Protagoras of Abdera and Prodicus of Ceos and a host of others have contrived to get the notion into the heads of their contemporaries that none of them will be able to manage either his own house or city unless *they* superintend their education, and on the strength of this skill have so entirely gained the affections of their associates that they are all but ready to carry them about on their heads.

Similarly Isocrates, in the next generation, of himself and his pupils, de Perm. § 285 τοὺς τὰ τοιαῦτα μανθάνοντας καὶ μελετῶντας ἐξ ὧν καὶ τὸν ἴδιον οἶκον καὶ τὰ κοινὰ τὰ τῆς πόλεως καλῶς διοικήσουσιν, ὧνπερ ἕνεκα καὶ πονητέον καὶ φιλοσοφητέον καὶ τὰ πάντα πρακτέον ἐστί.

Again, "a man's virtue," according to Meno, Gorgias' pupil, Meno 71 E, is ἱκανὸν εἶναι τὰ τῆς πόλεως πράττειν, "to be qualified to play a part in public life," and in so doing to be of service to one's friends, and to do injury to one's enemies, at the same time taking good care oneself to incur no risk of the like.

Similarly Prodicus is reported to have said of himself and the Sophists in general, Euthyd. 305 c, that they stood on the boundary line between the philosopher and the politician.

In Hipp. Maj. 282 B, the object of Hippias' instructions is defined in nearly the same terms as Protagoras uses: τὰ δημόσια πράττειν δύνασθαι μετὰ τῶν ἰδίων, "to attain the faculty of managing public affairs together with one's own."

So Evenus of Paros, the Rhetorical teacher and Elegiac poet, was a professor ἀρετῆς ἀνθρωπίνης τε καὶ πολιτικῆς. Apol. Socr. 20 в.

Of the early Sophists or teachers of rhetoric in general Isocrates says, κατὰ τῶν Σοφιστῶν, § 20, that they were worse than the dialecticians in that they ἐπὶ τοὺς πολιτικοὺς λόγους παρακαλοῦντες, ἀμελήσαντες τῶν ἄλλων τῶν προσόντων αὐτοῖς ἀγαθῶν, πολυπραγμοσύνης καὶ πλεονεξίας ὑπέστησαν εἶναι διδάσκαλοι. And of the same, Plutarch, Vit. Themist. c. 2, τὴν τότε καλουμένην σοφίαν, οὖσαν δὲ δεινότητα πολιτικὴν καὶ δραστηρίαν σύνεσιν...ἣν οἱ μετὰ ταῦτα δικανικαῖς μίξαντες τέχναις, καὶ μεταγαγόντες ἀπὸ τῶν πράξεων τὴν ἄσκησιν ἐπὶ τοὺς λόγους σοφισταὶ προσηγορεύθησαν.

The profession then of these early Sophists and teachers of Rhetoric implied nothing less than a complete training for all public and private duties, and the formation of the character of a good citizen and an honest man. How these lofty pretensions were actually carried out in practice and their assumed functions fulfilled we learn as well from the doctrines and views of life propounded by Polus and Callicles in this dialogue, and the thoroughly selfish objects which they propose to themselves as the end of a political career and of rhetoric its instrument, as also from the more direct statements of the gravest and most respectable authors, Xenophon, Isocrates, Aristotle, Plato and others, which I have quoted elsewhere (Journ. of Class. and Sacred Philology No. 2) and need not here repeat.

The real use that was made of this new art by its disciples was to avail themselves of its powerful aid in securing their own advancement by flattering and humouring the passions of the mob, or to prove that black is white in a law-court in defence of themselves or others by whom they might be employed. That the inculcation of these deceitful artifices was actually one of the objects of these teachers is shown by the extracts and notices that remain to us of the τέχναι or treatises upon rhetoric of the early writers on the subject, Corax, Tisias, and others, and by the Art now generally ascribed to Anaximenes, but at all events proceeding from the Sophistical school, which abounds with such immoral suggestions: the object proposed in them was to persuade at any price regardless of any considerations of truth and honour. The τὸν ἥττω λόγον κρείττω ποιεῖν is no mere calumny of Aristophanes, but the genuine profession of Protagoras, τὸ Πρωταγόρου ἐπάγγελμα, Arist. Rhet. II. 24. 11.

It is this assumption as contrasted with the actual practice of the Sophistical Rhetoricians and their pupils that justifies the terms applied to their art by Plato, when he speaks of it, Gorg. cc. XIX, XX. pp. 464 B—466 A, and Sophistic with which it is closely allied, as the spurious delusive unreal art of Politics, bearing the same relation to the true arts of the statesman, legislation and the administration of justice, as cookery does to medicine, or the art of adorning the outside of the person so as to produce a deceitful appearance of health and comeliness, the perfumer's, tailor's, and hair-dresser's arts, to gymnastics. And Aristotle, Rhet. I. 2. 7, describes it in precisely equivalent language, borrowing even his phraseology from Plato (Gorg. 464 D), "Hence rhetoric and those who lay claim to it assume the disguise of political science, partly owing to ignorance (on the part of its professors) partly to ostentation and quackery, and partly to other causes incident to humanity," and again, Eth. Nic. X. 10, "The sophists profess to teach politics but none of them practise it;" contrary to the habit of other artists, as physicians or statuaries, who usually combine theory and practice. "But of the Sophists, those who profess this are very far indeed from really teaching it; for they know absolutely nothing whatever of its nature and objects: for if they had, they would not have made it the same as rhetoric or even worse...."

Thus of the two Platonic dialogues in which Rhetoric plays a leading part, in the Gorgias it is looked at solely from the moral side and as the instrument of politics with which it was in fact confounded; it is the *object* of the rhetorician, and not the *method* or means by which he seeks to attain this object, that comes into consideration; see especially c. 58 foll. pp. 502 D—504 E, and the concluding words of the summary, 527 C, καὶ τῇ ῥητορικῇ οὕτω χρηστέον, ἐπὶ τὺ δίκαιον ἀεί. In the Phædrus on the contrary it is regarded technically as an art; its hollowness and insufficiency even for the purposes for which it was invented exposed, its technicalities and its method criticised and ridiculed: it is shown how an art which would really effect the object proposed to itself by rhetoric, viz. persuasion or conviction, must be based upon a thorough knowledge of all the varieties of human character, and the modes of appealing effectually to each variety studied and determined; but after all, even if the end be attained, no art or process which reaches no further than mere probability and temporary persuasion can be of the least value as compared with the true insight which comes by the study of philosophy and by dialectics its instrument. On the object and value of dialectics, contrasted with those of rhetoric, see likewise Phileb. 58 A—D. Upon the hints thus thrown out in the Phædrus, 271 C—272 B, 273 D, E, is based the method pursued by Aristotle in his treatment of Rhetoric; it is this doubtless that first suggested to him the elaborate and masterly analysis of human character motives and passions which constitutes the novelty and the peculiarity and the principal value of his great work, and occupies the larger portion of its two first books.

The fundamental difference of conception as to the province, functions and value, and proper mode of dealing with this art furnishes a curious and interesting illustration of the diversity of intellectual character and aim by which the two great philosophers of antiquity were so remarkably distinguished. The stern haughty[1] uncompromising Idealist, wrapped up in his sublime speculations and with his lofty unattainable ideal of truth and right ever present to his mind; holding scornfully aloof from the business and pursuits of a world which he disdained, and rebuilding society from its very foundations in the attempt to carry out his grand visionary scheme of a perfect Republic; acknowledging no pleasure but the contemplation of truth, and sternly banishing from his model state all the arts which minister merely to the gratification of the senses or the intellect; will not stoop to recognise the value of an art which falls short of perfection, and seeks to accommodate itself to human infirmity, and to serve the practical needs and uses of society; when conviction and full knowledge are impossible contents itself with probability and persuasion, and will accept something short of complete justice from the imperfection of human tribunals.

The shrewd observant sagacious Aristotle, the philosopher of experience and thorough man of the world, eschews all such Utopian and highflying notions; *he* is satisfied to take things as he finds them and make the best of existing circumstances. As the mountain will not come to Mahomet, Mahomet goes to the mountain. Assemblies must be held and governments carried on; crimes will be committed and disputes arise between man and man; and these must be submitted to courts of justice. Statesmen must speak in

---

[1] This conception of Plato's character is derived solely from his writings. It is however confirmed by the evidence of the Comic Poet Amphis, *Fragm. Dexidem.* in Diogenes, *Vit. Plat.* § 28:

ὦ Πλάτων,
ὡς οὐδὲν ᾖσθα πλὴν σκυθρωπάζειν μόνον,
ὥσπερ κοχλίας σεμνῶς ἐπηρκὼς τὰς ὀφρῦς.

And Heraclides reports (in the same Diogenes, § 26) that in his youth he was so modest and sober that he was never seen to indulge in a fit of boisterous or excessive merriment. In his mature years he preserved the same character; most of his laughter is of the sardonic kind, and his humour is shown chiefly in satire. How different from the loud hearty uproarious fun of Aristophanes!

the one, accusation and defence be carried on in the other:
it is well to be prepared for both these contingencies. If
we are *not* so prepared, innocence and right may be overcome
by fraud and injustice; the artificial aid of rhetoric allows
truth and right to assert their natural superiority (Rhet. I.
1. 12), which might otherwise be often endangered by human
artifice and ingenuity.   And further, as Gorgias is made by
Plato to plead in defence of his profession (Gorg. c. XI.), we
have no right to argue from the use to the abuse of anything.   Again, in the conflict of human passions and interests truth is often unattainable, probable evidence must be
accepted; mathematical demonstration belongs only to science, necessity which is essential to demonstration can *never*
be predicated of human actions and motives with which alone
rhetoric deals; and such as are the materials and elements
such must the reasoning be.   *The probable* is therefore assumed as the necessary basis and groundwork of his system.

     This premised, we now proceed to inquire whether rhe-
toric as thus explained may be regarded as the principal
subject of Plato's dialogue.   This view is very unceremo-
niously rejected by Olympiodorus, without however assigning
any reason whatsoever for that rejection except that those
who hold this opinion 'characterise the whole from a part;'
which assumes the very point in question.   I will venture to
say in addition, that what I know of Olympiodorus' commentary has not inspired me with a very high opinion of his
judgment, nor at all inclined me to accept his ipse dixit
upon any matter of this kind.   Next comes an authority of
a very different order.   Schleiermacher, Introd. to Gorg. pp.
1, 2, classes rhetoric with a number of other subjects previously suggested by others as containing the main gist and
purpose of the work; 'in all of which views' he says 'that
part of the whole which is brought so prominently forward
appears only in a very loose connection with the rest; so
that, if the whole be viewed in this light, the inquiry into
the nature of pleasure especially, can only be regarded as

an almost superfluous patch strangely stuck on to the rest
of the work.' This is no doubt true in the main if rhetoric
be understood exclusively in its narrower sense of the art of
speaking; though even in this case the exhibition of it as
one of the arts of flattery, and the classification of it with
the arts which seek only the gratification of those whom
they profess to serve without any consideration of their real
good, may be thought to connect it immediately with an inquiry into the nature of *pleasure;* but when it is taken in
its wider signification as above explained, as a training for
public life and private duty, its connection with the esta-
blishment of the rule of life and the choice of a course of
life—which if rhetoric is not, must I think be regarded as
the leading conception of the dialogue—is too apparent to
be mistaken or require further explanation. The inquiry
into the nature of pleasure I myself should regard as subordinate to the great moral object of the dialogue, the determination of the end aim and rule of life. It is shown inci-
dentally from the nature of pleasure, that, not being identical
with the good, it cannot be and ought not to be a man's sole
or principal aim.

In fact if the main purpose of the dialogue be the practical moral one of contrasting the true and the false objects
and rules of life[1], of exposing the vanity of the latter by a

---

[1] This view agrees very well with that of Bonitz—a writer from whom one
would not desire to differ—as to the object and main purpose of the dialogue.
Op. cit. p. 271. Schwerlich kann dann noch ein Zweifel sein, dass die mit
Kallikles verhandelte Frage: "ist Philosophie im Platonischen Sinne, oder ist
politische Rhetorik in ihrem damaligen thatsächlichen Zustande eine würdige
Lebensaufgabe?" den Kern und Zweck des ganzen Dialogs bezeichnet. Of
course the study and pursuit of Philosophy are in Plato's conception the highest
and worthiest object and aim of life: but as little is said of this during the
course of the dialogue and nothing at all at the conclusion, I would rather
instead of specifying philosophy and rhetoric as the contrasted members of the
antithesis, express the result in more general terms as I have done, as the true
and false object and rule of life, rhetoric being no doubt taken and put prominently forward as the representative of the latter. In Bonitz's favour is the
passage, 500 c, but philosophy is dropped in the final summary. The opinion

criticism of the popular views entertained upon this great question, and establishing the superiority of the former, it seems that no better representative of the false objects and rules by which men direct and regulate their conduct in life could have been selected than rhetoric, which stands for the career of politics as vulgarly understood and the pursuits of ambition, the most plausible and attractive and in some sort the highest of these false ends and aims; which may thus be fairly regarded as involving the conception of both. When we look at the dialogue alone, and apart from its enforced connection with other works of the author, which I must be permitted to say seems here as elsewhere to lead the acute Schleiermacher somewhat astray; when we consider that the three interlocutors who represent the three principal stages or general divisions of the argument are all rhetoricians professional or practical; that each of these three main divisions starts with and arises out of rhetoric and the views of life which accompanied the cultivation of it; that it recurs at every turn, and that at any rate no other *single* topic occupies anything like the amount of actual space that is assigned to this in the dialogue; that the entire dialogue begins and ends (see p. 527 c) with it; that it was a subject of the highest practical importance from the direct influence which it exercised upon the education, habits, principles, and moral conceptions of all those who aspired to distinction in the state and to the fulfilment of the highest functions of citizenship, and one thoroughly worthy to be so treated by Plato— all this may well make us pause before we reject the opinion that the correction of the immoral and ill-founded notions which prevailed upon this weighty matter was *not* the immediate object of the author in the composition of this work: at the lowest we are compelled to admit that it is the main

of Dr Whewell, who does not enter into the discussion of the question, seems to agree substantially with that which I have put forward, judging by the introductory note on the Title, *Platonic Dialogues*, II. 166, and the brief observation at the end, p. 258.

thread upon which the argument hangs, and the most prominent, if not the most philosophically important, of those
which occupied the mind of the writer of the Gorgias.

The only modern writer however with whom I am acquainted who adheres unreservedly to the most ancient
opinion upon this question is Van Heusde; who in his review
of this dialogue, Init. Phil. Plat. pp. 163—174, seems to take
it for granted that rhetoric is in reality. Plato's leading idea,
and traces the contrast between the true and false notions of
the perfection and proper office of the art through the various
stages of the discussion. But we want no other authority
than the work itself for the determination of the question[1].

It is singular that amidst all the controversy and variety
of opinion to which this question has given rise so little attention[2] should have been paid to a passage, already referred
to, in which the author himself seems to state clearly enough
what his intention was in writing the dialogue and what its
conclusions amount to. It occurs at p. 527 B, C. The results
arrived at as there stated are, that doing wrong is to be more
carefully avoided than suffering it; that sterling truth and
worth of character should be a man's study and not the mere
seeming and outside show; that whatever evil there be in
a man must be removed by correction, which is the use of
punishment; that next to being just and good it is desirable to be made so by correction and chastisement; that all
flattering *i.e.* the seeking to impart mere gratification by
any art or pursuit is to be shunned; and rhetoric as well as

---

[1] I may here observe that some of the most recent writers upon the history
of Greek philosophy, as Zeller and Butler, have treated the Gorgias with unde-
served neglect; the latter especially hardly ever alludes to it; I suppose because
they found more definite statements upon the same subjects in the constructive
dialogues. Still they have not dealt with the Theætetus in the same way.
Brandis bestows about four pages chiefly made up of quotations to this dialogue.
He considers the several arguments merely in their ethical bearings, and pronounces no direct opinion upon the point here in question.

[2] It is however noticed, but without any particular stress being laid upon
it, by Bonitz, *Op. cit.* p. 270.

every other action employed to promote the ends of justice
and to enforce the right. Another passage equally explicit
occurs, c. 55, p. 500 c.

What all this amounts to may be thus expressed: that
in spite of all plausible theories and views of life, (such as,
that might alone is right, that pleasure is the only good, and
so forth,) and all fallacious appearances, (as the happiness
for example of Archelaus and those who resemble him, or
the external semblance without the reality of virtue by which
society is often imposed upon,) truth justice and right are
alone to be aimed at, and to them all else is to be sacrificed
when they come into collision. In the pursuit of these pain
and danger, exposure and ridicule, are to be cheerfully encountered, and the remedial correction of legal punishment
to be eagerly sought, instead of shunned, with a view to the
attainment of these, the soul's only real good: and to this
end rhetoric like everything else is to be subordinate. Or
in other words, that right and justice are the only rule of
life, ambition and self-seeking only lead men to injustice and
wrong, that is to their own injury and ruin here and hereafter. And this I take to be the general conclusion scope
and purpose of Plato's dialogue.

We will now proceed to consider the argument in detail,
and trace the successive steps and stages of its progress towards these conclusions. It divides itself naturally and easily
into three[1] principal portions distinguished by the three
interlocutors who come successively into collision with So-

---

[1] Steinhart and Susemihl who appear to think that Plato constructed his
dramatic dialogue on the model of a five-act play, assume, after a short pro-
logue or introduction in cc. 1, 2, a fivefold division; cc. 3—20, 21—36, 37—46,
47—61, 62—83; and to make the resemblance complete, compare the myths
to the Deus ex machinâ which sometimes winds up an entangled plot, and the
summary of the principal results of the dialogue to "the anapæsts which at
the conclusion are wont to express in a few words the fundamental idea of the
Tragedy." The utter baselessness of this fanciful comparison, and of the
fivefold division to which it gives rise, is easily and at no considerable length
exposed by Bonitz in his essay, pp. 275—278.

crates and assist him by their opposition in carrying out his argument.

These three stages are distinctly marked, not only by the change of interlocutors, and the change of tone and feeling and expression and views of morality introduced with them, corresponding to which is a change of *form* in the *mode* of conducting the conversation (see Bonitz, u. s. pp. 265—268), but also by a retractation in the two latter of the principles previously admitted, and a resumption of the argument upon a new basis. 'The three principal divisions,' says Bonitz, p. 263, 'are distinguished by the character of the moral views of life therein subjected to criticism, by the depth of the principles adduced against them, and finally by the entire form and tone adopted in carrying on the conversation.'

In the person of Gorgias we have represented the virtual acknowledgement of moral right, essentially, though not formally, expressed; this appears in his hesitation to assert that it is not the duty of a teacher of Rhetoric to impart to his pupils correct notions of right and wrong if they come to him ignorant of such distinctions, though he is thereby involved in a contradiction, and seems, from other evidence, in reality to have differed from his sophistical brethren in abstaining from making the ordinary profession of teaching virtue.

In Polus is marked the unsteady wavering between the admiration of external power and splendour without regard to moral considerations, and yet on the other side a reluctance to deny that right is more fair and noble than wrong. Plato thus makes him the type of that compromising spirit which prevails so widely amongst the mass of mankind. Video meliora proboque, Deteriora sequor. He has never thought deeply and seriously upon any question and has no fixed principles of action; he is ready to take up with any popular notions, and allows himself to be imposed upon by the deceitful appearances of good: and it soon appears that he has not even distinguished between real and apparent power, between doing what one pleases or what seems fit, and doing that which is really good and of service to us, in which true power can alone consist. Accordingly in his answer Socrates deals with him dialectically without going deep into the questions raised, and refutes him merely by showing the inconsistency between his assumptions and the admissions he is obliged to make, and by the aid of the indefinite term καλόν, of which the signification in the common use of language is very vague and uncertain.

In Callicles' hands all this is changed; he impatiently flings aside all compromise and all conventional expressions, and boldly exposes the immoral theory in all its naked deformity. He, unlike his predecessor, has thought upon these questions, and is able to justify the self-seeking spirit which he avows by a theory which makes so called justice and right a mere convention established for the convenience of the majority, who are the weaker party, in order to shackle the stronger and prevent him from asserting his natural right, which is the supreme authority over his fellows; and when further pressed he maintains in accordance with these views that pleasure undistinguished and unlimited is the only good. Such thorough going opinions require an equally thorough examination of the principles on which they rest, and we accordingly find in the last stage of the argument a more fundamental and searching inquiry into the very nature of the conception on which Morality is based. The substance of the remarks immediately preceding is derived from Bonitz's Essay, pp. 263—268.

After a short preface, in which we are introduced to the scene—Callicles' house at Athens—and the characters of the dialogue, the argument opens at once with a question addressed by Socrates to Gorgias, the most distinguished living professor of the art of Rhetoric, who is now on a second visit to Athens and lodging with Callicles, as to the nature and meaning of his profession. The discussion which follows is conducted with the utmost politeness and decorum on both sides; until Gorgias who has at first defined his art merely as the art of persuasion—the received definition at the time, from which it appears that it deals only with what is probable or plausible, and is satisfied with the appearance without the reality of knowledge—is made to acknowledge that the Rhetorician is bound to teach justice, that is to impart some moral instruction to his pupils, though as we learn from the Meno as well as the present dialogue he not only made no such profession himself but laughed at those that did. The true rhetorician, is the conclusion of this first division of the argument, that is the master of the art, if it were what it professed to be, the art political, whose office is to train men for the duties of public and private life, must himself be a just and good man; that is, he must be acquainted with the justice and virtue which he undertakes to teach, and will then necessarily act in accordance with his knowledge[1]—at least so says Socrates, and Gorgias does not contradict him.

The same opinion of the necessity of virtue to the perfection of an orator was held by Quintilian. See Inst. Orat. Proœm. §§ 9, 18. In II. 15, 24—28, he refers to this discussion of the Gorgias, and argues that it is only ignorance of Plato's writings and the neglect of the distinction between the 'elenctic' and 'dogmatic' dialogues that could lead any one to suppose that his opinion of rhetoric was really unfavourable, concluding thus, § 28, ut appareat, Platoni non rhetoricen videri malum, sed eam veram nisi justo ac bono non contingere.

The author of the Rhetorica ad Alexandrum in a very absurd chapter, the 39th, likewise inculcates the union of virtue with rhetoric. He applies the rules of rhetoric to the conduct of life, and shows in detail how the principles which regulate a man's moral behaviour agree with or may be derived from the rules which determine the proper treatment of the five divisions of the speech and their contents, the προοίμιον, διήγησις, πίστεις, τὰ πρὸς ἀντίδικον, and

---

[1] On this reasoning and the Ethical theory it implies, see below, p. lxix.

ἐπίλογος; the object proposed to a man to encourage him
in the practice of virtue being, that you thereby acquire
a reputation for honesty and respectability which has a
powerful influence in gaining credit with an audience. § 2.

In making the above admission, which is extracted from
him by a short course of Socratic cross-examination, Gorgias
has allowed himself to be betrayed into an inconsistency with
a statement which he had previously made in defending his
art from the popular aspersions founded upon the frequent
abuse of it; that namely though it is quite possible to make
an improper use of rhetoric as of any other power acquired
by art, still the teachers of it and the art itself are not justly
chargeable with this, which is due solely to the wickedness
of those who pervert to evil uses the instructions intended to
be employed upon honest and virtuous objects alone. The
admission of the possibility of injustice and fraud in a well
qualified rhetorician is plainly inconsistent with that subsequently forced from him by Socrates, that a good rhetorician must also be a good man: this is gravely pointed
out by Socrates, and Gorgias who makes no attempt to
defend himself is allowed quietly to drop out of the discussion, in which he takes no further part except once or
twice as a deus ex machinâ to extricate the argument from
the dead-lock to which it has been brought by the obsti-
nacy of Callicles or some similar obstacle to its progress.
This carries us down to the end of the 15th chapter.

So far we have been occupied with the definition of
Rhetoric; the argument now enters upon its second stage
and is consigned to the custody of Polus, the youthful
disciple of Gorgias, who shows himself in the course of it
inordinately vain, hot headed, intemperate, prone to exaggerate and moreover devoid of any deep or true insight into
the questions which he professes to be thoroughly acquainted
with, but withal upon the whole candid and tractable: he
yields himself an easy victim to the Socratic dialectics. The
general subject of this second division is the *value* of Rhetoric:

what true power consists in, and what is the worth of that which may be obtained by rhetoric.

Breaking abruptly into the conversation in order to rescue his master from the contradiction into which he had fallen, and to show his own superiority to vulgar prejudice, Polus now asserts that teaching justice does not lie within the province of rhetoric at all; and after some preliminary sparring, and an awkward attempt on his part to get at Socrates' own definition of the art, the latter at length states, cc. 18, 19, 20, the famous distinction and classification of true and false art, which Schleiermacher takes to be the central idea and kernel of the dialogue; which, together with what is implied in it and arises immediately out of it, gives connection to the several parts of the dialogue itself and to this dialogue with the whole series, and justifies the position assigned to it at the head of his second division of the Platonic writings. The eight arts which are occupied with the treatment of the human body and soul may be divided in various ways. Four deal with the body, cookery[1], personal embellishment (the tailor's, hairdresser's, perfumer's, milliner's arts), medicine, and gymnastics; and four with the soul, rhetoric, sophistic, justice (the administration of justice), and legislation: the four last come under the general head of Politics: the first four have no collective name. Secondly, four of them, two genuine and two spurious arts, have a conservative and educational function, are employed in training or pretending to train the body and mind, κομμωτική, gymnastics, sophistic, and legislation: the other four, cookery, medicine, rhetoric and justice, are curative or remedial, their office is to correct imperfections and restore

---

[1] ὀψοποιϊκή, cookery, is not the art of the simple preparation of food, plain roasting and boiling, to fit it for man's use, but it professes to *correct* the imperfections of the food provided by nature by condiments and seasoning so as to flatter or gratify the palate. Plato seems to be of the opinion with regard to Cooks expressed in the familiar English proverb, that they are sent by the author of all evil to spoil the good meat which God has provided.

body and soul to their normal state of health and vigour. Lastly, which is in fact the object of the entire classification, four of them are true and genuine having the real good of that which they profess to treat constantly in view, gymnastics, medicine, legislation, justice; and four are mere counterfeit spurious delusive arts of 'flattery' or cajolery, aiming only at the outward show and not the substantial reality of good; assuming the mask of the others to which each severally corresponds, and deceiving by that assumption those whom they pretend to serve. Hence we get the following proportion:

1. Arts conservative, aiding growth and development of,		2. Arts remedial or corrective of,	
Body.	Soul.	Body.	Soul.

κομμωτική : gymnastics :: sophistic : legislation :: cookery : medicine :: rhetoric : justice.

Some of these terms speak for themselves, and require no explanation. νομοθετική, legislation, is the principal branch of the duty of a statesman or πολιτική, whose proper office it is, as subsequently appears in this dialogue, to train and educate the citizens committed to his charge to the practice of all intellectual and moral virtue: this is (imperfectly) effected by the *laws* and *institutions* of the state, supplemented by a general system of education which it is likewise the statesman's business to establish and superintend. See Aristotle's Politics, Bks. VII. VIII. (Bekk.), Plato's Republic and Politicus, &c. &c. Of this true and genuine art σοφιστική is the εἴδωλον, unreal image or counterfeit. This *pretends* to effect what legislation really does, to lay down moral rules for the regulation of life and conduct: and the distinction *here taken* between this and rhetoric, is, as Schleiermacher observes, Introd. to Gorg. p. 8, that sophistic is represented as a sham philosophical art which lays down and recognises first principles, by which the mind is shaped and moulded as the body by gymnastics ; where as rhetoric only applies these to individual cases, that is, as a remedial art to the cure of a given corruption. Of Justice, δικαιοσύνη,

standing here for δίκη, or rather δίκη διορθωτική, I have
spoken in the note to the translation p. 465, c. 20. Compare Gorg. 478 A, B, which determines the precise meaning.
Stallbaum points out in his note on p. 464 B, that δικαιοσύνη
is elsewhere spoken of as an 'art'; Rep. I. 332 C, D, and
Erast. 137 D.

Polus in his bungling attempt to carry on the argument
by putting questions to Socrates had been very anxious to
get him to admit that Rhetoric is a very fine thing because
it confers great power upon its possessor; he now endeavours
by the same argument to invalidate the contemptuous judgment which his opponent has just pronounced upon it : how
can an art be a mere 'flattery' and a sham which may be
made the instrument of acquiring the supreme power in a
State? which enables its possessors to do what they please like
tyrants, and gratify all their passions and caprices at the
expense of their fellow-citizens? The answer to this question depends upon the proper definition of 'power.' True
power consists not in doing what we like or what we *think*
fit, but in doing what is really good for us: now what we
like and what we *think* fit is often not really beneficial but
injurious to us, and therefore to do that without consideration of consequences indicates not strength or power, but
weakness. The mistake arises from a confusion of means
with ends. The only true and universal end of all action is
Good. The acts that Polus mentions as constituting power,
putting to death, robbing, banishing any one at pleasure, are
not in themselves good but only means to attain that end :
now if owing to want of wisdom or true insight the particular end which a man has in view in doing such acts be
a bad and not a good one, the acts are not desirable; he is
doing what he *pleases,* but not what he *desires,* which is good
alone, the end of all human action. But to do from ignorance
or want of self-control what one does not desire is a sign not
of strength but of weakness. Consequently unless the Rhetorician or the tyrant has a thorough knowledge of what is

good and evil, and knows how to choose the one and avoid
the other, his apparent power is a mere delusion, and a
despot may be in reality the weakest man in the realm,
.cc. 21—24. Polus though unable to make any direct answer
to this, yet remains unconvinced and returns to the charge by
demanding whether Socrates himself would not be a tyrant
if he could; explaining tyranny as before to mean the licence
to commit any arbitrary act at his pleasure. Socrates again
reminds him that regard must be had to consequences—that
such acts if followed by punishment for example are not desirable, which Polus at once admits: and by the same rule
universally nothing is really desirable which is not attended
with good results, and that power like everything else must
be measured by this standard : good in this case means just
and right; if acts are right they are good, if wrong evil :
c. 25. Polus now as a final and conclusive argument tri-
umphantly quotes the case of Archelaus the usurper and
tyrant, who had earned by a series of the most atrocious
crimes not punishment but the throne of Macedonia, on
which he was then seated in the enjoyment of the greatest
happiness, that is splendour and prosperity, c. 26. Upon
this case issue is now joined, Polus asserting that happiness
is compatible with injustice and wrong, Socrates on the other
hand maintaining that the wrongdoer and unjust man is in
every case miserable, less miserable if he be brought to
justice and corrected by punishment, but most miserable
of all if he escape with impunity and so be encouraged to
continue in his wickedness, c. 28 init.: but in the following
argument the question is made to assume the form, in which
Socrates had already expressed it (c. 24, p. 469 B, C), whether
doing wrong or suffering it be worse.

To supply a basis for the reasoning that follows Polus
the half-thinker is first made to admit, that although to
suffer wrong is *worse*, κάκιον, to do wrong is fouler, uglier,
more disgraceful, αἴσχιον. This he is quite ready to do ; for,
not having examined the grounds of his own opinions, and

being in fact the representative of the popular unphiloso-
phical views of happiness in its relation to morality, though
he is persuaded that success in life however attained is the
highest good in one sense and man's highest aim, he is yet
not prepared to reject in terms those deeply rooted sentiments inherent in the human heart by which we approve of
what is right and condemn what is wrong, as such, and
irrespective of their consequences : though at the same time
he seems quite unconscious of what they really imply, and
does not allow them to exercise the smallest influence upon
the views of life which he adopts and recommends : and
secondly he accepts a definition of καλόν and αἰσχρόν proposed by Socrates and established by a brief induction, which
makes the former consist in what is pleasant or profitable or
both, and the latter in the opposites. c. 30. Armed with
these two admissions Socrates speedily proves his point, that
since doing injustice is not more painful than suffering it, and
yet is fouler, i. e. by the definition either more painful or injurious, it must be more injurious, and therefore worse : and
that consequently in saying that he himself or Polus or any
one else would prefer suffering wrong to doing it he was
maintaining no glaring paradox as Polus had supposed but
following the dictates of simple common sense. cc. 30, 31.

On the general moral bearings of this argument the
principles therein appealed to and the terms employed, see
Dr Whewell's observations, Platonic Dialogues, II. 195—197.

The validity of it rests upon the definition of καλόν and
αἰσχρόν, and also upon the admission of a real distinction
between right and wrong and of the authority of those
sentiments of moral approbation and disapprobation with
which we instinctively regard them. When these are admitted the rest follows of course. The standard of 'good'
and 'bad,' ἀγαθόν and κακόν, on the other hand is utility or
one's own interest. Socrates in Xenophon's Memorabilia,
III. 8. 5, 6. IV. 6. 9, goes so far as to identify ἀγαθόν and
καλόν in this sense. But utility or one's own interest may

be regarded in two different aspects. There is an enlightened self-interest which leads men to seek their real and abiding good; and it is in this sense, as afterwards appears, p. 477 A, and elsewhere in this dialogue, that justice is better than injustice, however it may be attended with impunity and crowned with success and worldly prosperity, because this alone constitutes the soul's health, and is alone in conformity with its real nature, being the principle of order harmony strength and stability in the human constitution—as is more largely set forth in the Republic —: and there is another and a lower kind of it which looks merely to the acquisition of power wealth station and other worldly advantages. The latter is evidently Polus' notion of utility or self-interest, as appears from what he had just before said; and therefore when he admits that to do wrong is ugly or base he is, so far as his *conscious intention* goes, merely using the current popular language without observing the inconsistency with his previously expressed views which the admission involves : and when he assents so eagerly to the definition of καλόν which describes it as pleasure or advantage, it is plain that the advantages that he contemplates are such as those which he has described with such gusto as enjoyed by Archelaus, and not those which are understood by Socrates, the only sense in which the definition is really applicable : and so he drifts on unconsciously, entangled in the meshes of Socrates' dialectical net, under this misunderstanding, to the conclusions by which his assertions are upset and the other's point established. The argument thus though logically sound involves an essential unfairness. "Plato," as Mr Grote somewhere says, "is playing both games upon the chess-board," and arranges the men and the moves at his pleasure. If Polus had had his eyes open, like his successor Callicles, he never would have admitted without distinction the positions that lead to his discomfiture. He however serves the purpose for which he is introduced into the dialogue, to represent the opinion based upon no real knowledge or insight enter-

tained by the vulgar upon happiness the rule of life and
moral obligation, and the inconsistency of the principles which
men instinctively approve with those by which their practice and conduct are actually regulated : and it is left for his
successor Callicles to justify this selfish practice by theory,
and in so doing to reject all notions of duty and morality.

The second 'paradox' that Socrates undertakes to prove
(476 A) is that impunity in wrong doing is the greatest
of all evils, greater than suffering punishment, or being
chastised and corrected (κολάζεσθαι), for one's offences. It is
first shown by induction, c. 32, that when any act is performed it is performed upon some person or thing, that agent
necessarily implies patient, and that the quality or properties
of the act are the same in agent and patient, or that the
effect is of the same nature and character in the patient as
the action in the agent ; consequently if a judge inflicts a
just punishment upon an offender the punishment as received by the patient is likewise just, and if so καλόν, and if
καλὸν, ἀγαθόν. Punishment therefore if just is good for the
recipient. The good or benefit which he receives, c. 33, is
correction and moral improvement which is effected by the
removal of the evil that had lodged in his soul and corrupted
it ; and of the three restorative arts that apply a remedy
to the diseased condition of a man's mind body and estate,
trade medicine and corrective justice, as injustice and vice,
the disease of the soul, are far 'fouler' than poverty and sickness, the diseases incident to a man's fortunes and body, and
yet not so painful, it follows again, from the definition of
καλόν, that the soul's disease must be an enormously greater
evil than the other two and the justice or punishment which
rids us of it infinitely to be preferred to all other blessings.
So far therefore from shunning and trying to escape justice,
the wicked man should eagerly have recourse to the judge,
as the sick man to the physician[1], in order to be rid of his

---

[1] On this false analogy, which in fact vitiates the entire reasoning, for if
punishment does *not* cure or eradicate vice, as the physician's art disease, if no

wickedness the greatest of all calamities which must needs
render him miserable. And the general conclusion now is,
c. 35, 479 D, that injustice and wrong-doing is only second in
the degrees of evil, "to do wrong and escape the penalty
is the first and greatest of all ills," and by this we may
estimate the amount of real happiness enjoyed by Archelaus
and those who like him have committed the most enormous
crimes without repentance and atonement, and the value
of the maxims and principles by which Polus thought that a
man's conduct and pursuits in life should be guided.

Or the result may be stated thus: Vice and injustice are
the disease of the soul—comp. Rep. x. 608 E, foll.—the
noblest part of man, and therefore, as corruptio optimi fit
pessima, the worst thing that can happen to a man: 'justice'
is the natural remedy for this: accordingly just as a man in
good health is in the best case, but if he be afflicted with a
disease the next best thing is to apply a remedy and get rid
of it, so that man is to be most envied whose soul and moral
condition are sound and healthy; he is happy in the next
degree who is cured of his vice by correction and punishment; he most wretched of all who having a soul polluted
and depraved with crime remains undetected and unpunished
until the ulcer and the disease have become inveterate and
incurable. Finally the only legitimate use of rhetoric is not
as Polus maintains to excuse and palliate iniquity and avert
from oneself and friends its due penalty, but rather to bring
our hidden crimes to light and expose the guilty to the
correction which may operate as a cure[1]. Comp. Rep. IX.
591 A, B.

moral improvement is really affected thereby, the argument fails, I have elsewhere quoted Renouvier, *Manuel de Phil. Anc.* Vol. II. p. 31. See note on
Translation, p. 54.

[1] In the interpretation of the passage, 480 E—481 B, we must be careful
not to do Plato the injustice of construing his words too literally, and attributing to him the horrible and revolting meaning which at first sight may seem
to be conveyed by the text, that in order to punish an enemy we may encourage and foster in him all wickedness and depravity until he becomes incur-

This brings us down to the end of c. 36, p. 481 B, and concludes the second division of the argument.

Polus being thus reduced to silence Callicles now steps forward to the rescue, and the argument enters upon its third stage. He first accuses Polus in his turn of timidity and over deference to popular prejudices, and then turning upon Socrates charges him with wilful sophistry in availing himself of the ambiguity of the word 'right,' which is employed in two different significations according as 'natural' or 'legal and conventional' right is thereby intended. When Socrates declares that wrong doing is an evil and worse than wrong suffering he is speaking 'according to law' or 'convention;' whereas 'by nature' the opposite is true. In explanation of this he propounds his theory. All distinctions which imply moral approbation or disapprobation are now swept away; 'by nature' every thing is 'fouler' more disgraceful which is also 'worse' more injurious, and therefore suffering wrong: to endure injury or insult without the power of helping oneself is unmanly and fit only for a slave; for such an one it is better to die than to live. The notion that to suffer wrong is better and nobler than to inflict it and such like are the inventions of the weaker majority who constitute society; these have agreed amongst themselves to encourage such opinions, and to frame their laws in accord-

---

able, and thus ruin him body and soul. It is true that the Greek moralists generally admitted the principle of doing good to one's friends and evil to one's enemies as a maxim of their moral code; and this is one of the most striking of all the points of difference between heathen and Christian morals; but none of them it may safely be affirmed would have ventured to go such lengths as to include the promotion of injustice and vice amongst the allowable injuries that might be inflicted on an enemy. The case is merely a supposed one. *If* we desired to do an enemy all the mischief in our power, this is the way in which we should proceed. If any doubt remained on the point, it would be removed by the following passage of the *Republic*, I. 335 B, D: ἀνθρώπους δὲ μὴ οὕτω φῶμεν βλαπτομένους εἰς τὴν ἀνθρωπείαν ἀρετὴν χείρους γίγνεσθαι;...καὶ τοὺς βλαπτομένους ἄρα τῶν ἀνθρώπων ἀνάγκη ἀδικωτέρους γίγνεσθαι;...οὐκ ἄρα τοῦ δικαίου βλάπτειν ἔργον, οὔτε φίλον οὔτ' ἄλλον οὐδένα, ἀλλὰ τοῦ ἐναντίου, τοῦ ἀδίκου.

ance with them, in order to protect themselves against the superior or stronger, whose natural right it is to be their lord and master, to gratify all his impulses and passions, and in short to do as he pleases: and this is *natural* justice. c. 38. The rest of his speech is occupied first in defending this position and in depicting the triumph of this natural right when the stronger has shaken off the chains imposed upon him by society and its conventions, when like a horse that has broken loose he has burst his bonds and flung his rider and escaped from human control, and rises in his might to assert his natural superiority, and trample under foot the feeble restraints that bound him, c. 39; and secondly, cc. 40, 41, with a graphic description of the consequences of a life devoted to philosophy and the utter helplessness, the liability to every insult and death itself, which attends it; and an earnest recommendation to Socrates (who here stands for Plato himself) to renounce this childish study and betake himself to more manly and useful pursuits, the career of the rhetorician or politician.

The theory of society and of morals here set forth seems to agree substantially with that propounded by Thrasymachus in the Republic, Book I. Mr Grote however, Hist. of Greece, VIII. 537 (Ed. 2), maintains that it is 'essentially different;' but I think the difference between them lies rather in the point of view from which 'conventional' right and justice are looked at, and the terms in which the theories are stated, than in the principles on which they are based and the views of society and moral obligation which they imply. Thrasymachus, it is true, says nothing about 'right.' His theory is—I will adopt the terms in which Mr Grote himself expresses it, p. 536—'that justice is the *interest* of the superior power; that rule, which in every society the dominant power prescribes as being for its own advantage. A man is just for the advantage of another, not for his own: he is weak, cannot help himself, and must submit to that which the stronger authority, whether despot oligarchy or commonwealth, commands.' But surely this implies a 'natural right' in the stronger or superior to avail themselves of the advantages thus offered to them: right must reside somewhere; and by Thrasymachus' theory it resides in the governing body, whatever its special form may be, which enacts laws establishes institutions and inculcates notions in accordance with its own interests, that is, for the maintenance of its authority. It is true again that according to Thrasymachus the conventions which dictate the opinions and rules by which man's conduct is regulated proceed from the stronger, and are established for the purpose of ensuring the obedience of the weaker or governed: whereas in Callicles' view they arise out of the fears of the weaker majority to hold the stronger in check and prevent him from breaking loose and asserting his natural right to their obedience; in the one justice, conventional justice, is the interest of the stronger, in the other the interest of the weaker: still the fundamental conception of law and right and the effect produced is the same in either case; justice and right as men commonly conceive them are equally delusive equally devoid of any natural and inherent claim to respect and observance; the stronger overrides them, establishes and alters them at his pleasure, either by natural right which renders him superior to all conventions, or (which seems in fact to come to much the same thing) because he has himself introduced and can deal with them as he pleases: in both alike they are mere human inventions and result in the established order of society[1]. Thrasymachus' views are stated and discussed in

---

[1] A question of this kind must be decided by reason and not authority. But it may be as well to observe that at least three writers on this subject whose opinion is deserving of the very highest consideration and respect seem to agree, if not in identifying the two theories, at any rate in tracing in them a very close resemblance. Brandis in his *Handbuch*, Vol. II. p. 464, note kk, places *Rep.* I. 338 c side by side with *Gorg.* 482 E, 483 A, without comment, as authorities for the following words of his text. Da aber der verwegenere Kallikles Polus' Zugeständniss verwirft und das der Natur nach Schöne und Gerechte von dem nach Satzung Schönen und Gerechten unterscheidend,

the Republic, I. p. 338 to the end; resumed in a more moderate tone enlarged and corrected by Glaucon and Adimantus
at the beginning of the second, and summed up in a single
sentence, p. 367 C.

In Xenophon's Memorabilia, IV. 4. 14, Hippias argues
similarly about justice and law, that they vary at different
times and places, and are therefore purely arbitrary and conventional; compare also the doctrines attributed to Protagoras in the Theætetus, pp. 167 C, 172 B. The same views
are ascribed to the Sophists (as I have endeavoured to show,
Journal of Classical and Sacred Philology, No. 2, pp. 153—
157) in a mass, Plat. Legg. 889 E.

The same theory, that justice in the ordinary acceptation
is a mere convention, invented for the convenience of societies and therefore liable to change according to the different
circumstances of time and place, that there is no natural
right, unless it be that of the stronger, and that consequently
every one has a right to get what he can and keep what he
can get—" the simple plan, that they should take who have
the power and they should keep who can "—was revived by
Carneades, the most celebrated of the Sceptical philosophers
of the New Academy, in a famous argumentation delivered
during his embassy at Rome in B.C. 156, and reported by
Cicero in the third book of his treatise de Republica, of which

ersteres auf das Recht des Stärkeren zurückführt, &c. And again, p. 470, in
examining the theory as stated by Thrasymachus in the *Republic*, he speaks of
die ähnliche Behauptung des Kallikles im Gorgias. And Schleiermacher, *Introd. to Republic*, p. 8, has, Und wenn allerdings das Thema des Thrasymachos
auch sehr bestimmt an den Gorgias erinnert, and immediately afterwards
speaks of the ähnlichkeit between them. As one of Schleiermacher's principal
objects in his Introductions is to show how the later dialogues were developed
out of germs already contained in the earlier ones, or carry on the same trains
of thought, these expressions are at all events sufficient to show that he could
not have found an 'essential difference' between the two theories in question.
Lastly Zeller, *Phil. der Griechen*, Vol. I. p. 260, 1st ed. Die Sophistik, after
referring to the doctrine of Thrasymachus in the *Republic*, proceeds thus, am
bestimmtesten endlich wird diese Ansicht, und namentlich…von dem Sophisten-
schüler Kallikles entwickelt.

a few fragments still remain. Fragmm. VIII—XVIII. The summary of it is supplied by Lactantius in these terms. Fragm. XV. " That men established for themselves a system of law or rights in conformity with their interests, that is to say, varying according to their habits and customs, and often changed as circumstances required amongst the same people : natural right there is none. All men as well as other living creatures are impelled by the very guidance of nature to seek their own advantage; therefore either there is no such thing as justice, or if there be any, it is the height of folly, since it hurts itself in consulting the interests of others (here he is in entire agreement with Thrasymachus). All people who ever enjoyed a flourishing empire, in fact the Romans themselves, who hold the sovereignty of the whole globe, if they mean to be just, that is to make restitution of what belongs to others, must return to their original cabins and lie prostrate in poverty and misery." And further, Fragm. XIV. "As one man and one order is afraid of another, and again no one can rely upon himself, a sort of compact is made between the mass of the people and the powerful, from which arises the association of civil society. For it is weakness and not nature nor free will that is the mother of justice. For whereas our choice has to be made out of three things; either to do wrong and not suffer it, or to do and suffer it, or neither; the best of all is to do wrong with impunity if you can; the second best neither to do nor to suffer it; the most wretched of all lots is to be in a perpetual conflict of inflicting and suffering injuries."

Similar doctrines of the origin and nature of justice law and right were reasserted in the seventeenth century by Hobbes of Malmesbury, whose theory is absolutely identical with that laid down by Callicles. He maintained in his Leviathan that right and wrong have no independent existence: that the natural state of mankind is one of mutual war; and that consequently the notions of right and wrong, just and unjust, have there no place: these spring from the union

d

of individuals in society, whence proceeds positive law, a convention which establishes right and wrong in and for that society. Right is the power of enforcing; duty the necessity of obeying. See further in Dr Whewell's Hist. of Mor. Phil. in Engl. p. 17. Compare p. 52. "Hobbes had maintained that the state of the nature of man is an universal war of each against all; and that there is no such thing as natural right and justice (that is, of course, in the ordinary sense); these notions being only creations of civil society, and deriving their sanction entirely from the civil ruler." See likewise Mackintosh, Dissert. on the Hist. of Eth. Phil., p. 122 (Ed. Whewell); and on Spinosa's Views, Ibid. p. 124.

In the following chapter, 42, Socrates is occupied chiefly in quizzing Callicles for the uncompromising freespokenness with which he has stated his theory, and the judicious advice which he has so kindly and gratuitously bestowed upon him. Fun to all appearance is its principal, if not sole, object; and it seems to require no other justification than the humour that pervades it of its introduction here, though the argument be not directly advanced thereby. There be however Teutonic writers who see in it a deeper meaning; and conceive that we are to understand by the compliments which Socrates pays to Callicles on his candour, wisdom, and kind feeling towards himself, that he has now found a worthy antagonist with whom he can go deeper into the questions proposed for discussion.

The argument is resumed in chapter 43,.and the examination of Callicles' theory commenced. But first it is necessary to state it a little more distinctly, and explain the meaning of the terms in which it is expressed. What for instance does κρείττων 'superior' mean? Callicles first says, ἰσχυρότερος, meaning doubtless to include all the resources of ability and power in the notion of strength. Socrates however confines it to its literal sense; and in this limited application to mere strength of body it immediately appears that the many or individually weaker are superior to the one stronger in whom the natural right resides, and therefore according to this view of the case *they* have the right and not he. Callicles at once abandons this, c. 44, and proposes ἀμείνων as a substitute, but this is just as vague as the word κρείττων or βελτίων which it proposes to explain; and he then suggests φρονιμώτερος, that the superiority which gives the natural right resides in practical wisdom and sagacity, skill and knowledge. It is soon found, c. 45, that neither do these qualities entitle their possessor to an advantage over his fellows or an undue share in any of the good things of this life; and then Callicles finally pronounces that the strength and superiority that he really means lies in a union of the highest qualities of the statesman, the knowledge and skill to form plans (for the public good and his own) or to frame a policy, and the energy and vigour to carry them into execution. "These are the men that have a right to bear rule, and justice consists in this, that these should have the advantage over the rest, the governors over the governed." c. 46, p. 491 D. Socrates takes occasion by this to inquire who these governors and governed are? whether the notion of *self-government* is included? and thus the subject of σωφροσύνη or self-control is introduced, and the transition made to the next question, the contrast between this and the unrestrained and unlimited indulgence of the appetites and desires, and which of the two conduces to virtue and happiness. Hereupon Callicles abandons all reserve, and plainly states that a man's duty and happiness consists in the gratification of all his desires[1], which he is therefore bound to foster and encourage, provided only he have the means of satisfying them, and this is to be sought in absolute power.

Socrates, c. 47, after commending Callicles' frankness in speaking so boldly out what other people often think but don't usually choose to express, first, cc. 47, 48, in two fables or allegories, derived most probably from the Orphics and

---

[1] This is what Demosthenes calls, τῇ γαστρὶ μετρεῖν τὴν εὐδαιμονίαν, *de Cor.* § 296.

Pythagoreans (see note B. in the Appendix), draws a picture
of the condition of a man who thus passes his life in the constant and unlimited indulgence of all his appetites and passions, like the daughters of Danaus, ever engaged in pouring
water into a vessel which he can never fill: but finding as
he anticipated that Callicles is proof against conviction by
any such means, and indeed laying no great stress on these
allegorical representations himself, he next proceeds, c. 49, to
a comparatively serious and searching examination of the
question virtually involved in the original theory put forth
by Callicles, but now more immediately raised by his recent
explanations, that is, the nature of pleasure and its relation
to the good.

The treatment of this subject however in our dialogue is
still dialectical and somewhat popular and negative. Plato's
maturer views upon the question are to be found in the
Philebus, to which the argument of the Gorgias may be
regarded in some sort as introductory, where pleasure is
submitted to a more thorough and fundamental analysis,
its true nature and distinctions determined, and its relation
to the ultimate good and the rank which is consequently to
be assigned to it in the scale of goods finally and definitively
settled.

It follows immediately from what Callicles has already
said that he regards pleasure as the only good, and it now
appears, c. 49, that he makes no distinction between the different kinds of pleasure; all alike are good, every appetite
and desire is alike worthy of satisfaction.

The views here put forward in the person of Callicles are
in fact those of Aristippus and the Cyrenaics, upon whom
see Zeller, Phil. der Gr. I. 120, foll. Some of them seem to
have pushed their theory to the same extreme lengths as
Callicles does here, for Diogenes Laert. II. 87, says that they
held μὴ διαφέρειν ἡδονὴν ἡδονῆς μηδὲ ἥδιόν τι εἶναι: though
he afterwards ascribes to Aristippus, § 90, the milder doctrine of a gradation of pleasures. The same is spoken of

as the popular view, Rep. VI. 505 B, τοῖς πολλοῖς ἡδονὴ δοκεῖ
εἶναι τὸ ἀγαθόν. It is often by modern writers ascribed to
the Sophists: and though we have I believe no direct ancient
authority for this, still it is an easy deduction from the moral
theories and views of life which they entertained. The
ancient authorities for the doctrines of Aristippus may be
seen in Stallbaum's Introd. to Phileb. p. 23. Ed. 1.

The first argument against the identity of pleasure and
good occupies cc. 50, 51, and part of 52, to p. 497 D. It is to
this effect. Good and bad, it is admitted, like health and
disease, strength and weakness, speed and slowness, are
opposites, and as such mutually exclude one another, that is,
they cannot reside together in the same subject and the same
part of it at the same time and place and under the same
circumstances. Now from the nature of pleasure, that is
sensual corporeal pleasure which alone is here in question,
this cannot be asserted of pleasure and pain. On the contrary, the gratification of a bodily appetite consists in the
relief of a want, the filling up of a gap, the supply of a
deficiency of a certain part of the body, or of the entire
bodily constitution, and the restoration of the whole system
to the normal harmony of its condition. But we relieve
distress, and a want is painful, and therefore in gratifying
an appetite we feel pain and pleasure together; and not only
so, but the two cease simultaneously, as in drinking the thirst
or pain and the pleasure that arises from drinking by which
that pain is relieved, 497 A; and therefore pleasure and pain
since they coexist in the same subject and the same part of
it cannot be identical with good or evil.

The same view of the nature of the pleasures of sense is
expressed in a more dogmatic form in the Philebus, p. 31 D.
Pain is there made to consist in the λύσις τῆς ἁρμονίας of the
bodily frame, pleasure in the restoration of this balance or
harmony, in the filling up of the void produced by this dissolution. Compare 32 B, 42 C, D: and Timæus, p. 64 D, where
pain is similarly referred to a violent disturbance of the

natural order, τὸ παρὰ φύσιν καὶ βίαιον γιγνόμενον ἄθροον παρ' ἡμῖν πάθος ἀλγεινόν; and pleasure to a return to 'nature,' that is the restoration of the natural order and harmony; and some further details are added on the same subject. Compare also Republic, IX. 585 A, πεῖνα καὶ δίψα καὶ τὰ τοιαῦτα κενώσεις τινές εἰσι τῆς περὶ τὸ σῶμα ἕξεως. 584 C, μὴ πειθώμεθα καθαρὰν ἡδονὴν εἶναι τὴν λύπης ἀπαλλαγήν. In the entire passage on this subject Rep. IX. 583 B—586 C, the conclusions of the Philebus seem to be assumed. In the scale of goods which is the general result of the discussions of the Philebus, 66 A, to the end, the pure and painless pleasures of the intellect and imagination—and affections, which might have been added, but are not (comp. p. 52 C)—in which sense has no direct share, except in certain cases as a medium, occupy the fifth and lowest place; sensual pleasures, which belong to the ἄπειρον or indefinite, the fleeting shifting unstable element of the greater and less, the principle therefore of all excess and defect—as opposed to the μέσον or μέτριον, the highest of all goods—are the causes only of excess and disturbance, and therefore excluded altogether from the catalogue of good things.

The second argument, cc. 52 p. 497 D, and 53, is as follows. If pleasure is the only good and pain the only evil, good and bad men will be distinguished only by the amount of pleasure and pain they feel. But experience shows that bad men, as fools and cowards, feel quite as much or even more pleasure—as a coward for example in escaping danger—that is, by the hypothesis, are as good or better, than the wise and brave who are good: which is absurd. The same reductio ad absurdum is thus briefly stated, Phileb. 55 B: "How absurd it would be for a man when he feels pain to be obliged to say that he is then a bad man, though he may be the most virtuous person in the world, and vice versâ."

Again, when Callicles abandons his former ground and endeavours to avoid the conclusion by accepting the dis-

tinction of good and bad pleasures, Socrates immediately
shows him that if some pleasures are to be avoided because
they are useless or injurious, it is not pleasure per se that
men seek when they indulge themselves, but profit or advantage; or, that if they are persuaded that the evil consequences of an indulgence overbalance the pleasure they feel
in it, they abstain. Consequently it is not pleasure that is
men's real object, but good, τὸ ἀγαθόν, the ultimate end of
all human action. c. 54.

In the following Chapter, 55, p. 500 B, these conclusions
are connected by another link with the general subject of
the dialogue, and employed in confirmation of the positions
laid down in the course of the arguments with Gorgias and
Polus. The distinction just established between pleasure and
good justifies that which was previously *assumed* without
proof between the spurious and genuine arts, and is now
directly applied to these, and to politics in general under
the name of rhetoric, the thread on which the entire argument is made to hang, cc. 56—58. Socrates is now enabled
to reassert more confidently and with a deeper meaning the
views then put forward rather tentatively and hypothetically.
The spurious art of politics, as it was interpreted by Callicles
and the Sophists, aims only at pleasure, that is, at gratifying
the passions and vanity of him who practises the art—this
may be included in the notion of 'flattery,' though it is
not expressly mentioned—and tickling the ears of the mob
to whom it is addressed, humouring them like children
(ὥσπερ παισὶ χαριζόμενον, 502 E); and this has been shown
not to be the good. Whence it appears that its aim must
be a wrong one, and requires to be rectified by the study
of philosophy or dialectics, the only true art of words
(Phædr. 261 E), and the only genuine qualification for
public life.

This is to be taken together with a great deal of what
follows, as Schleiermacher first pointed out, as an implied
justification of Plato's own abstinence from public affairs,

or rather neglect of his public duties, and exclusive devotion
to philosophical speculation, with which his enemies seem
to have reproached him[1], and may accordingly be compared
with the two more celebrated passages of a similar tendency,
Theætetus, 172 c—177 c, and Republic, VI. 488 A—497 A (and
the following), especially 496 c—E, where Plato is manifestly
drawing a picture of himself, his own feelings and position;
and also with the 7th Epistle in which either himself or
some one well acquainted with him and his history describes
the motives by which he was led to abstain from politics and
the feelings which he entertained towards all existing governments.   The duty of a philosopher in this particular, and the
reasons, founded upon the views of justice and happiness and
man's moral constitution previously developed in the course
of the dialogue, which will determine his choice of a career
in life, are stated still more explicitly, Rep. IX. 591 E, to the
end.   And in Politicus, 299 A, the young Socrates seems to
express Plato's own sentiments when he exclaims after hearing the Eleatic Stranger's description of certain existing institutions, οὐκοῦν ὅ γ' ἐθέλων καὶ ἑκὼν ἐν τοῖς τοιούτοις ἄρχειν
δικαιότατ' ἂν ὁτιοῦν πάθοι καὶ ἀποτίνοι.

It must be owned that in all this the great Moralist
exhibits a somewhat singular unconsciousness that all these
fine motives and reasons are mere selfishness very thinly

---

[1] This apology which Plato here makes for himself, and the announcement
of his determination to persevere in the course of life which he had marked
out, combined with other reasons, have led Schleiermacher to refer the composition of the dialogue to Plato's return from his first journey to Sicily in 389 B.C.,
at the age of 40, after which he settled in Athens and opened his philosophical
school, as the period most suitable to such a defence and statement of his
intentions.   Schleiermacher thinks that Plato did not return to Athens "for
any long time at least" after his residence at Megara.   Professor Thompson
(quoted by Dr Donaldson, *Continuation of Müll. Hist. Gr. Lit.* II. 51—54) in
accordance with the usual opinion, derived from Diogenes Laertius, that Plato
returned to Athens, after his first absence, in 395 B.C., fixes the date of composition at an earlier period, between his return from his travels after his
residence at Megara and his first journey to Sicily in 389.

disguised; a simple unwillingness to sacrifice his own ease comfort and pursuits to a possible public duty, with a considerable admixture of spite and scorn for the existing government and policy of his native country. Not that I would affirm that he was not in reality better employed, and conferring more benefit on the world at large, in speculating on the true the good and the beautiful than in humbling the pride of the great King, or invading Laconia (for which however it would seem from the allusion, Gorg. 515 E, and his expressions elsewhere, he would have had no particular inclination) at the head of a combined force of Athenians and Thebans, or in arguing with some Callicles before the public assembly about ships long walls docks and such like 'nonsense;' but that he seems to overlook the possibility of a man's being *obliged* by his duty as a citizen and a patriot to make the sacrifice of his own inclinations and prepossessions to the interests of his country, to serve which he himself tells us so often is paramount over all other obligations; or again that if the state of society at Athens was really as corrupt as he deemed it to be, it *might* be his business actively to aid in improving it, even at the risk of destroying the balance or dissolving the harmony (Rep. IX. 592 A) of his soul thereby. This appears in fact to be one of the numerous instances in which great philosophers—need I refer to the case of Bacon?—see clearly enough what duty requires in others, but are unable to apply their own rules to their own individual circumstances.

With rhetoric are included in the same category as arts of flattery other highly esteemed and popular arts, as the various kinds of music, dithyrambic and even tragic poetry, which have pleasure only for their object: and here again we seem to have an anticipation of the discussions of the Republic, Books II. III. and X., which end in the exclusion from the model state of poetry and music, with the exception of the simplest and gravest branches of those arts. Gorg. 502 D.

Continuing, c. 58, to apply the principles thus gradually established to the solution of the main question, what is the true rule of life, Socrates, after having shown that the real end and aim of human action is not pleasure nor external advantage, and therefore not power, but good, now infers that this must likewise be the end and aim of all education, and with it of political education or the statesman's art. A man's private duty is therefore to aim at becoming good himself, and his public duty to endeavour to make others so. And herein lies the explanation of the failure of past and present statesmen alike in fulfilling the true object of their profession, which is to make men better, that they have been ignorant of this great truth that good is to be preferred to immediate gratification and external power and splendour, and so have mistaken their end and followed a wrong course and left the citizens as bad or worse than they found them.

Next follows, c. 59, an inquiry into the means by which men are to be made good, and what it is that constitutes soundness, health, goodness in man's moral constitution. It appears, by the analogy of the arts as usual, that every artist in dealing with his materials and shaping them to his end, has in his mind a certain order and arrangement or settled plan to which all that he uses and all that he does is subordinate and made to conform; it is this order and harmony and right arrangement that constitutes the 'goodness' of a house, a ship, the strength and health of the human body, and so by analogy, the virtue or excellence of the soul. The result of this order in the soul is obedience to law, by it men are made observant of law and orderly; and this is δικαιοσύνη and σωφροσύνη, justice and self-control, 504 D. To the same rule, c. 60, the rhetorician or statesman must likewise conform. The true, scientific, orator and statesman, one who really understands his profession its ends and obligations, must before all things seek to implant these virtues in the souls of those who are entrusted to his charge.

Accordingly he must control their inclinations, correct and chastise them, which is the only way in which their character can be really improved, instead of trying to gratify, humour, and indulge them, which Callicles thought to be the politician's object; and so it is not ἀκολασία unlimited unrestrained indulgence of the appetites and desires, but the opposite, κολάζεσθαι, correction and control, which is a man's true object, alike as a statesman or a private citizen, 505 C. Here Callicles, who is fairly silenced and can no longer find any argument or subterfuge to serve his purpose, becomes sulky and obstinate, and flatly refuses to continue the discussion. He now suggests, c. 61, that Socrates should carry it on by himself, which after a show of modest hesitation and reluctance, and earnest entreaties to his friends to be very hard upon him and carefully to note and criticise any error he falls into, and by the intervention of the Deus ex machina (Gorgias), he at length is persuaded to do.

In chapter 62 he next proceeds to recapitulate in a summary way the results of the preceding argument; and the first general conclusion is that σωφροσύνη, the principle of order and of harmony, of due subordination and arrangement in the human soul, which has been shown to be the soul's highest good, rightly understood involves every virtue; piety and justice, which consist in doing what is right, one's duty, τὰ προσήκοντα, to Gods and men[1], and courage or fortitude, which consists in seeking and avoiding the right things and men, pleasures and pains, and enduring either

---

[1] The reasoning here depends upon the interpretation of the words σώφρων, σωφρονεῖν. σωφροσύνη is here regarded as soundness of mind, in accordance with its derivation, and 'soundness of mind' it is argued necessarily implies the notion of doing what is proper and fitting to every one, men and Gods; and therefore of doing one's duty to them, which is the meaning of piety and justice. Schleiermacher accordingly renders σώφρων der Besonnene. The same may be said of the following argument to show that it implies bravery as well as justice and piety. And by this interpretation σωφροσύνη will also necessarily imply φρόνησις, the fourth of the cardinal virtues, and so include *all* the four.

pain or danger when a man is bound to do so. Consequently one who has the virtue of temperance or self-control must be in all respects a good man, and a good man will 'do well,' and one who 'does well' will be happy: and the opposites of this, intemperance licentiousness self-indulgence, must therefore be the soul's vice and lead to misery instead of to happiness, as Callicles maintained. p. 507 c.

Accordingly the general conclusions of cc. 62, 63, may be thus summed up. In opposition to Callicles' position that happiness consists in intemperance licentiousness self-indulgence, it has been shown (by induction) that order harmony due subordination and arrangement are necessary to, or rather constitute, the well-being and perfection of everything in art and nature; by these principles heaven and earth, the Gods and human society, are held together, and from this the whole universe receives its name ($\kappa\acute{o}\sigma\mu o\varsigma$). In man these principles are called $\kappa o\sigma\mu\iota\acute{o}\tau\eta\varsigma$, $\sigma\omega\phi\rho o\sigma\acute{v}\nu\eta$; and this is that temperance or self-control which necessarily brings with it the other virtues, and unites all our faculties, physical mental and moral, in an orderly and harmonious co-operation, tending to one end, the supreme good. Hence it appears that orderliness and subordination, 'due measure' proportion or 'law,' are necessary to the development and maintenance of the integrity and perfection of the human nature, as of all other things; and that licentiousness, which introduces disorder and is accompanied by $\pi\lambda\epsilon o\nu\epsilon\xi\acute{\iota}a$, a grasping rapacious dissatisfied spirit, a desire for inequality, and a principle of insubordination, and thereby thwarts and mars this harmonious development, so far from being good and contributing to happiness, is in fact the worst evil that can befal a man; and that any remedy or correction however painful must be resorted to by which we may be relieved of it: and hence also those paradoxes, as they appeared when first stated, are now shown to be really true, that to do wrong is a greater calamity than to suffer it, that the only use of rhetoric is to *accuse*, not to defend, oneself or one's child or friend of any secret crime which would otherwise pass undetected and unpunished; and so we now come round again to the conclusion of the original argument with Gorgias, that the genuine rhetorician or true statesman must be just himself and acquainted with the principles of justice and of virtue. 508 C.

Σωφροσύνη, which stands in this dialogue for the principle of order, the supreme regulative and controlling authority in man's moral constitution, takes here the place which is assigned to δικαιοσύνη in the psychological analysis of the Republic. There Justice (that is, distributive Justice) is the principle which orders and harmonises that constitution, introduces a right arrangement of the several parts, keeps the desires and appetites and the lower elements in general in due subordination to the higher, the reason or νοῦς, governs the whole and regulates the action of the entire machine. Compare also, Rep. IX. 591 A—E, where this effect is described as the ἁρμονία, ξυμφωνία, of the soul, ἡ ἐν αὐτῷ πολιτεία; and the same views of man's nature in its perfection, of the aim of life conduct and education, are expressed in terms derived from the conclusions moral and psychological previously established in the course of that dialogue. Here again therefore the arguments of the Gorgias may be regarded as anticipatory of or introductory to the more advanced and dogmatic statements of the Republic. To use Dr Whewell's words, Platonic Dialogues, II. 222, "So given, the discourse (Socrates' recapitulation) becomes a statement of Plato's philosophy at this period; that is, at a stage of his doctrines preceding that which the Republic presents; namely, when he regarded the soul of man as a *constitution*, but had not yet discerned clearly what were the component elements of that constitution."

The high value which Plato attached to this conception of order harmony, proportion, law, and the important place which it fills in the entire scheme of his philosophy, may be further estimated by the prominent part assigned to it in the discussions of the Philebus. It first appears there as the πέρας, or τὸ περαῖνον, or πεπρασμένον. Borrowing the notion from the Pythagoreans Plato commences that dialogue by laying down three original elements in the entire constitution of things, together with a fourth, the first cause, which is independent of the rest. The ἄπειρον, or indefinite matter, assumes a definite shape and a positive existence by the introduction of the πέρας, the limit, the principle of the defi-. nite or determinate, or, in a wider sense, of order symmetry harmony organization, which the Pythagoreans represented under the form of numbers, but may be conceived more definitely and expressed in one word as 'law.' The third element is the mixture of these two; and besides these as a fourth, there is the cause of the mixture, or independent first cause. The ἄπειρον per se is the principle of evil. In it is included all that is susceptible of degree, τὸ μᾶλλον καὶ ἧττον, all excess and defect. This evil tendency is corrected by the introduction of the πέρας, and from the blending of the two proceeds all that is good. Thus in the human bodily constitution, the ἄπειρον is the principle of the excess or defect in which consists disease: the πέρας corrects this, and the union of the two produces health, the normal or perfect state of the constitution of the body. In sounds, the indefinite materials sharp and flat, quick and slow, which are naturally and in themselves devoid of musical harmony, are harmonized by the πέρας and become music. Similarly in hot and cold, the πέρας brings with it the due temperature of the seasons; and so on in other things. And in the classification of the various forms of good which concludes the dialogue, p. 65 C, the first place is assigned to τὸ μέτριον καὶ τὸ καίριον, the general principle of harmony proportion and measure, or in other words of 'law' and 'order,' in place and time. In the Laws, IV. 716 C, God himself is called μετριότης, μέτρον πάντων χρημάτων.

It is hardly necessary to observe that from the principles thus set forth in the Philebus Aristotle has derived two of the most prominent and leading doctrines of his Metaphysical and Ethical system. The ἄπειρον appears amongst his four causes as the ὕλη, the material cause or element, the indefinite shapeless matter of things, having only a potential existence, δυνάμει; the πέρας becomes the λόγος, or τὸ τί ῆͺν εἶναι, which gives the formless matter a definite shape and substantial existence, ἐνεργείᾳ, and makes it what it *is*, or *was to be;* fulfils, that is, its idea, the end or τέλος of its being. It is equally plain that the ἄπειρον with its excess and defect, and the πέρας, which by limiting and defining these converts them into good, furnished his Ethical philosophy with the notion of the mean, τὸ μέσον, in which virtue resides, and the ὑπερβολή and ἔλλειψις which constitute vice and error.

To return to the Gorgias. In c. 64 Socrates first replies to the taunts which Callicles had thrown out against his lifelong devotion to philosophy, which it now appears were misdirected and baseless; and then proceeds to recapitulate his previous assertions which have at length been established by argument and become conclusions. And now Callicles is again enticed back into the discussion: but his spirit is by this time broken and his objections exhausted, and though still secretly of the same mind as before he shows no further fight, and does little more than express assent until the end of the dialogue.

The comparative value of a defence against doing and suffering wrong is now therefore determined, since it has been proved that doing wrong is undoubtedly the greater evil of the two. A defence against this is to be found only in the knowledge of right and wrong, what is just and what is unjust (in the study, that is, of Ethical Philosophy), since no one does wrong intentionally and with his eyes open, c. 65; protection against suffering wrong, c. 66, can be secured only by making oneself like the ruling powers; by setting oneself from one's earliest youth to copy their manners, adopt their feelings and opinions, and in short assimilate one's mind and character

in every point as nearly as possible to theirs: this is the only
way of ingratiating oneself with them and thereby ensuring
one's safety. Callicles here objects that this is a necessity;
one who sets himself in opposition to the powers that be will
be put to death; but this makes no difference to the question;
it still remains true that to conform oneself to a vicious pat-
tern and so become wicked is a greater evil than to suffer
any calamity: and again, cc. 67, 68, if rhetoric is of that
high value which Callicles attributes to it in virtue of its
being the art of self-preservation, the same must be true of a
number of other arts, swimming, navigation, fortification or
military engineering, which are equally necessary in many
cases to the preservation of a man's life and fortunes, and yet
none of them assumes the consequence or gives itself the
pretentious airs of self-importance which are exhibited by
the Rhetorician, or Politician as Callicles understands it. (In
the connection of the argument in the last paragraph I have
followed Bonitz, u. s. p. 258.)

In proving the first point in the above argument Plato
has recourse to the axiom which is elsewhere expressed in
the phrase οὐδεὶς ἑκὼν κακός: a principle which, Socrates
observes, has been already admitted in the course of the discussion with Polus. He refers to c. 24, p. 468 c. foll., where
it is argued that good is always a man's real object, or that
when a man does what he really wishes, he does what is
good. This principle, directly or indirectly stated, and whatever its exact meaning may be, is asserted through the entire
series of Plato's works from the Protagoras to the Laws, and
therefore must have been held by him in some sense or other
at all periods of his philosophical career. It occurs Protag.
358 c, it is implied and argued upon, Meno, 77 B—78 B, and,
to refer only to his later writings, is found in the Philebus,
22 B (indirectly stated), Rep. IX. 589 c, Timæus, 86 D, Laws,
v. 731 c, 734 B, IX. 860 D, where it is discussed at length.
Various meanings may be attached to the axiom. It may
signify, as in the Timæus, 86 D, that all vice arises from an

imperfect faulty bodily organization, an evil nature, and defects of education, public and private, which prevent men from seeing and following what is good. κακὸς μὲν γὰρ ἑκὼν οὐδείς· διὰ δὲ πονηρὰν ἕξιν τινὰ τοῦ σώματος καὶ ἀπαίδευτον τροφὴν ὁ κακὸς γίγνεται κακός. These vices of bodily constitution are explained to be the various bad humours which produce all sorts of diseases in the soul, generating ill-temper and peevishness and rashness and cowardice and forgetfulness and stupidity. (Of course these must be understood as mere hindrances, not as *insurmountable* obstacles to the attainment of virtue and good, otherwise what is here said would be absolutely irreconcileable with the passages quoted below from the Republic, X. and Laws, X. in which the entire freedom of the will in the choice of our path in life, of virtue and vice, is most explicitly affirmed.) And further, Tim. 87 A, "and besides all this...when the forms of government, and the doctrines current, and the language held in public and in private through our cities are all so bad, and the studies pursued by the young are by no means calculated to correct these influences, thus it is that from these two causes all those of us that are bad are made so most involuntarily."

Again it may be a deduction from the ethical theory that virtue is nothing but knowledge: and in this sense it stands doubtless in the Protagoras, which was written while Plato was still under the immediate influence of the teaching of Socrates, who as is well known from Xenophon Aristotle and and other authorities held this view of the nature of virtue. From this theory it follows at once as a necessary consequence that vice being mere ignorance is unintentional; "for," as Socrates himself says in Xenophon, Memor. III. 9, 4, "all choose out of the possible courses of action those which they think most advantageous to themselves, and neither can those who are acquainted with virtue and justice choose anything else in preference to them, nor can those who do not understand them act in conformity with them." In this sense the maxim is criticised and rejected by Aristotle, Eth. Nic. III. 7

(Bekk.), VI. 5 ult., Metaph. Δ. 29, 1025, a. 9, compare Magn. Moral. I. 1. 6. The criticism in one word amounts to this, that in pronouncing vice to be involuntary Socrates overlooked the freedom of the will; the ἀρχή of all moral action resides in ourselves; *until the habit has become confirmed*, and *then* perhaps vice may be said in a sense to be unintentional. Plato's opinion upon the subject, the connection of wisdom or knowledge and virtue, gradually underwent a change as his knowledge widened and his views became enlarged. In the Gorgias 495 D, ἀνδρεία is expressly distinguished from ἐπιστήμη, (with which it is identified in the Protagoras, and perhaps also the Laches,) and therefore from virtue in general; and in Meno, 98 D, E, the identity of virtue and φρόνησις is explicitly denied. Still he continued to maintain to the end of his career the inseparable union of the two, that virtue in the highest sense without philosophical insight was impossible. See especially the passage of the Phædo 68 B—69 D and the references given by Stallbaum in his valuable note on p. 68 C, in which he distinguishes three kinds or degrees of virtue recognised by Plato. The highest form of virtue based upon and springing from philosophical knowledge, and due in part to a happy organisation of body (compare the curious passage of Timæus, 86 D), and soul (Republic) is of course beyond the reach of vulgar mortals and cannot be imparted by precept or training *alone* (Meno) Rep. VII. 518 B, C. However, the freedom of the will in the determination of a man's conduct is most distinctly asserted in two remarkable passages of his latest works. Rep. X. 617 E, ἀρετὴ δὲ ἀδέσποτον, ἣν τιμῶν τε καὶ ἀτιμάζων πλέον καὶ ἔλαττον αὐτῆς ἕκαστος ἕξει. αἰτία ἑλομένου· θεὸς ἀναίτιος. And Laws X. 904 C, τῆς δὲ γενέσεως τὸ ποίου τινὸς ἀφῆκε ταῖς βουλήσεσιν ἑκάστων ἡμῶν τὰς αἰτίας. ὅπῃ γὰρ ἂν ἐπιθυμῇ καὶ ὁποῖός τις ὢν τὴν ψυχήν, ταύτῃ σχεδὸν ἑκάστοτε καὶ τοιοῦτος γίγνεται ἅπας ἡμῶν ὡς τὸ πολύ.

As regards the communicability of virtue, εἰ διδακτὸν ἡ ἀρετή, Plato's expressions in his earlier dialogues, particularly the Meno, are very various and puzzling, and might seem even to be contradictory. Writing late in life, he attributes the greatest importance to education in the formation of character. In the Timæus, p. 86 D, he says διὰ πονηρὰν ἕξιν τινὰ τοῦ σώματος καὶ ἀπαίδευτον τροφὴν ὁ κακὸς γίγνεται κακός, and again 87 B, ὧν (i.e. τῆς κακίας) αἰτιατέον μὲν τοὺς φυτεύοντας ἀεὶ τῶν φυτευομένων μᾶλλον καὶ τοὺς τρέφοντας τῶν τρεφομένων, προθυμητέον μὴν ὅπῃ τις δύναται καὶ διὰ τροφῆς καὶ δι᾽ ἐπιτηδευμάτων μαθημάτων τε φυγεῖν μὲν κακίαν τοὐναντίον δὲ ἑλεῖν. Another important passage on the nature and effect of education occurs in Legg. II. 653 A foll., which is however too long to quote. He seems in this to be speaking of virtue in its popular and ordinary sense, ἡ δημοτικὴ καὶ πολιτικὴ ἀρετή as he elsewhere calls it, not of the highest or philosophical form of it.

To reconcile the various and apparently conflicting expressions of Plato upon the subject of virtue and especially upon the possibility of imparting it, is a task of great difficulty, and I know not if I have anywhere seen it thoroughly and satisfactorily executed in detail. The distinction of philosophical and popular virtue which he recognised may go some way towards helping us out of the embarrassment; and perhaps the following account may in some degree represent his ultimate views upon the conditions of virtue and the possibility of teaching or imparting it. The Sophists by their unlimited professions of teaching virtue seem first to have raised the question whether it really could be taught. This *in their sense*, that is that it could be sown like a seed or planted like a tree and made to grow in any soil or under any conditions, is disproved in the Meno; compare Isocr. ἀντίδ. § 274: and especially the impossibility of transmitting virtue in the sense of skill and ability is shown by the failure of all the famous statesmen of Athens to impart it to their children, because we may fairly assume that they would have done so if it had been possible. The perfection of virtue requires first a happy natural organization even of

e 2

body, Tim. 86 D already quoted, and mind[1] (Republic); and
favourable antecedents, as of the form of government and
state institutions, virtuous parents and capable instructors.
Tim. u. s. 86, 87. In its *highest perfection* it cannot exist
without a full knowledge of the realities of things, and therefore requires a thorough philosophical training and insight
into truth (Phædo and Republic). Philosophy and education
it is true cannot impart virtue when no favourable conditions
of temper and knowledge exist. All that they can do in any
case is to encourage and stimulate, guide and direct the soul
in the pursuit of virtue, by diverting it from fleeting trans-
itory phenomena and things of sense, together with the
pleasures and passions which cling to this lower world of
phenomena, and so by raising it to the contemplation of
truth and reality and revealing to it the excellence of virtue
and real good, to inspire it with a passion and a desire to
attain to it. See Republic VII. and especially the passage
already referred to 518 B, C, D, foll. which seems to furnish
the key to the solution of the riddle of the Meno, by contrasting the pretensions of education—οἵαν τινὲς ἐπαγγελλό-
μενοί φασιν εἶναι. φασὶ δέ που οὐκ ἐνούσης ἐν τῇ ψυχῇ
ἐπιστήμης σφεῖς ἐντιθέναι, οἷον τυφλοῖς ὀφθαλμοῖς ὄψιν
ἐντιθέντες—with its true meaning office and capacity[2].

---

[1] Aristotle likewise admits this, at all events as far as the mind is concerned. To the attainment of complete virtue, or the perfection of character,
a certain εὐφυΐα, a happy constitution or natural capacity of mind, and probably of body too, is essential.

[2] Compare Dr Whewell's excellent observations upon the philosophical
meaning and purpose of the Meno, *Platonic Dialogues*, I. 255, 6. It is thus
briefly stated in the Introductory note upon the second title, p. 196: "the
conclusion, in which it is implied that the Virtue which does not involve
knowledge is not what the philosopher seeks." The same writer, p. 255, inti-
mates that the doctrines upon the connection of virtue and knowledge, which
the dialogue is really intended to convey, represent the opinions held by Plato
at this period, i. e. at the very early period of Plato's literary career, while he
was still under Socratic influences, to which Dr Whewell assigns it. But if
the opinions intended amount to nothing more than that true virtue must be
based on philosophical knowledge of the true and good and cannot exist with-

But, returning to the Gorgias, from which we have perhaps strayed too far away, all that seems to be meant *here*,
and generally in the later dialogues, by saying that those who
do wrong do it unintentionally is that as good is the universal aim, and moral good the only real good, when once a man
has acquired a knowledge of the true nature and excellence
of virtue it will exercise an overpowering attraction upon his
conduct, and he will be irresistibly impelled to the pursuit
of it; as upon the same principle it was argued in the conversation with Gorgias, p. 460 B, C, that those that have
learnt justice are just, and the just will always act justly; not
meaning that justice is nothing but knowledge and a kind of
skill to be acquired by teaching like any of the arts, nor
amounting like the Socratic doctrine to a total suppression
of the will, but implying merely that, as the will is in-
fluenced by motives, the good or virtue, which supplies an
overpowering motive, cannot fail to attract the enlightened
will and determine it to the pursuit of virtue.

And now we are brought to the final judgment and con-
demnation of the views of life and the course of conduct set
forth by Callicles as those which alone lead to happiness,
cc. 69—78. As the starting point and basis for this last stage
of the argument, Socrates first reminds his opposite, now no
longer his active opponent, that of the two varieties of modes
of dealing with body and soul all those that aim exclusively at
pleasure are to be rejected, and consequently that the object
of the genuine statesman must be to promote the good, that
is, the moral improvement, of the citizens, compared with

---

out it, we need not thus limit the period at which the author held them to the
early part of his life: the terms in which Dr Whewell describes these opinions,
in the sentences beginning "over against this stands the opposite opinion, &c."
present a most curiously exact parallel (considering that it is to all appearance
accidental) to the passage from the Republic, Bk. VII. quoted in the text, which
he does not refer to: and there can be no doubt that this must represent the
views entertained upon the question by Plato in the fully developed matu-
rity of his philosophical creed.

which every other service real or supposed that he can render them, as the acquisition of wealth power dominion, is
absolutely worthless. There is accordingly an art of Politics
in which the would-be statesman ought to be thoroughly
versed and his skill tested before he enters upon any public
duties; just as the state physicians, shipwrights, architects,
and so forth, are obliged to give some proof of their qualifications before they are entrusted with any public functions;
and this is in fact moral science or ethical philosophy,
which teaches what are the true objects and rule of life, and
by what means this moral improvement may be attained.
cc. 69, 70. Tried by this standard the shortcomings of
the Athenian statesmen, even the most famous of the past
ages, are brought to light. Their claim to admiration and
respect as statesmen must be estimated by the moral progress made by the citizens whilst under their care: without
this all mere external embellishments, all accession of power
wealth and splendour provided by their administration, weigh
as nothing in the balance. But it is precisely in this point
that their deficiences are most manifest. Even Pericles the
most celebrated of them all is acknowledged to have left the
citizens more lazy and garrulous and effeminate and greedy
than he found them by the system of fees that he was the
first to introduce. But just as we should charge a herdsman
or horsebreaker with utter ignorance of his business if the
animals which he received free from vice had learnt under
his hands to butt or kick or bite, so by the same rule a
statesman who is charged with the care and training of men
must be pronounced incompetent if the animals that *he* has
to deal with become worse under his management. And
this is shown by the conduct of the citizens themselves to
these their supposed benefactors. Cimon they ostracised;
Themistocles they treated in the same way, and banished to
boot; Miltiades narrowly escaped being thrown into the Pit;
and Pericles was found guilty of embezzlement and nearly
condemned to death. But had they been really trained in

justice and virtue they never could have been guilty of such flagrant ingratitude. cc. 71, 72. These men it is true were most skilful and able ministers to the city's vanity and ambition, which they pampered by providing her with docks fleets long walls and other such non-essentials, but they are no more entitled for this to the credit of genuine statesmanship than the baker the tavern-keeper or the cook can properly claim to fulfil the office of the trainer and physician in the development of the strength and comeliness and the maintenance of health in the body, c. 73: although, as popular approbation is no test of truth, the men who are the real authors of disease in the body corporate will very likely escape all censure from those whom they have corrupted, and all the blame will be thrown upon the advisers who are called in, like a physician in a fever, when the complaint has reached its crisis. However in any case it is just as absurd for a statesman to complain of the ingratitude of the citizens by whom he has been ill treated as it is for a sophist to accuse those whom he has proposed to educate in justice and virtue of cheating him of the fee that he has earned: for such ingratitude only shows that the work has not been properly done. c. 74. In fact the teacher of virtue is the only artist who can safely leave the remuneration of his services to the gratitude of those whom he has instructed; and this is why for this particular service, that namely which the Sophists proposed to render[1], for giving instruction in public and private virtue, the *previous* demand of a pecuniary compensation is condemned by public opinion, because in this case if the service is really performed the reward is certain. cc. 75, 76, to p. 520 E.

---

[1] Compare the well-known definition of these Professors and their profession in Aristotle, *de Soph. El.* 165 a, 21: ἔστι γὰρ ἡ σοφιστικὴ φαινομένη σοφία οὖσα δ' οὔ, καὶ ὁ σοφιστὴς χρηματιστὴς ἀπὸ φαινομένης σοφίας ἀλλ' οὐκ οὔσης, and 171 b, 25, foll. Sophistic in the latter passage is distinguished from the kindred arts and pursuits by two specific characters; 1. the mercenary object, and 2. the ostentatious exhibition of unreal knowledge or wisdom.

"The man convinced against his will Is of his first opinion still," says Hudibras: and it now appears that Callicles'
recent acquiescence has been a mere pretence; for upon being
asked by Socrates whether he still recommends the same
course of political conduct as before, he replies that he does.
c. 76.

The two directions of public life and conduct are now
finally contrasted. Socrates now claims to be the only man
in Athens, or nearly so, past and present who has true notions of what Politics are and what public duty means. Any
one however who like him really aims at the improvement
of his fellow-citizens must expect unpopularity, if not perse-
cution and death: he will be like a physician on his trial
before a jury of children to whom he has given much necessary pain in the course of his medical practice; all his pleas
of having acted for their advantage in what he did will be
set at nought or misunderstood; he will be accused (as Socrates actually was) of corrupting the young and slandering
the old, and his ultimate fate will not be doubtful. But
armed with the consciousness of his innocence he will fear
neither danger nor death: death is terrible to none but the
fool and the coward; the only real evil and the real object of
dread is injustice and wickedness, and to go with a soul laden
with crimes to the world below. cc. 77, 78.

The dialogue concludes with a myth in which the condition of the soul in the other world after its separation from
the body, together with the doctrine of a future judgment
and retribution, are represented in accordance with the current popular and traditionary belief. Then the true nature
of justice and injustice will be finally and fully revealed;
then when the soul is stript bare of all the adventitious accomplishments and worldly advantages, rank wealth splendour talents personal beauty, by which men's eyes are daz-
zled and her true condition disguised, when she stands thus
naked face to face before her Judge and all her corruption
and depravity is brought to light, then it will be the turn

of Callicles and those who with him have preferred wrong and injustice in this life to stand amazed and abashed, 'dizzy and open-mouthed,' in the presence of their Judge—like Socrates the philosopher before a human tribunal—and then they may chance to meet with the same insults that Socrates was threatened with by Callicles if he neglected the cultivation of rhetoric as an instrument of self-defence, whilst the philosopher who has "minded his own business and not meddled with other people's affairs" will be approved by the Judge and sent to dwell in the Isles of the Blest.

And so with a brief summary of the conclusions to which the argument has led them, and renewed exhortations to Callicles to abandon those views of life which have now been shown to be false and delusive, and to follow the path of duty which alone leads to true and abiding happiness, with a genuine Platonic simplicity which reminds us of the celebrated opening of the Republic, the conversation is brought to a close.

The myth of which the general moral purpose has been thus briefly expressed is one of four, or five if we include the Cosmogony of the Timæus, that occur in Plato's writings upon a similar subject, the condition of the souls of men in another state of being[1]. The immortality of the soul, which is necessarily involved in the doctrine of a retribution after death, is here assumed, not proved. These conceptions are invested with this fabulous character doubtless as conveying doctrines which agree indeed with the conclusions of a sound philosophy, and being based upon the inmost convictions of the human mind itself have existed in some form or other at all times and in all places, but cannot be made to rest on a scientific basis, and therefore may be allowed to assume this fanciful half-poetical shape, and to fall in with the traditions

---

[1] The myth of the Timæus should perhaps hardly be included amongst those which shadow forth the destiny that awaits men after this life. The passage that relates to this subject, 42 B, C, is very short and only incidental to the main subject.

of the mythologist and the fictions of the poet. The notions that they embody of a future state of retribution, happiness and misery, however they may have been acquired—whether derived from primeval tradition, or inherent in the human heart and conscience—were at all events current in Greece from the earliest period of which the records remain to us; they appear in the most ancient of her literary monuments, the Homeric poems.

The representation of the soul's future state assumes in accordance with the general scope and intention of the dialogue the most purely *moral* aspect in the myth of the Gorgias, and there is here little that is original in the scenery and concomitant circumstances of the judgment in the world below, these being derived with only slight alteration from the traditions of the Poets and Mythologists: it is mixed up with no cosmical speculations as in the Phædo and Republic, no physical theories or scientific calculations derived from Geometry Harmonics and Astronomy as in the Timæus, no metaphysical and psychological allegorizing as in the Phædrus, no Pythagorean or Orphic[1] metempsychosis as in the Phædrus Phædo and Republic. From these two points of difference an argument might be derived—if any such were necessary—for assigning an earlier period to the composition of the Gorgias than to the other four: but the whole dialogue is animated by a youthful spirit of fun, here and there, one might almost say, of levity; and not only the tone, but the matter and the mode in which it is dealt with, and the state of knowledge and progress in the development of the author's system which it presents—for example there is no hint of the Ideal Theory—all seem to imply that the writer was a comparatively young man, and to agree perfectly well with the date which has been determined by other considerations (see above p. lvi. note), the period, that is, intervening between Plato's return from his first travels in 395 B. C. and his first journey to Sicily in 389 B. C.

---

[1] See Renouvier, *Manuel de Phil. Anc.* I. p. 68, Bk. II. § I.

As to the degree of faith which Plato himself reposed in these representations of a future state, whether they are to be regarded as speculations, or traditions, or the natural and universal but indemonstrable convictions of the human conscience, his own somewhat contradictory expressions hardly enable us to pronounce with certainty. In the Gorgias, 523 A, he speaks of the story that he is going to tell as 'a true tale,' though Callicles will probably regard it as a mere myth, ὡς ἀληθῆ γὰρ ὄντα σοι λέξω ἃ μέλλω λέγειν. At the conclusion of it he expresses himself with less certainty, 527 A. "All this very likely seems to you to be a mere fable, like an old wife's tale, and you look with contempt upon it. And there would be no wonder in your doing so, if by any research we could find anything truer and better." And in the Phædo, 114 D foll., he says that no man of sense would maintain the exact truth of the description of the other world that he has been giving; still he thinks that such a state of things is in conformity with reason and what ought to be, and the probability of such reward of virtue and punishment of vice is sufficient for a man to stake his hopes of the future upon. And much the same kind of conviction of the general, though not particular, truth of such representations, as sufficient to determine a man's conduct in life, is expressed at the beginning and end of the myth of the Republic, 614 A and 621 C. From a comparison of these passages it seems that an inference may be drawn as to Plato's views upon the subject such as I have already intimated: that these doctrines harmonising as they do with the conclusions of philosophy as to the immortality of the soul, the aim and end of life, and the true nature of virtue and vice, and likewise with the universal popular belief upon the subject— see upon this a striking passage, Rep. I. 330 D, and compare Epist. VII. 335 A—may in some form or other be accepted as sufficiently certain to supply a solid ground of action: against the supposition that the particular mode of representation adopted is meant for the *literal reality*, the mythical form in which they are clothed, and the statements already quoted, Phæd. 114 D, Gorg. 523 A, seem expressly intended to guard. See the observations of Zeller on this subject, Phil. der Griechen, II. 266, and Brandis, Handbuch, II. 442, foll.: also Prof. Thompson's note in Butler's Hist. Phil. II. 246, whose interpretation of Plato's meaning appears to coincide exactly with my own.

On the foundation of the universal belief in a future state, the proofs of it, and the arguments derivable from it, see Cicero, Tusc. Quæst. I. 12—15.

OF the DRAMATIS PERSONÆ,

GORGIAS is a pompous and dignified but courteous old gentleman of about 75 or 80—as to the exact date of his birth the authorities vary; Clinton, Fast. Hell., sub annis 427 and 459, inclines to the year 485 B.C.; Foss, De Gorgia Leontino, and others place it five years later—with a great deal of simple and harmless vanity, fully alive to the splendour of his own reputation and the extent of his acquirements, of which he reminds us ever and anon in the course of conversation, but at the same time with a most gracious condescension for the ignorance and infirmities of his inferiors—that is, of all the rest of the world. He is treated with great respect by Socrates in consideration of his venerable age and distinction, and after a short conversation, in which he defends his art by the ordinary arguments and finally contradicts himself, is allowed to sink into a dignified repose, from which he only emerges for an instant whenever a *dignus vindice nodus* calls for the interposition of such a godlike personage. On the hypothesis which fixes the scenic date of the dialogue in the year 405 B.C. he is now staying at Athens on a *second* visit.

POLUS is his disciple and famulus, young hot and impetuous, νέος καὶ ὀξύς, forward and conceited to the very verge of presumption—extremely like Thrasymachus in the Republic, whose general views of life and conduct coincide pretty nearly with his own—and quite unable to understand a distinction or see a difficulty. He has caught all the graces and affectations of his master's new prose style, and has all Gorgias' ostentation without his courtesy and moderation in expressing himself. And so he plays his part[1].

---

[1] Of Polus' intellectual character and opinions something more has been said in the Introduction, pp. xxxvi. and xl. foll.

CHÆREPHON is the familiar and constant attendant of Socrates, whose pale face and slovenly exterior are so well known to us from Aristophanes' Clouds, where his manners habits and pursuits are caricatured for the amusement of the Athenian play-goers. His part in this dialogue is confined to a very few short sentences. In the Charmides, the only other of Plato's dialogues in which he is introduced, he is treated in the same way, and is little more than a κωφὸν πρόσωπον. All that we learn of him from that work is that he was of an eager and enthusiastic temper, which procures for him the epithet of μανικός.

The character of CALLICLES is much more fully exhibited to us, and is therefore of a more composite order than any of the preceding. He is a man of good family and position in Athenian society, which entitles him to look down with a very lofty scorn upon all professional people and mechanical occupations; see p. 512 C. He seems to be a young man from the half patronising politeness and affectionately derisive tone with which Socrates occasionally addresses him. His temper is ambitious; he regards honour and distinction and power as the highest good; thinks that a man's own advancement is the true object of life, and that this is to be sought at his country's expense by ingratiating himself with the governing mob and thus obtaining office and authority. As a means of attaining this end he vaunts the new art of Rhetoric, the artificer of persuasion, as the only study worthy of a man of sense; philosophy, the rival pursuit recommended by Socrates, he deems only fit for a child, as a training and preparation for the more serious business of public life. He is much clearer-headed and sharper-witted than the juvenile and half-educated Polus, though eventually he has to succumb to the irresistible cogency of the Socratic dialectics. He dislikes contradiction and defeat, and is apt to turn sulky and stubborn, as well as to have recourse to underhand subterfuges, (so Bonitz, op. cit. p. 267) when shown to be in the wrong, and always displays a good deal of petulance and a bold freedom sometimes almost amounting to effrontery. Finally he has imbibed either from his master Gorgias, or rather perhaps (for we have no evidence for the former supposition) from the Athenian freethinkers of the day[1]—see Rep. II. 358 E. foll., where the exposition of these doctrines is prefaced with a φασί,—the ethical theory that might is the only right, that a man's own interest and advantage is the only true end and rule of life, to which he gives expression in its most undisguised and offensive form and in the most uncompromising terms.

Lastly, SOCRATES is————the Platonic Socrates; perhaps the completest and most highly finished portrait in the entire range of dramatic literature of one of the most extraordinary men, hero, saint (saint after the fashion of the fifth century before Christ), philosopher, that ever dignified human nature and puzzled his contemporaries; and no where more graphically and skilfully represented than in this dialogue with all his odd peculiarities, his humour, his never-failing good-temper, his mock humility, his pretence of ignorance, his scrupulous politeness and affected deference for those whom he is all the while turning into ridicule, his 'irony' in a word—a term which as Aristotle hints took its special sense from these very peculiarities in Socrates' ordinary manner—lastly with his real heroism, his unyielding firmness and strength of resolution, and above all that gigantic intellectual power which enabled him as Xenophon says, (Memor. I. 2. 14) "to do just what he pleased with any body in argument."

This is not the place to enter into any details about the person manners and character of Socrates, which have been so often and so ably described by others, by none more ably

---

[1] The word φασί in the Republic is perfectly indefinite and we are not told whether it was any particular class of persons that held and propagated these doctrines; but all the evidence we have upon the subject induces me to believe that they were originated by one of the Sophists, the Freethinkers of the day in religion and morals, Protagoras or Thrasymachus or others, one of whom actually states the theory as I have endeavoured to show, whilst it agrees perfectly with the known opinions of Protagoras and others of the early Sophists.

than by Mr Grote, Hist. of Greece, Vol. VIII. 68, and I will therefore only add one single observation; what must be thought of the genius of the writer who could place such a character in all its strength so fully and vividly before us that the Socrates of two thousand years ago is to us as one whom we have seen and heard and conversed with? who has presented the scenes in which he always plays the principal part with such perfect liveliness and fidelity that we seem ourselves to be looking on and listening to the argument as it turns and winds through its devious course, and find it hard to believe that such a drama as the Phædo, or the Symposium, or the Phædrus, or the Gorgias, is after all nothing but a fiction, and a 'Philosophical Dialogue'?

PLATO'S GORGIAS.

Callicles. THIS is the time, they say, Socrates, to come p. 447 c. 1. in at a fight and a fray[1].

Socrates. What? are we come at the tail of a feast, as the saying is, and too late?

Cal. Yes indeed, and a very dainty feast it was. For Gorgias has just been treating us to a fine long declamation.

Soc. Aye but for *that*, Callicles, my friend Chærephon here is to blame, because he forced me to stay loitering in the market-place.

Chærephon. No matter, Socrates: as I was the cause so I'll find the cure. For Gorgias is a friend of mine, and therefore he'll declaim for us, if you like at once, or if you prefer it by and by.

Cal. How's that, Chærephon? Is Socrates anxious to hear Gorgias?

Chær. To be sure, that's precisely the object of our being here.

Cal. Well then if you please to come home to my house— For Gorgias is staying with me, and he'll favour you with one of his addresses.

Soc. Thank you, Callicles. But do you think he wouldn't mind *conversing* with us? for I want to learn from the

---

[1] *Henry IV.* Part I. Act IV. Sc. 2, v. 74.

Fal. Well,
To the latter end of a fray and the beginning of a feast
Fits a dull fighter and a keen guest.

1

What Socrates wants us to know

gentleman what is the real meaning of his art, and what it is that he professes to teach. The rest of his address he may deliver, as you say, at some future time.

Cal. There's nothing like asking him, Socrates. That in fact was one of the points in the address that he gave us. At all events he invited just now every one of the present company[1] to ask him any question he pleased, and he said he was ready to answer them all.

Soc. I am so glad to hear it. Ask him, Chærephon.

Chær. Ask him what?

Soc. Who he is.

Chær. What do you mean?

Soc. Why suppose he had been a maker of shoes, he would have answered, I presume, that he is a shoe-maker. You understand what I mean, don't you?

c. 2.   *Chær.* I understand, and will ask him the question. Tell me, Gorgias, is it true, as Callicles here says, that you profess to answer any question that may be put to you?

448   *Gorgias.* Quite true, Chærephon; in fact, that was the very profession that I was making just now, and I tell you that for many years nobody has ever yet asked me any new question.

Chær. Then I presume you find no difficulty in answering, Gorgias.

Gor. You may try the experiment if you please, Chærephon.

Polus. Yes, 'egad, and upon me too, if you like, Chærephon. For I am afraid Gorgias must be quite tired by the long speech which he has just been delivering.

Chær. How say you, Polus? do you think that you can answer better than Gorgias?

[1] τῶν ἔνδον ὄντων. The dialogue opens in the street where Socrates and Chærephon, who are hurrying from the market-place to Callicles' house to see the distinguished foreigner, meet Callicles and his party who are just quitting it. Upon Callicles' invitation they turn back together: and the words τῶν ἔνδον ὄντων show that they are supposed by this time to have reached the house, where the rest of the dialogue is carried on.

Pol. And pray what does that matter, if I do it well enough for you?

Chær. Not at all. Well then, since such is your wish, answer me.

Pol. Ask away.

Chær. I will. If Gorgias had been master of the same art as his brother Herodicus, what name would it have been proper to give him? Would it not have been the same as the other?

Pol. No doubt it would.

Chær. Then in calling him a physician we should have given him his right name.

Pol. Yes.

Chær. And if he had been skilled in the art of Aristophon son of Aglaophon, or his brother (Polygnotus), what would it have been proper to call him?

Pol. Plainly a painter.

Chær. And as it is, what is the art in which his skill lies? and what would be the proper name to give him in consequence?

Pol. Chærephon, there are many arts amongst mankind from experiences experimentally invented : for it is experience that makes our days proceed by rule of art, the want of it by chance: and in each of these men participate various in various variously, the best of them in the best: of whom in fact Gorgias here is one, and so is a member of the noblest of all professions[1].

---

[1] This is no caricature, as Dr Whewell (*Platonic Dialogues,* II. 171), who adopts Mr Grote's views about Plato's relation to the early Sophists and their followers, insinuates: it is a literal quotation from Polus' *Art of Rhetoric.* The first clause is quoted by Syrianus, *Schol. ad Hermog.* ap. Spengel, *Art. Script,* p. 87; and the second by Aristotle, *Metaph.* A. 1. It appears probable from the former passage that these were the words with which the work commenced. It is characterised by the symmetrical and highly artificial structure which Gorgias introduced into his prose compositions, and even reproduces another of his peculiarities in the use of the poetical word αἰῶνα for βίον. It displays besides a rhetorical figure, of which Polus seems to have been him-

c. 3.   *Soc.* Rarely indeed to all appearance, Gorgias, is Polus provided for making speeches; still however he is not fulfilling his promise to Chærephon.

Gor. What in particular, Socrates?

Soc. He doesn't seem to me exactly to answer the question put to him.

Gor. Well then, if you please, do *you* ask him.

Soc. Not if you wouldn't mind answering yourself, but I should much prefer asking you. For it is plain to me even from what Polus has already said, that he has studied rather what is called the art of rhetoric, than that of (dialectical) conversation.

Pol. How so, Socrates?

Soc. Because, Polus, when Chærephon asks you what art Gorgias is master of, you pronounce an eulogium upon his art, just as if any one found fault with it; without answering what it is.

Pol. Why, didn't I answer that it was the noblest of all?

Soc. Yes indeed you did. But no one asked you what sort of art Gorgias' was, but what, and by what name Gorgias ought to be called; just as Chærephon traced out the line for you before, and you answered him fairly and in few words, so now in the same way tell us what the art is, and what we are to call Gorgias. Or rather, Gorgias, do you tell us yourself what *is* the art you are master of, and what we are to call you in consequence.

449

Gor. The art of rhetoric, Socrates.

Soc. Are we then to call you a rhetorician?

Gor. Aye a good one, Socrates, if you please to call me what 'I boast myself to be,' as Homer says.

Soc. Well, I will with pleasure.

Gor. Then pray do.

self the inventor: for the reduplication of the words ἐμπειριῶν ἐμπείρως, and ἄλλοι ἄλλων ἄλλως, is doubtless an exemplification of the διπλασιολογία which Plato, *Phædr.* 267. B...mentions as having been treated of by Polus in his art.

Soc. So then are we to say that you have the power of making others besides yourself the same?

Gor. Yes, I certainly make this profession, not only here but elsewhere as well.

Soc. Would you then be good enough, Gorgias, to finish the conversation in the way in which we are now talking together, in alternate question and answer, and lay aside that lengthy style, in which Polus just began, for a future occasion? Come now, keep your promise, and don't disappoint me; but consent to answer briefly the questions put to you.

Gor. There are some answers, Socrates, which are obliged to express themselves at great length: not but that I will do my best to make them as short as possible. For in fact this again is one of the things that I lay claim to, that no one could ever express the same meaning in fewer words than myself.

Soc. That's exactly what we want, Gorgias. This is precisely what I should like you to give us a specimen of, your short style; your lengthy one you can reserve for some future time.

Gor. Well, I will do so; and you shall say that you never heard any one use fewer words.

Soc. Come then. Since you say that you are master c. 4. of the art of rhetoric, and can make any one else an orator —what of all things is it that rhetoric deals with? as weaving for instance is employed upon the production of clothes; isn't it?

Gor. Yes.

Soc. And music, again, upon the composition of tunes?

Gor. Yes.

Soc. Faith, Gorgias, I *do* admire your replies. You are indeed answering in the very fewest possible words.

Gor. (*Complacently.*) Yes, and I think I do it very tolerably well, Socrates.

Soc. You are perfectly right. Come, then, answer me

in the same way about rhetoric again; what *are* the things
to which its knowledge is applied?

Gor. To words.

Soc. To what sort of words, Gorgias? Do you mean those
that point out by what course of treatment the sick may
recover their health?

Gor. No.

Soc. Then rhetoric does not deal with all words.

Gor. Certainly not.

Soc. But still it makes men able to speak.

Gor. Yes.

Soc. And to understand what they talk about as well?

450   *Gor.* Of course it does.

Soc. Well, but doesn't the art we were just now speaking of, medicine I mean, make men able to understand as
well as to speak about the sick?

Gor. Necessarily.

Soc. Then medicine too, it seems, deals with words?

Gor. Yes.

Soc. Those which are about diseases?

Gor. Precisely.

Soc. Well and doesn't the gymnastic art too deal with
words, those namely which relate to the good and bad condition of bodies?

Gor. Certainly.

Soc. And moreover the case is the same, Gorgias, with
all other arts besides: each of them deals with words—
those, that is, that belong to the thing which is the object of
each particular art.

Gor. So it appears.

Soc. Then why in the world don't you call all the rest
of the arts rhetorical, when they are about 'words,' if you
give the name of rhetoric to every one which deals with
words?

Gor. Because, Socrates, in all the other arts the knowledge is, so to speak, entirely confined to manual operations

and such like actions, whereas in rhetoric there is no such manual process involved; but of all that it does and all that it effects words are the vehicle. That is why I claim on behalf of rhetoric that it is the art that deals with words; and I maintain that I am right.

Soc. I wonder whether I quite understand what sort c. 5. of art you mean to call it? (Never mind.) I shall know better by and by. Pray now answer me. We have such things as arts, haven't we?

Gor. Yes.

Soc. But of all these arts, some I believe have production for their chief object, and require few words—some indeed none at all; in fact, the objects of the art might be carried out even in silence; such as painting and sculpture and many others. That is the kind which you seem to have in view, when you say that rhetoric has no connection with them. Isn't it?

Gor. You take my meaning perfectly, Socrates.

Soc. But other arts there are which perform all their operations by means of words, and as to acts, require either none at all, as one may say, in addition, or only in a very trifling degree; such as numeration for example, and reckoning, and land-measuring, and draughts, and a number of other arts, some of which have their 'words' pretty nearly equal in amount to their actions, most of them indeed more numerous; or even altogether their processes are carried on and their effects produced entirely by means of words. It is to this class, I believe, that you understand rhetoric to belong.

Gor. Quite true.

Soc. But I don't at all suppose that you mean to call any one of these rhetoric, although this *was* implied by the expression you used, in saying that the art whose effects are produced by words is rhetoric; and one might suppose if one chose to be captious in arguing, so then you mean arithmetic by rhetoric, do you, Gorgias? But I don't believe you

do mean either arithmetic or geometry when you speak of
rhetoric.

451   *Gor.* And quite right too, Socrates; your supposition is
perfectly just.

c. 6   *Soc.* Then let us begin at once, and do you do *your* part
in dispatching the answer to my question. For as rhetoric
is found to be one of those arts which chiefly employ words,
and there are others also of the same kind, try to explain
to me what it is in words upon which rhetoric operates in
producing its effects; suppose, for instance, any one were
to ask me about any one you please of the arts I just now
mentioned—what is the art of numeration, Socrates? I should
tell him, as you said just now, that it is one of those that
produce their effects by words. And if he were further to
inquire, what are those about? I should say that it is one
of those which are about (have for their object) the even
and odd, the whole series of each of them, whatever the number may amount to. And if again he were to ask, And
reckoning, what art do you call that? I should reply that
this likewise is one of those that effects all its operations by
words. And if he were to ask still further, what is its object? I should say, in the language of the framers of bills
drawn for the assembly, 'in all else' the art of reckoning
is 'like the foregoing';' for its object is the same, the even
and the odd; but there is just this amount of difference between them, that the art of reckoning or arithmetic takes
into consideration the relative as well as the absolute properties and relations of the even and the odd in point of
number. And if the same question were repeated about

---

1 This refers to the formula employed when a προβούλευμα of the Council
was altered and modified in the general assembly. It was open to any citizen
when a measure was sent down by the former body to the latter for its rati-
fication, either to oppose it by a counter-proposition, or, accepting some of its
provisions, to add others of his own, or to cancel or alter such as he dis-
approved. In the latter case, to avoid repetition, the proposed ψήφισμα usually
commenced with the words τὰ μὲν ἄλλα καθάπερ τῇ βουλῇ ἔδοξε.

astronomy, and upon my replying, that this again effects all
its processes by words, the questioner were to say, And what
are the 'words' (calculations, the science) of astronomy about,
Socrates? I should tell him that they are about the motion
of the stars and the sun and moon, that is to say, their
relative velocities.

Gor. And you would be quite right, Socrates.

Soc. Come then, in your turn, Gorgias. It so happens,
you see, that rhetoric is one of those arts that effect and
give force to all their operations by words. Isn't it?

Gor. It is so.

Soc. Then tell me what they deal with. What of all
things in the world is that which is the object of the words
which rhetoric employs?

Gor. The most important of all human things, Socrates,
and the best.

Soc. Nay, Gorgias, here again what you say is open to c. 7.
question, and by no means clear as yet. For I think you
must have heard at parties after dinner people singing this
catch, in which in the words of the song the good things of
this life are enumerated, how that health is best of all, the
second best thing is to be born handsome, and the third, as
the author of the catch says, to be rich without fraud.

Gor. To be sure I have; but what is your object in
mentioning this?

Soc. Because those whose business lies in all those things 452
that the composer of the catch spoke so highly of would
straightway present themselves, physician and training-master
and tradesman; and first of all the physician would say,
My dear Socrates, Gorgias is deceiving you: for it is not his
art that is employed upon mankind's greatest good, but mine.
If then I were to ask him, And who are you that say this?
he would reply probably, A physician. What say you then?
Is it your art that has the greatest good for its object? How
can health, Socrates, he would say very likely, be anything
else? What greater blessing *can* men have than health?

And if again after him the trainer were to say, I should be surprised too myself, Socrates, if Gorgias can point out to you any greater good in his own art than I in mine; I should make answer to him again as to the other, And who may *you* be, my friend, I should like to know? and what's *your* business? A professor of gymnastics, he would say; and my business is to make men strong and handsome in their persons. And next to the training-master the tradesman, I dare say, would tell us with a lofty scorn of them all, Do pray consider, Socrates, whether you think that there is any blessing superior to wealth, either in the eyes of Gorgias or of any one else whatsoever. We should say to him accordingly, What's that pray? are you the man that makes that? He would say yes. And what's *your* name? A man of business. How then? do you judge wealth to be the greatest blessing to mankind? we shall say. Of course I do, he will reply. Aye, but Gorgias here contends that his own art is the source of greater good than yours, we should say. Plainly then his next question would be, And what is this good? let Gorgias make answer. Come then, Gorgias, consider yourself to be questioned by them as well as me, and answer us what is that which *you* say is the greatest good to mankind, and that you can produce it.

Gor. That, Socrates, which really is the greatest good and the cause at once of freedom to men in general in their own persons, and no less to the individual man of acquiring power over others in his own city.

Soc. What name then pray do you give to this?

Gor. The power of persuading by words, I should call it, the judges in a court of law, or the councillors in a council-room, or the assembly men in an assembly, or any other kind of meeting which is convened for a public purpose. And yet (in spite of all you have said) by the aid of this talent you may make the physician your slave, and the trainer your slave: and for your famous man of business, it will turn out that *he* makes his money for somebody else and not for himself, but _for you who_ have the power of speaking and gaining the ear of the multitudes.

Soc. Now, Gorgias, I think you *have* come very near c. 8. to an explanation of what you understand by the art of rhetoric, and, if I at all enter into your meaning, you define 453 rhetoric to be the artificer of persuasion, and you say that / its entire business and the whole sum and substance of it results in this. Or have you any power to mention that rhetoric possesses beyond that of producing persuasion in the minds of the hearers?

Gor. None at all, Socrates; your definition seems to me to be sufficient; this *is* no doubt the sum and substance of it.

Soc. Then listen to me, Gorgias. I flatter myself, you may be quite sure, that if there be any one else[1] in the whole world that engages in a discussion from a genuine desire to know just what the argument is about and no more, *I* too am one of that sort; and I make no doubt that you are another.

Gor. Well, what then, Socrates?

Soc. I'll tell you directly. What your view is of the exact nature of the persuasion produced by rhetoric, and of the subjects to which it is applied, I assure you I by no means clearly understand; though at the same time I have a kind of suspicion of what I suppose you to mean by it, and what it deals with. Still I will ask you nevertheless what you *do* mean by the persuasion that proceeds from rhetoric, and what are the objects on which it is exercised.

---

[1] The word 'also,' just like the Greek ἄλλος, with which it may be etymologically connected, as well as 'other' 'the rest' and so on, are frequently found in the best English writers where they are redundant or involve a logical and grammatical inconsistency. I have elsewhere quoted *Macbeth*, 'Of all men else I have avoided thee.'

The explanation of this logical blunder, and the false grammar which expresses it, in the two classes of idioms in which it appears in Greek, I reserve for a more appropriate occasion than that which is offered by the notes to a mere translation.

Now why when I have a suspicion about the matter myself am I going to ask you instead of myself stating it?
It is not on your account (not to refute or annoy you),
but for the sake of the argument, that it may proceed in
such a way as may make the subject of our conversation
most clear to us. For see now if you don't think I am
right in repeating my question. Take a parallel case. If
my question had been, to what class of painters does Zeuxis
belong? had you replied, he is a figure-painter, would it
not have been quite fair in me to ask you, what sort of
figures he paints, and on what occasions?

Gor. Quite so.

Soc. And is not the reason this, that there are besides
him other painters employed upon a number of other figures?

Gor. Yes.

Soc. But if no one else were a painter but Zeuxis,
your answer would have been right enough?

Gor. Of course it would.

Soc. Well then tell me about rhetoric in the same
way; whether it is your opinion that rhetoric is the only
art that produces persuasion, or others besides it. What
I mean is something of this sort: when any one teaches
anything, does he persuade in teaching it? or do you think
otherwise?

Gor. Certainly not, Socrates; on the contrary, he most
assuredly does persuade.

Soc. And again, if we apply our question to the same
arts as we mentioned just now, does not numeration, or the
man conversant with that science, teach us all the properties
of number?

Gor. Yes, no doubt.

Soc. And so likewise persuades?

Gor. Yes.

Soc. Then numeration also is an artificer of persuasion?

Gor. It seems so.

Soc. So then if we are asked what kind of persuasion

and what about, we shall reply I presume, that which conveys instruction, which deals with the amounts of all 454 the odd and even numbers. And we shall be able to show that all the rest of the arts that we were just now referring to are artificers of persuasion, and what that is, and what it is about. Shan't we?

Gor. Yes.

Soc. It follows that rhetoric is not the only artificer of persuasion.

Gor. True.

Soc. Since then it is not the only one that effects c. 9. this object, but others besides it, we should be entitled next to put a further question to the speaker, as we did in the case of the painter, What sort of persuasion then is it of which rhetoric is the art, and what is that persuasion about? You think it would be fair, don't you, to put such a further question?

Gor. Oh, yes.

Soc. Answer me then, Gorgias, since you agree with me in this view.

Gor. Well then I mean that kind of persuasion, Socrates, which is exercised in law-courts and any other great crowds, as indeed I said just now; and it is about everything that is just and unjust.

Soc. I had a suspicion myself, to tell you the truth, Gorgias, that that was the kind of persuasion you meant, and that those were its objects: but that you may not be surprised if I ask you by and by some such question as seems to be quite clear, though I repeat it—for, as I say, I do so in order that our argument may be brought regularly to a conclusion; not on your account (for the pleasure of annoying or refuting you), but that we may not get into the habit of snatching up an over-hasty conclusion as to one another's meaning founded on a mere guess, but that you may state your views as you think fit according to your own notions.

Gor. Indeed, Socrates, in my opinion you are doing quite right.

Soc. Come then, let this be the next thing we examine. There is such a thing as what you call 'to have learnt'?

Gor. There is.

Soc. And again 'to have believed'?

Gor. Oh, yes.

Soc. Do you think then to have learnt and to have believed, and learning and believing, are the same thing, or something different? ·

Gor. Different, *I* should think, Socrates.

Soc. And quite right too: and you may be sure of it from this. If you were asked, Is there such a thing, Gorgias, as false as well as true belief? you would say yes, I presume.

Gor. I should.

Soc. But again, is there false as well as true knowledge?

Gor. Certainly not.

Soc. To be sure, because it plainly appears a second time that they are not identical[1].

Gor. True.

Soc. But still those that have learnt are persuaded, as well as those that have believed.

Gor. It is so.

Soc. Would you have us then assume two forms of persuasion, the one conveying belief without knowledge, the other knowledge?

Gor. Yes, by all means.

Soc. Then which of the two kinds of persuasion is it that rhetoric effects in law-courts or any other large assemblies on the subject of right and wrong? Is it that

---

[1] In this sentence γάρ has reference to Gorgias' decided οὐδαμῶς. 'You deny it so readily and so positively, *because*, here again, by this second process (αὖ), it is quite plain that they are not the same.'

which gives rise to belief without knowledge, or that from which knowledge springs?

Gor. Plainly, of course, Socrates, that which gives rise to belief.

Soc. Rhetoric then, it seems, is an artificer of persuasion 455 productive of belief but not of instruction in matters of right and wrong.

Gor. Yes.

Soc. Nor consequently is the rhetorician qualified to instruct law-courts or any other large masses of people on questions of right and wrong, but only to persuade them. For surely he never could be able to instruct such a great crowd in things of such importance in a few minutes.

Gor. Certainly not.

Soc. Come, then, let us see what we do actually mean c. 10. by rhetoric: for to tell you the truth, I can't yet distinctly make out even myself what my own opinion is. Whenever the city holds a meeting for the election of state-physicians or shipwrights or any other class of craftsmen, will not on such occasions the rhetorician refrain from offering his advice? plainly because in every election we are bound to choose the most skilful practitioner. Or, again, as to the building of walls, or the construction of harbours or docks, it is not he that will give advice, but the master-builders. Or, again, when advice is to be given upon the election of generals, or the disposition of troops to meet an enemy, or the occupation of military positions, on such occasions it is the military men that will advise, and not the rhetoricians. Or what say you, Gorgias, to such cases? For as you profess to be a speaker yourself and to qualify others for speaking, it is right to learn your opinion upon the matters of your own art. So pray suppose that *I* am acting now with a view to your interests. For very likely one of the present company here may be desirous of becoming a pupil of yours—as in fact I think I see some, and I dare say a good many—who perhaps might be ashamed to trouble you with repeated

questions. And so when I repeat mine, suppose yourself to
be questioned by them as well. What good shall we get,
Gorgias, by frequenting your society? On what subjects shall
we be able to offer advice to the city? is it about right and
wrong alone, or all those things besides which Socrates was
just now mentioning? Try then to give them an answer.

Gor. Well, Socrates, I will try to reveal to you clearly
the entire force and meaning of rhetoric : in fact you pointed
out the way very well yourself. You know, I presume, that
yonder docks and walls, the pride of your city[1], and the
construction of your harbours, are due to the counsels of
Themistocles, and partly to those of Pericles, but not to the
masters of the several crafts.

Soc. So I am told, Gorgias, of Themistocles; *Pericles* I
heard myself when he gave us his advice about building
the 'middle wall[2].'

456 ⟋ *Gor.* And so you see, Socrates, that wherever there is an
⟋ election of such officers as you were just speaking of, it is
the orators that give advice, and carry their opinions in
such matters.

Soc. It is exactly because I was so surprised at this that
I have been asking ever so long what the virtue of rhetoric
can possibly be. For regarded in this light its grandeur
and importance appear to me to be something quite supernatural.

Gor. Aye, if you knew all, Socrates, how it embraces

---

[1] On the difference between τὰ νεώρια καὶ τὰ τείχη τὰ 'Αθηναίων and τῶν
'Αθηναίων, see Stallbaum's note.

[2] τὸ διὰ μέσου τεῖχος is the interior or southern of the two 'long walls,'
of 40 stadia each, which connected Athens with the Piræus. A third wall,
shorter than the 'long walls,' of 35 stadia, led to the harbour of Phalerum.
The 'middle wall' was built last of the three, in 457 B.C., during the administration of Pericles. It is called by Æschines, *de Fals. Leg.* τὸ νότιον τεῖχος—
the exterior of the two μακρὰ τείχη being styled by way of distinction τὸ
ἔξωθεν, or τὸ βόρειον τεῖχος. Thuc. I. 107, 108, II. 13, with Arnold's note;
Thirlw. *Hist. of Greece*, III. 62, and note, 1st Ed. ; Grote, *Hist. of Greece*, Vol.
v. p. 440, VI. 26; and the article 'Athens' in Smith's *Dict. of Geography.*

under it every kind of power, as one may say. I will give
you a convincing proof of it. I myself have often ere now,
in company with my brother (Herodicus), or any other
physician, gone into the house of one of their patients, and
upon his refusing to take their medicines, or to submit to be
operated upon either by the knife or the cautery, when the
physician failed to persuade him, I succeeded, by the aid
of no other art than that of rhetoric. And I maintain too
that if a physician and a rhetorician went together into any
city you please, supposing they had to argue out the question before a general assembly or any other kind of meeting
which of the two was to be elected, orator or physician,
the latter would be totally extinguished (totally eclipsed, altogether distanced), and the able speaker elected if he chose.
And if the contest lay between him and the master of any
other craft you please to name, the rhetorician would carry
his own election sooner than any one else whatever: for
there is no subject in the world on which the rhetorician
could not speak more persuasively than the master of any
other art whatsoever, before a multitude. Such then is the
extent and such the quality of the power of this art. We
are bound however, Socrates, to employ rhetoric in the same
way as every other kind of exercise. For in fact all other
exercises are not to be employed against every body indis-
criminately merely because a man has become such a pro-
ficient in boxing and wrestling or the use of arms as to have
the advantage over friend and foe: this does not entitle him
to knock his friends down or stab or assassinate them. No
by my faith, nor again if any one were to frequent a
wrestling-school until he had got his body into prime condition, and become an expert pugilist, and then go and strike
his father and his mother or any other of his relations or
friends, would that be any reason for conceiving an aversion
to trainers and fencing-masters, and expelling them from our
cities. For they no doubt gave their lessons to these pupils
of theirs with a view to the proper employment of them

2

against enemies and wrong-doers, in self-defence, not aggres-
457 sion: whereas the others pervert their strength and their
art to an improper use. Yet it does not follow that the
teachers are rogues, nor that their art is either to blame
for all this, or bad in itself; but those that misuse it, in my
opinion. For it is true that the orator is *able* to speak against
every body and upon every question in such a way as to find
greater acceptance with all large assemblies, on any subject
in a word he chooses. But he is none the more entitled on
that account to rob either the physicians of their due credit,
because he could do it if he liked, or artists of any other
kind; but he is bound to use his rhetoric fairly, like skill in
any other exercise. But it seems to me that, supposing a
man to make himself a rhetorician and then to use this
faculty and this art to commit wrong, it is not the teacher
that ought to incur odium and to be banished from our cities.
For he gave his lessons to be turned to a fair use, but the
other perverts them. It is therefore he that abuses the art
that may fairly be held in aversion and banished or put to
death, and not the teacher.

c. 12   *Soc.* I believe, Gorgias, that you like myself have had a
good deal of experience in arguments, and in the course of
them have arrived at the discovery of something of this sort,
that it is no easy matter for people to come to any definite
agreement upon any questions they may have undertaken to
discuss, and after giving and receiving instruction so to bring
the conversation to an end; but on the contrary, if a dispute
arises between them upon any point, and the one declares
that the other expresses himself either incorrectly or indistinctly, they get angry, and suppose that what is said proceeds from jealousy of themselves, from a spirit of mere
rivalry, and not from a wish to sift the question proposed for
discussion. And in fact occasionally this results at last in
the most indecent scenes, in mutual abuse and recrimination
of such a kind that even the bystanders are vexed on their
own account that they ever condescended to listen to such a

set of fellows. What then is my motive in saying this? It is because your present statements don't seem to me quite consistent or in harmony with what you said at first about rhetoric. Now I am afraid to refute you, for fear you should suppose that I speak with a disputatious object, not with a view to throw light upon the subject under discussion, but aiming at you personally. Now if you are one of the same 458 sort of persons as I am myself, I should be glad to continue my questions, but if not, I would rather let it alone. And what sort of person am I? I am one of those that would be glad to be refuted when I assert[1] anything that is untrue, and glad to refute any one else supposing he fall[1] into any error; but just as glad to be refuted as to refute, because I consider it a greater benefit, in proportion as the benefit is greater to be delivered oneself from the greatest evil than to deliver another. For I think that there is no evil that can befall a man so great as a false opinion upon the subjects which we now have under discussion. Now if you as well as myself profess yourself to be one of this sort let us go on with the conversation: but if on the other hand you think we had better drop it, let us at once dismiss it and break off the argument.

Gor. Nay, Socrates, I myself like you pretend to be one of that sort of persons whose character you are sketching: perhaps however we ought also to have consulted the convenience of the company present. For to say the truth, for some time before you came I had been delivering a long address to our friends here, and now again if we go on with our discussion we shall very likely protract it to a considerable length. We ought therefore to consider their inclina-

---

[1] Observe here the politeness of Socrates. In speaking of his own liability to error he uses the indicative mood, making a definite and positive supposition, and assuming the probability of the occurrence. In speaking of a similar infirmity in others the optative is substituted for the indicative, implying the uncertainty of the event, and avoiding the assertion that such a thing is at all likely to happen. There is the same distinction in our own language between the indicative and subjunctive after 'if.'

tions as well as our own, and not to detain them when they may be wanting to do something else. (*Sensation*).

c. 13   *Chær.* You hear yourselves, Gorgias and Socrates, the applause of our friends there, how anxious they are to hear any thing you have to say. For my own part however, God forbid that I should ever be so busy as to give up an argument so important and so well treated because I preferred doing anything else.

Cal. Yes, by my faith, Chærephon. And indeed for myself, though I have been present ere now at plenty of discussions I don't know that I ever in my life was so much gratified as on the present occasion; and therefore as far as I am concerned, if you choose to go on talking all day long you will do me a favour.

Soc. Well you may be sure, Callicles, there is nothing to prevent it on my part, if Gorgias consents.

Gor. After this Socrates, it would indeed be a shame for *me* to hang back, when I myself challenged the company to ask me any question they pleased. But if our friends here are of this mind, go on with the conversation and ask me what you like.

Soc. Then let me tell you, Gorgias, what surprises me in the words you used: to be sure I dare say you are right and it is I that misunderstand you. You say you are able to qualify any one for speaking who chooses to become your pupil.

Gor. Yes.

Soc. Does that mean then that he is qualified to gain the ear of a crowd on any subject, not by way of instruction but persuasion?

459   *Gor.* Just so.

Soc. You said just now if I mistake not that in sanitary matters too the orator will be more persuasive than the physician?

Gor. I certainly did, in a crowd that is to say.

Soc. Well and doesn't 'a crowd' mean the ignorant? for

surely amongst the well-informed he wont carry more weight than the physician?

Gor. Quite true.

Soc. And so if he is to be better able to persuade than the physician, he becomes better able to persuade than the man of real knowledge?

Gor. Yes certainly.

Soc. Not being a physician though, is he?

Gor. True.

Soc. But one who is not a physician is unversed I presume in the art of which the physician is master.

Gor. Plainly so.

Soc. It follows then that the ignorant man will be more persuasive among the ignorant than the man of real information, supposing the orator to be more persuasive than the physician. Does this follow, or any thing else?

Gor. In *this* case no doubt it does.

Soc. And so likewise in respect of all the rest of the arts the case is the same with the orator and with rhetoric; there is no occasion, that is to say, for them to be acquainted with the things themselves, but it is enough for them to have discovered some instrument of persuasion which may enable them to present the appearance to the ignorant of knowing better than the well informed.

Gor. Well and isn't it a great comfort, Socrates, without learning any of the other arts, but with this one alone, to be at no disadvantage in comparison with the professional people?

Soc. Whether the rhetorician is or is not at a disadvantage with the rest of the world by reason of this state of things [or, in consequence of this character, these qualifications of his] we will examine by and by, if we find that our argument requires it; but just at present let us consider this first, whether the rhetorician stands in the same relation to what is just and unjust and base and noble and good and bad, as to what is wholesome and the several objects of all the

other arts; that is to say, that he is ignorant of what is good
or bad or honourable or disgraceful or just or unjust, in itself,
but has devised the means of persuasion about them, so as
with no knowledge at all to get the credit amongst the
ignorant of knowing better than the man of real knowledge?
Or is this knowledge absolutely required? and must any one
who means to learn rhetoric be prepared with all this before
he comes to you? or if not, shall you the master of the art
give one who does come no instruction at all in these
matters—for it's no business of yours—but make him in the
eyes of the vulgar *seem* to know things of this kind when he
doesn't, and *seem* to be good when he isn't? or will you be
altogether unable to teach him rhetoric unless he have a
previous acquaintance with the truth in these matters? or
460 what are the real facts of the case, Gorgias? Do in heaven's
name, as you said just now, draw aside the veil and tell us
in what the virtue of rhetoric really does consist.

Gor. Well I suppose, Socrates, if he does not know all
this already I shall have to teach him this as well.

Soc. Hold there (don't say any more), for that is well
said. If you make a man a rhetorician he must needs.be
acquainted with what is just and unjust either beforehand, or
afterwards from your instructions.

Gor. Just so.

Soc. How then? one who has learnt the art of building
is a builder, isn't he?

Gor. Yes.

Soc. And so one who has learnt music a musician?

Gor. Yes.

Soc. And one who has studied medicine a physician?
and so on for all the rest upon the same principle; every one
who has studied any particular subject acquires that character which is imparted to him by the knowledge of it?

Gor. No doubt.

Soc. And so likewise by the same rule one that has
learnt justice is a just man?

Gor. Most undoubtedly.

Soc. But the just man it is to be presumed does just things.

Gor. Yes.

Soc. So then must the rhetorician needs be a just man, and the just man desire to act justly ?

Gor. Yes, so it appears.

Soc. Consequently the just man will never desire to do wrong.

Gor. Necessarily.

Soc. And it follows from what we said that the rhetorician must be a just man.

Gor. Yes.

Soc. Consequently the rhetorician will never desire to do wrong.

Gor. No, it seems not.

Soc. Then do you remember saying a little while ago c. 15 that we have no right to find fault with the training masters nor expel them from our cities if a boxer makes an unfair use of his boxing and does wrong ? and so in like manner if an orator employs his rhetoric unfairly, we are not accuse the teacher or expel *him* from the city, but the man that does the wrong and misuses his rhetoric ? was that said or not ?

Gor. It was.

Soc. But now it appears that that very same person, the rhetorician, never could have been guilty of any wrong at all, doesn't it ?

Gor. It does.

Soc. And at the beginning of our conversation, Gorgias, it was stated that rhetoric deals with words, not words about even and odd numbers, but about what is just and unjust; wasn't it ?

Gor. Yes.

Soc. Well I supposed at the very time when you made that remark that rhetoric never could be an unjust thing,

when all the speeches that it makes are about justice; but,
461 when you told us shortly after that the orator might make an
unjust use of his rhetoric, *then* I *was* surprised, and thinking
that the two assertions did not harmonize with one another I
said what I did, that if you thought it like myself an advantage to be refuted it was advisable to continue the conversation, or if not to let it drop: and now that we afterwards
come to examine the point, you see yourself that we are come
again to the conclusion that it is impossible for the rhetorician to make an unjust use of his rhetoric or consent to do
wrong. Now to sift this matter thoroughly and satisfactorily
to make out what the exact truth of it may be, by the dog,
Gorgias, is a thing not to be done in a short interview.

c. 16　　*Pol.* How's that, Socrates? is that your real opinion
about rhetoric that you are now stating? Or do you suppose
because Gorgias was ashamed not to admit that the rhetorician is acquainted with justice and honour and good, and if a
pupil come to him without knowing all this that he will
teach it himself—and then from this admission there followed
I dare say some slight inconsistency in the expressions he
used—just what you are so fond of, when it was you yourself
that turned the conversation upon questions of that sort[1]?

---

[1] In the foregoing sentence, if ὅτι is rendered 'because,' as it probably
should be, there is an anacoluthon. Stallbaum in his 3rd ed. supposes that
Polus means to deny that there *is* any inconsistency, and therefore thinks that
the anacoluthon resides in the change of συμβῆναι, which should follow οἴει,
into συνέβη: and that the note of interrogation should be removed after διδάξειν
and a comma substituted. As I believe that the supposition upon which this
rendering is based is incorrect, I prefer following the Zurich Editors and retaining the note of interrogation. The entire sentence down to ἐρωτήματα is
irregular; and this irregularity is very likely meant to express, as Stallbaum
conjectures, the impetuosity and precipitation by which Polus' language is characterised. I have rendered it as if the apodosis were wanting after οἴει ὅτι.
This would naturally be, 'think you because......that this is really his opinion,
and that you have any right to triumph over him!' and this is implied in what
follows. If ὅτι is rendered 'that,' the meaning is, 'or rather, think you,
that...' i.e. don't you rather think that. Heindorf's version is 'an (quod res
est) pudore deterritum Gorgiam putas...' which is tantamount to the preceding.

For who do you think is likely to deny either that he is acquainted with justice himself, or can teach it to others? Nay, it is very unmannerly (ill bred, bad taste in you) to turn the conversation upon such things as these.

Soc. Well to be sure, fairest Polus, it is precisely for this reason that we provide ourselves with friends and children that as soon as the advance of age has made our footing uncertain you youngsters may be there to set our life on its legs again in word as well as in deed. And now if Gorgias and I are making any false step in our argument there you are to set us right again : indeed you are bound to do so. And I on my part am ready if you think any of our conclusions are wrong to retract any one of them you please, provided only you do me the favour (μοι) to observe just one thing.

Pol. What thing do you mean ?

Soc. To keep that discursive style of yours in check, Polus, which you made the attempt to indulge in at first.

Pol. How? Mayn't I be allowed to say as much as I please ?

Soc. It would indeed be hard upon you, my admirable friend, if you were to have come to Athens, where there is the greatest freedom of speech in all Greece, and then *you* were to be the only person there who was debarred from it. But just set my case against yours. If you make a long speech and refuse to reply to my questions, wouldn't it be equally hard upon me not to be allowed to go away and not listen to you ? No, no, if you have any regard for the argu- 462 ment we have been holding and want to set it right again, as I said just now take back any thing you please, and in your turn questioning and questioned, like myself and Gorgias, refute or submit to refutation. For you claim to be acquainted with all that Gorgias knows, I believe, don't you ?

Pol. Yes to be sure I do.

Soc. Then I suppose you like him invite people on all occasions to put any question to you they like as one that knows how to find an answer?

Pol. No doubt I do.

Soc. Well then *now,* either put the questions or answer them, whichever you like.

c. 17   *Pol.* Well, so I will. Answer me then, Socrates. Since you seem to think that Gorgias is at a loss about rhetoric, what do you say it is yourself?

Soc. Do you ask me what art I say it is?

Pol. Yes I do.

Soc. None at all, it seems to me, Polus, to tell you the exact truth.

Pol. Well what do you take rhetoric to be then?

Soc. A thing which you tell us in the work that I lately read gave rise to art.

Pol. What *thing* do you mean?

Soc. I mean a kind of acquired habit (or 'routine,' *Cousin*).

Pol. So you take rhetoric to be an acquired habit?

Soc. Yes I do—if you have no particular objection.

Pol. A habit of what?

Soc. Of the production of a sort of gratification and pleasure.

Pol. Well and don't you think rhetoric a very fine thing, to be able to oblige one's fellow creatures?

Soc. Hallo, Polus, have I told you yet *what* I say it is, that you think yourself entitled to ask what follows that, whether I don't think it very fine?

Pol. Why, haven't you told me that you call it a sort of habit?

Soc. Will you please then, since you set such a high value on 'obliging,' to *oblige* me in a trifling matter?

Pol. To be sure I will.

Soc. Ask me now what art I take cookery to be.

Pol. I ask you then, what art is cookery?

Soc. None at all, Polus.

Pol. Well what is it? tell us.

Soc. I tell you then, a sort of habit.

Pol. Of what? let us hear.

Soc. What *I* say is, of the production of gratification and pleasure, Polus.

Pol. Do you mean to say then that cookery and rhetoric are the same thing?

Soc. Oh dear no, but a branch of the same kind of pursuit.

Pol. What pursuit do you mean?

Soc. I fear it may be somewhat rude to say the truth: for on Gorgias' account I am reluctant to speak out, for fear he should suppose that I am satirizing his professional pursuits. At the same time whether this *is* the kind of rhetoric 463 that Gorgias practises, I really don't know; for in fact from our argument just now we arrived at no distinct notion of his views on this matter. But what *I* mean by rhetoric is a branch of a particular set of things which have nothing 'fine' about them at all.

Gor. What is it, Socrates, pray let us know; don't hesitate on my account.

Soc. It seems to me then, Gorgias, to be a sort of pur- c. 18 suit not scientific at all, but of a shrewd and bold spirit, quick and clever in its dealings with the world. And the sum and substance of it I call flattery [coaxing or wheedling]. Amongst a great number of branches of this kind of study one in particular I take to be cookery: which has indeed the appearance of an art, but according to my view is no art, but a habit and a knack. Of this I call the art of rhetoric a branch, as well as that of dressing and adorning oneself and of sophistic, four branches of it applied to four varieties of things. If then Polus wishes to make any inquiry, let him do so: for he has not yet heard which sort of branch of flattery I pronounce rhetoric to be; but without observing that I have not yet answered that question, he goes on to ask further whether I don't think it a very fine thing. But I wont answer him whether I think rhetoric a fine thing or a foul one until I have first made answer what it is. For it is not fair, Polus: but if you want to learn (what my opinion is), ask me what kind of branch of flattery I pronounce rhetoric to be.

Pol. I ask you then, and do you answer me, what kind of branch?

Soc. I wonder whether you will understand me when I *do* answer. Rhetoric is according to my view the unreal image (counterfeit presentment) of a branch of Politics.

Pol. Well then, do you say it is a fine thing or a foul one?

Soc. A foul one, I should say, for all bad things I call foul; since I *must* answer you as though you already understood my meaning.

Gor. No upon my word, Socrates; why I myself don't understand what you say either.

Soc. Like enough, Gorgias, for I have not yet explained myself distinctly; but Polus (Colt) here is so young and hot.

Gor. Well never mind him; but tell *me* what you mean by saying that rhetoric is the unreal image of a branch of Politics.

Soc. Well I will try to tell you what rhetoric appears to me to be: and if I am wrong Polus here will refute me. There is such a thing I presume as what you call body and soul?

464   *Gor.* Of course there is.

Soc. And in these again you believe that there is a good condition of each?

Gor. To be sure I do.

Soc. And again, an apparent but not real good condition? Take a case like the following: there are many that appear to have their bodies in good condition in whom it would not be easy for any one but a physician or one of your professors of gymnastics to discover that they are not so.

Gor. Quite true.

Soc. Something of this sort I say there is in body and in soul, and that is what makes the body and the soul *seem* to be in good condition when they are not really so never-theless.

Gor. It is so.

Soc. Let me see then if I can explain my meaning more c. 19 clearly to you. Two classes of things have I say two arts corresponding to them; that which has the soul under its direction (or, that which is applied to the soul) I call Politics; and though for that which has charge of the body I can't find you just on the spur of the moment any single name, still the care of the body is one and has as I reckon two divisions, the one gymnastics and the other medicine. In Politics against gymnastics I set legislation, and as the counterpart to medicine I assign justice. In each of these pairs, how-ever, medicine and gymnastics, justice and legislation, there is a good deal of intercommunication seeing that they deal severally with the same objects; yet still there is a difference between them. Well then of these four, which always have the highest good the one of the body the other of the soul in view in their treatment of them, the art of flattery takes note, and I don't say with a full knowledge but by a shrewd guess divides herself into four branches, and then smuggling herself into the guise of each of those other divisions pre-tends to be that of which she has assumed the semblance, and cares not one jot for what is best, but with the bait of what is most agreeable for the moment angles for folly and deludes it to such a degree as to get the credit of being something of the highest value. • And so I say cookery has assumed the disguise of medicine, and pretends to the knowledge of the kinds of food that are best for the body, so that if a cook and a physician had to go through a contest before a set of boys, or men as silly as boys, to de-cide which of the two understood the subject of good and bad kinds of food, the physician or the cook, the physician would die of starvation. • Now *I* call it flattery, and I say that 465 such a thing as this is base and contemptible, Polus—for now I am addressing you—because it aims solely at what is agreeable without considering what is best: and an art I do *not* call it but a habit, because it can render no account of the exact nature of the things which it applies, and so cannot tell the cause of any of them. But to nothing which is irrational can I give the name of art. If you contest any of

c. 20 these points I am ready to stand an examination. Now as I say cookery has taken the disguise of medicine, and the art of dressing in just the same way that of gymnastics, a knavish and cozening and ignoble and illiberal art, cheating people so by the aid of forms and colours and polish and dress as to make them in the endeavour to assume a borrowed beauty neglect the native and genuine beauty which comes by gymnastics. However not to be tedious, I will state the thing like the geometers—for by this time I dare say you will be prepared to follow me—as the art of dressing is to gymnastics so is cooking to medicine: or rather thus, as dressing to gymnastics so is sophistic to legislation, and as cookery to medicine so is rhetoric to justice[1]. However as I say, though such is the natural distinction between them, still, as these arts are so nearly allied, sophists and rhetoricians and the things with which they deal are a good deal jumbled

---

[1] The 'justice' here spoken of is the *principle* of δίκη ἐπανορθωτική or διορθωτική, remedial or corrective, one of the branches of Political Justice, which governs the decisions of courts of law; see c. 34. p. 478 A. It redresses the disturbed balance of society, heals the diseases which injustice and wrong have introduced into the body corporate, and so corresponds to medicine which operates similarly upon the individual human body. Of this rhetoric, which pretends to maintain the right and redress wrong, is the spurious and counterfeit copy, the unreal unsubstantial image (εἴδωλον).

The other branch of Political Justice is the distributive kind, δίκη διανεμητική. This assigns to every citizen his due position and rights, functions and authority, in the society of which he is a member. A third variety is distinguished from these two by the author of the fifth book of the *Nicomachean Ethics*. This he calls τὸ ἀντιπεπονθὸς ἐν ταῖς ἀλλακτικαῖς κοινωνίαις, c. 8. It establishes a due proportion in the transactions of barter or exchange, or more generally, is the regulating and controlling principle of commercial morality. It seems to me to be a mere variety of 'distributive justice' understood in its widest sense.

together, and they don't know either themselves what to
make of their own profession, or any body else what to make
of them. ⌐For in fact, if it were not the soul that had the
control of the body, but the latter were its own master, and
so cookery and medicine were not surveyed and distinguished by it, but the body itself were the judge, weighing
and estimating them by the gratifications that they procure
for it, the state of things described in the saying of Anaxagoras
would prevail far and wide, my dear Polus—for you understand these things—every thing would be jumbled together
in a mass (there would be an universal chaos) and things
sanitary and wholesome and the cook's sauces and condiments
undistinguishable. ⌐You have heard now what I affirm rhetoric to be, the counterpart of cookery in the soul corresponding to that in the body. Now perhaps I have done
rather an odd thing in expatiating at such length myself
when I refused to let *you* make a long speech. However I deserve to be excused; for when I spoke in short
sentences you didn't understand me, nor could you make any
use of the answer I then gave you, but required a detailed
explanation.   Now if I on my side don't know what to
make of any of your answers you may expatiate in your 466
turn, but if I can make good use of it, let me do so : for that
is fair.   And now if you can make any thing of this answer
of mine, there it is for you.

   Pol.   What say you then ? Do you take rhetoric to be a c. 21
sort of flattery ?

   Soc.   Nay I said a *branch* of flattery. Why, have you
no better memory at *your* age, Polus ? What will you do by
and by ?

   Pol.   Then is it your opinion that good orators are
esteemed worthless in their cities as flatterers ?

   Soc.   Is that a question you are asking, or the beginning
of a speech ?

   Pol.   A question to be sure.

   Soc.   Then I don't think they are *esteemed* at all.

Pol. How not esteemed? Are they not all-powerful in their cities?

Soc. No, if at least you mean that power is a good to its possessor.

Pol. Why of course I mean that.

Soc. Then it seems to me that the orators have of all citizens the least power.

Pol. How? Don't they like tyrants put to death any one they please, or strip of his property or banish from their cities any one they think proper?

Soc. By the dog, Polus, I am really quite in doubt at every word you say whether you are making an assertion yourself and delivering your own opinion, or asking me a question.

Pol. Why I'm asking you to be sure.

Soc. Very good, my friend: and then do you ask me two questions at once?

Pol. How two?

Soc. Didn't you say just now something of this sort, that the orators put any one they please to death, like the tyrants, or rob of his money, or banish from their cities any one they think proper?

Pol. Yes I did.

c. 22   *Soc.* I tell you then that these questions of yours are two, and I will give you an answer to both. For I maintain, Polus, that the orators and the tyrants have the smallest possible power in their cities, as I said just now; for they don't do anything at all that they desire, so to speak: however I admit that they do anything that they think best.

Pol. Well and isn't that great power?

Soc. No, at least according to what Polus says.

Pol. *I* say no? I beg your pardon, I say yes.

Soc. No by—indeed you don't, for you said that great power is a good to its possessor.

Pol. Well and so I do.

Soc. Then do you think it a good for a man to do any-

thing he thinks best, supposing he has no understanding?
and do you call *that* great power?

Pol. No not I.

Soc. Then you must prove to me that the orators are
men of understanding, and that rhetoric is an art, and not a 467
mere flattery, and so refute me. But if you leave me un-
refuted, your orators who do what they think proper in their
cities, and your tyrants, will find no advantage in *that*, if
indeed power is as you say a good, and doing what one
thinks fit without understanding you too admit to be an
evil. You do, don't you?

Pol. Yes I do.

Soc. Then how can orators or tyrants have great power
in their cities unless Socrates be forced by Polus to own that
they do what they desire?

Pol. Here's a fellow—

Soc. I say they don't do what they desire—There now,
refute me.

Pol. Didn't you admit just before that they do what
they think best?

Soc. Well and so I do now.

Pol. Why then they do what they desire.

Soc. I say no.

Pol. What? whilst they do what they think fit?

Soc. Yes.

Pol. This is abominable, Socrates, quite monstrous.

Soc. Don't be abusive, most polite Polus, to address you
in your own style[1]: but if you have any question to put to
me prove that I am wrong, or if not answer yourself.

---

[1] Polus' ' own style' has been already partially exemplified at p. 448 c.
He was a disciple of Gorgias and had adopted the rhetorical figures introduced
by the other into prose composition, which he disfigured by the lavish excess to
which he indulged in them. See further on this subject, *Journal of Classical
and Sacred Philology*, No. VII. pp. 69—72, where these figures are classified
and illustrated. ὦ λῷστε Πῶλε is referred by Plato to the class ταρίσωσις, as
we may see from the similar example in *Symp.* 185 c, where Παυσανίου παυ-

Pol. Well I will answer, to find out what really you do mean.

c. 23   *Soc.* Is it your opinion then that people in doing any thing on any occasion desire simply what they do [i.e. the means to their end] or that which is the object of their doing what they do? As in the case of patients for instance who take medicine prescribed by the physicians, think you they desire merely what they do, to swallow the medicine and suffer pain, or that, health to wit, which is the object of their taking it?

Pol. Plainly health, which is the object in taking it.

Soc. And so with foreign merchants or those that are engaged in any other branch of trade, what they *desire* is not what they are habitually doing; for who desires to incur all the risk and trouble of a voyage? what they desire I presume is that which is the object of their voyage, wealth: for it is for wealth they undertake it.

Pol. Yes certainly.

Soc. And isn't the same true in all other cases? If a man do any thing for an object, he doesn't desire that which he does, but that which was his object in doing it?

Pol. Yes.

Soc. Well then, is there any thing existing that is not either good or bad or indifferent, neither good nor bad?

Pol. Most decidedly, nothing, Socrates.

Soc. Well do you call wisdom and health and wealth and every thing else of that sort good, and the opposites of these bad?

Pol. Yes I do.

Soc. And by things neither good nor bad do you mean
468 things like these, such as sometimes partake of the nature of the good and sometimes of the bad and sometimes of neither, as sitting for example and walking and running and sailing,

σαμένου is afterwards described as ἴσα λέγειν. It would however usually be regarded as a case of παρομοίωσις or παρήχησις, or the subordinate variety παρονομασία.

or again things such as stones or sticks or any thing else of that sort? These are what you mean, are they not? or is there any thing else to which you give the name of neither good nor bad?

Pol. No, these are what I mean.

Soc. Do people then do these indifferent (intermediate) things when they do them for the sake of the good, or the good for the sake of the indifferent?

Pol. The indifferent for the sake of the good to be sure.

Soc. Consequently it is in pursuit of good that we either walk, when we do walk, because we think it better for us, or, the contrary, stand still, when we do stand, with the same object, the good, don't we?

Pol. Yes.

Soc. And so likewise don't we put a man to death if we ever do such a thing, or banish him, or deprive him of his property, because we think it is better for us to do it than not?

Pol. Yes no doubt.

Soc. So then it is for the sake of what is good that people do all these things that do them.

Pol. I allow it.

Soc. Well but didn't we admit that when we do things c. 24 with an object in view we don't desire those things, but that which is the object of our doing them?

Pol. Quite so.

Soc. Then we don't desire to massacre people or expel them from our cities or rob them of their money merely in the abstract, but if these things are advantageous we desire to do them, but if mischievous we do not. For we desire what is good, as you allow; but what is neither good nor bad we do not desire, nor what is bad, do we? Do you think what I say is true, Polus, or not? [*a pause*]. Why don't you answer?

Pol. (*Sulkily.*) True.

Soc. Well then admitting this, if a man puts any one to

death or expels him from the city or strips him of his property, whether he be tyrant or orator that does it, because he thinks it is better for him, when it is really worse, *he* I presume does what he thinks fit, doesn't he?

Pol. Yes.

Soc. But does he also do what he desires, supposing these things to be bad for him?—Why don't you answer?

Pol. No, I don't think he does what he desires.

Soc. Can it be said then that such an one has great power in that city, if great power means something good according to your admission?

Pol. It can not.

Soc. I spoke the truth then in saying that it *is* possible for a man to do what he pleases in a city and yet not to have great power nor to do what he desires.

Pol. Just as if you, Socrates, would not choose to have the liberty of doing what you please in your city rather than not, and don't envy a man when you see one that has either put some one to death or robbed or imprisoned him because he thought proper to do so.

Soc. Do you mean justly or unjustly?

469 *Pol.* Whichever it be, is it not enviable either way?

Soc. Hush, hush, Polus.

Pol. Why so?

Soc. Because we musn't envy the unenviable nor the miserable, but pity them.

Pol. What? Is this your opinion of the condition of the men that I speak of?

Soc. How can it be otherwise?

Pol. Then do you think a man who puts any one he pleases to death if he does it justly is wretched and an object of pity?

Soc. No I don't; but not enviable either.

Pol. Didn't you say just now that he was wretched?

Soc. Nay I said if he did it unjustly, my friend, and an object of pity into the bargain; but if justly, unenviable.

Pol. Oh no doubt a man who is put to death unjustly is pitiable and wretched.

Soc. Less so than the author of his death, Polus, and less so than one who deserves to die.

Pol. In what way pray, Socrates ?

Soc. In this, that to do wrong is the greatest of all evils.

Pol. What ? *this*.the greatest ? is not to suffer wrong a greater ?

Soc. No by no means.

Pol. Would you prefer then suffering wrong to doing it ?

Soc. I should *prefer* neither for my own part; but if I were obliged either to do wrong or to suffer it I should choose suffering rather than doing it.

Pol. Then I suppose you wouldn't accept despotic power ?

Soc. No, if you mean by despotic power the same as I do.

Pol. Well *I* mean what I said just now, to have the liberty of doing anything one pleases in one's city, the power of death or banishment or, in short, doing anything according to one's own will and pleasure.

Soc. My worthy friend, let me tell you something and c. 25 then when it comes to your turn to speak you may criticise it. If in a crowded market[1] I were to take a dagger under my arm, and whisper to you, Polus, I have just come into possession of quite a despotic power, perfectly amazing; for if I think fit that any one of those men that you see there should die this instant, he'll be a dead man, any one of them I please ; or if it seems to me that any one of them ought to have his head broken, it'll be broken on the spot, or to have his coat torn in two, it'll be done : so great is my power in this city— If I say on finding you incredulous I were to show you

---

[1] ἐν ἀγόρᾳ πληθούσῃ is not used here as a note of time to signify the forenoon; but, as in Thuc. VIII. 92, it denotes simply the crowded state of the market-place. See Arnold and Poppo's *Notes.*

my dagger, you would say probably when you saw it, why, Socrates, at this rate every body would have great power, for in this fashion any house too you please might be set on fire, aye and the Athenian docks as well and their men of war and all their other vessels public as well as private. But surely *this* is not the meaning of having great power, to do anything one pleases. Do you think it is?

Pol. No certainly not, in that way.

470   *Soc.* Can you tell me then why you disapprove of power of this kind?

Pol. Yes I can.

Soc. Why is it then? say.

Pol. Because punishment is the inevitable consequence of doing such things as that.

Soc. And is not punishment a bad thing?

Pol. To be sure it is.

Soc. And so, my fine fellow, you have come round again to the opinion that great power is a good provided the doing what one pleases be accompanied by some advantage in doing it, and that this alone really is great power; otherwise it is a bad thing and mere weakness. And next let us consider *this* point. We admit, don't we, that it is sometimes better to do such things as we were just speaking of, to put men to death or banish them or deprive them of their property, and sometimes not?

Pol. Yes certainly.

Soc. Well then, it seems, you and I agree in admitting this.

Pol. Yes.

Soc. Then when do you say it is better to do them? Tell me where you draw your line?

Pol. Nay, Socrates, do *you* answer this same question yourself.

Soc. Well then I say, Polus, if you prefer hearing it from me, that it is better to do these things when they are done justly, and when unjustly then worse.

Pol. Very hard[1] indeed it is to refute you, Socrates. c. 26
Why, couldn't any child prove you to be in the wrong?

Soc. Then I shall be very much obliged to the child,
and equally so to you, if you refute me and deliver me from
my absurdity. Pray now don't shrink from the trouble of
doing a friend a kindness, but refute me.

Pol. Why really, Socrates, there is no occasion to go
back to stories of old times to refute you; for the events of
only the other day[2] are quite enough to prove you in the
wrong and to show that many wrong doers are happy.

Soc. What are they?

Pol. You see I presume that the famous Archelaus son
of Perdiccas is king of Macedonia?

Soc. Well if I don't, I *hear* of it at any rate.

Pol. Do you take him then to be happy or wretched?

Soc. I don't know, Polus, for I haven't the honour of his
acquaintance.

Pol. How's that? Do you mean to say you could dis-

---

[1] Polus' irony is here directed against the opinion which prevailed amongst
the friends of Socrates that it was impossible to refute him.

[2] 'Only the other day' really means eight years ago. The dramatic date
of the dialogue is fixed by the passage 473 E, πέρυσι βουλεύειν λαχὼν κ.τ.λ. in
the year 405 B.C., and Archelaus usurped the throne of Macedonia in 413. Stallbaum's arguments (*Introd.* pp. 56—72) are quite conclusive in favour of the
year 405, and against an earlier date. He is also very fairly successful in
explaining away all the historical references, such as the present passage,
which seem to clash with this supposition. But it may reasonably be doubted
whether it is worth while to bestow any great amount of pains and labour upon
such an attempt. All great writers of fiction such as Shakespeare and Walter
Scott allow themselves great licence in this particular; and I strongly suspect
that Plato was no more careful to avoid such lapses than his literary brethren.
This seems to me to be proved by the great difficulty which is almost invariably
found in fixing the dramatic date of any of his dialogues, arising partly from
the numerous inconsistencies and historical inaccuracies which we seldom fail to
find in them. These most easily escape detection on the part of the author
and the reader, both of them having their attention occupied with more
important matters; a fact which seems to show how slight and excusable such
blemishes are in a work of fiction; at all events, how little they interfere with
the real interest of this kind of composition.

cover it by making his acquaintance? Dont you know without that at once (or, instinctively, Heind.) that he is happy?

Soc. No by my faith I don't.

Pol. Then it's plain, Socrates, that you will say that you don't *know* that the great king is happy either.

Soc. And if I do I shall say the truth : for I don't know what is his condition in respect of his mental cultivation and moral character[1].

Pol. How then? does happiness consist solely in this?

Soc. Yes according to my view, Polus : for an honest man or woman I say is happy, and one that is unjust and wicked miserable.

471　　*Pol.* Then according to your account the great Archelaus is miserable?

Soc. Yes, my friend, if he is unjust.

Pol. Why of course, how can he be otherwise? He had no claim whatever to the throne which he now occupies, being the son of a woman (Simiche) who was the slave of Perdiccas' brother Alcetas, and in strict justice was Alcetas' slave; and if he had desired to do what was right he would have been the slave of Alcetas and happy according to your account. But now it is really amazing how miserable he has become, for he has done the most enormous wrong. First of all he invited this very same master and uncle of his to his court as if he meant to restore to him the dominions of which Perdiccas robbed him, and after entertaining him and his son Alexander, his own cousin, about the same age as himself, and making them drunk, he stowed them away in a carriage, carried them off by night, murdered them both and made away with them. And after all this wickedness he never discovered that he had made himself the most miserable of men, nor repented of what he had done, but he did not choose to make himself happy by bringing up as he was bound to do his brother the legitimate son of Perdiccas, a

---

[1] Cicero, *Tusc. Disp.* v. 12, renders this, quam sit doctus, quam vir bonus.

boy of about seven years old, to whom the throne came by right, and restoring to him his kingdom, but shortly after he threw him into a well and drowned him, and then told his mother Cleopatra that he had tumbled in as he was running after a goose and so come by his death. Doubtless therefore now as he is the greatest criminal in Macedonia he is the most miserable of all the Macedonians, and not the happiest, and I dare say there are a good many people in Athens, with yourself at their head, who would rather take the place of any other Macedonian whatever than that of Archelaus.

Soc. I complimented you before at the beginning of our c. 27 conversation, Polus, upon your being as it seemed to me so admirably instructed in the art of rhetoric, though at the same time I thought you had somewhat neglected the dialogue. And so now, this is the famous argument, is it, with which any child could refute me? and this is the sort of talk by which in your opinion I now stand convicted when I assert that the wrong doer is not happy? How can that be, my good friend? And yet I don't admit a single word you say.

Pol. No because you won't; for I'm sure you think as I say.

Soc. My dear creature, that's because you try to refute me in rhetorical fashion, as they fancy they do in the law courts. For there indeed the one party is supposed to refute the other when he brings forward a number of respectable witnesses in support of any statements he happens to make, whilst the opponent produces only a single one or none at all. But refutation of this kind is absolutely worthless for the purpose of 472 ascertaining the truth: for it may even happen sometimes that a man may be overborne by the false witness of numbers and apparent respectability. And now if you want to bring forward *witnesses* to prove that I am wrong on the points you speak of, you will find nearly every body, Athenians and foreigners, agree with you. You may have for witnesses Nicias, if you please, son of Niceratus with his brothers,

whose tripods are standing in a row in the Dionysium, or if
you please Aristocrates son of Scellias, the donor of that
splendid offering again at Delphi[1], or if you like, the whole
house of Pericles or any other family you choose to select
out of those of this place. But I, alone as I stand here,
refuse to admit it: for you can't convince me, but you try by
bringing forward a number of false witnesses against me to
dispossess me of my substance[2] and of the truth. But for
my part, if I don't produce yourself for one as a witness in
confirmation of what I say, I think I have effected nothing
of the least importance in advancing the object of our discussion; nor you either I think, unless I singly and alone bear
witness in your favour, and you leave all the rest of those
people entirely out of the question. This then is one kind of
proof, as you and a good many others besides you imagine it
to be; and there is also another which I on my side deem to
be such. Let us then compare them together and see if we
shall find any difference between them. For in truth the

(margin note: majority*)*

---

[1] This is one of the passages which has been supposed to disagree with the
date 405 B.C. assigned as the dramatic date of the dialogue: and even Schleiermacher who adopts it conceives that Nicias and Aristocrates, who died in 413
and 406 respectively, are spoken of as living witnesses, and that this is therefore an anachronism. I have already expressed my belief that Plato thought
little of historical consistency in writing his dialogues; but in the present
instance we are not driven to any such supposition. Ast has pointed out that
it is the evidence of the *monuments* that is here appealed to. *They* testify
to the wealth and splendour of those who dedicated them, and also to their
opinion upon the advantages of such things by the desire they evince for the
perpetuation of the memory of them. They are "the bricks" in short "that be
alive to this day to testify" to their regard for worldly advantages. In fact,
unless this *were* Plato's meaning, there could be no conceivable reason for mentioning their offerings at all.

[2] This is what I may call the 'received' translation of οὐσία, which of
course has a double meaning 'property' and 'reality' or real truth. It is open
however to the objection of being too technical in its philosophical sense. The
Aristotelian 'substance' was unknown to the Platonic terminology. I believe
the lawyers have a word 'realty' or 'realties,' used as an alternative for real
property. If so, this I think would render the original better, as coming much
nearer to the Platonic conception of οὐσία; though from its technicality I have
hesitated to introduce it into the text.

subject we are debating is one of by no means slight importance, nay it is one might almost say that on which to know
is noblest and not to know most disgraceful : for what it all
amounts to is, either to know or to be ignorant who is a
happy man and who is not. First of all for instance, to take
the particular point we are now discussing, *you* conceive it
possible for a man to be happy in wrong doing and in wickedness, supposing that you think Archelaus to be a wicked
man and yet happy. Are we not to suppose that this is
your opinion ?

Pol. Yes certainly.

Soc. And I say it's impossible. Here is one point on c. 28
which we differ. So far so good. But will then a man be
happy in wrong doing if he be overtaken by justice and
punishment ?

Pol. No, by no means ; in that case he would be most
miserable.

Soc. But if the wrong doer chance to escape justice,
according to your account he will be happy ?

Pol. That is my view.

Soc. And in my opinion, Polus, the wrong doer and
the wicked man is in every case miserable; more miserable however if he escape justice and evade punishment for his iniquity, but less miserable if he pay the
penalty of his crimes, and be duly punished by Gods and
men.

Pol. A strange paradox this, Socrates, that you under- 473
take to maintain.

Soc. Aye and I will try to make you too maintain the
same, my friend, for as a friend I regard you. So now, the
points on which we differ are these. Look at them yourself.
I told you I believe before that doing wrong is worse than
suffering it.

Pol. No doubt you did.

Soc. You on the contrary thought suffering it worse.

Pol. Yes.

Soc. And *I* said that the wrong doers are miserable, and you refuted me.

Pol. Yes, egad, that I did.

Soc. At least in your own opinion, Polus.

Pol. And my opinion is right I should rather think.

Soc. But you said on the other hand that the wicked are happy, provided they escape justice.

Pol. No doubt of it.

Soc. And *I* say they are most miserable, and those that are brought to justice less so. Will you refute that too?

Pol. Why that's still harder to refute than the other, Socrates.

Soc. Not only so, Polus, but impossible; for the truth can never be refuted.

Pol. How say you? If a man be detected in a criminal design of making himself absolute, and thereupon be put to the torture or mutilated or have his eyes burnt out; or, after having been himself subjected to every possible variety of the severest torments and been forced to look on whilst his own children and wife endured the like, then last of all be crucified or burnt to death in a coat of pitch— will *he* be a happier man than if he were to escape and make himself tyrant, and pass his life as supreme ruler in his city in doing whatsoever he pleases, an object of envy and congratulation to his own citizens and all foreigners to boot? Is *this* what you say it is impossible to refute?

c. 29   *Soc.* *Now* you are trying to scare me with bugbears, my brave Polus, instead of refuting me; just now you were citing witnesses against me. However never mind that, but just refresh my memory a little: "in a *criminal* design upon the tyranny," you said?

Pol. Yes I did.

Soc. Then neither of them will ever be *happier* than the other, neither he that has unjustly compassed the tyranny nor he that is punished for his misdeeds: for of two miserable men neither can be said to be *happier:* still the *more*

miserable is he that remains undiscovered and secures himself on the throne. [*Polus smiles.*] What does that mean,
Polus? Are you laughing? Here's another new kind of
refutation; when an assertion is made to refute it by grin-
ning instead of argument[1].

Pol. Don't you think, Socrates, you are confuted already,
when you assert such things as no human being would maintain? Only ask any one of the company there.

Soc. Polus, I am not one of your public men; in fact
only last year when I was elected member of the Council,
and, my tribe having the Presidency, it became my duty
to put a question to the vote, I made myself ridiculous by
not knowing how to do it[2]. So don't ask me again this time 474

---

[1] "And coxcombs vanquish Berkeley with a grin."—Pope. ✓

[2] This is the passage by which the dramatic date of the dialogue is determined. It is so precise and positive that there can I think be no doubt that
Plato really intended it as a mark of time: and whereas the chronological indi-
cations and allusions which have suggested an earlier period can all be made
very fairly to harmonise with this by merely allowing a very reasonable latitude
in the use of indefinite expressions, such as νεωστί and ἐχθὲς καὶ πρῴην, the definite and precise πέρυσι absolutely precludes any other date than the year 405
B.C.—except upon the most improbable supposition that Socrates twice held the
office of ἐπιστάτης: a notion which to say nothing of other arguments, is directly contradicted by Socrates' own assertion, *Apol. Socr.* 32 B, that he never
engaged in public business but once in his life.

The real circumstances of the case are related by Xenophon, *Hellen.* I. 7.
15, and alluded to *Memor.* I. i. 18, and Plat. *Apol. Socr.* 32 B. Mr Grote,
Hist. of Greece, Part II. ch. lxiv. Vol. VIII. p. 271, note, expresses a doubt as to
the correctness of Xenophon's statement in the *Memorabilia* that Socrates was
ἐπιστάτης on this occasion. He omits however to refer to the present passage
of the *Gorgias*, where the use of the technical term ἐπιψηφίζειν, expressive of
the special function of the ἐπιστάτης, seems fully to confirm Xenophon's statement and to remove all doubt upon the point.

The reason here assigned by Socrates for not putting the illegal question to
the vote in the memorable trial of the generals after Arginusæ, and his attributing to ignorance what was in fact an act of heroic firmness and resolution
which has few, if any, parallels in history, is a most curious and striking example of that form of 'dissimulation' which as Aristotle tells us, *Eth. Nic.*
IV. 7. 14, from Socrates' constant use of it, came to be distinguished as εἰρωνεία
in a proper or special use, the 'mock humility' or 'self-disparagement' in
which in fact Socrates' 'irony' mainly consists. In another aspect, it is hardly

to take the votes of the present company; but, as I said just now, if you have no better argument than those you have used hand the matter over to me in my turn, and try the sort of proof that *I* think ought to be employed. For I know how to produce one witness in support of my assertions, and that is the man himself with whom I am arguing, the many I utterly disregard; and there is one whose vote I know how to take, whilst to the multitude I have nothing whatever to say. See then whether you will consent to submit to be refuted in your turn by answering my questions. For I think, you know, that you and I and every one else believes doing wrong to be worse than suffering it, and escaping punishment for one's transgressions worse than enduring it.

Pol. And I, that neither I nor anyone else in the world believes it. For would *you* rather suffer wrong than do it?

Soc. Yes, and so would you and every body else.

Pol. You are quite wrong; on the contrary neither I nor you nor any one else.

Soc. Then will you answer?

Pol. By all means, for in fact I am quite curious to know what you can possibly have to say.

Soc. Then tell me that you *may* know, just as if I was beginning my questions all over again, which of the two seems to you to be worse, Polus, doing or suffering wrong?

Pol. Suffering it to be sure.

Soc. But what say you to 'fouler'?' Which of the two is *that?* .

distinguishable from that form of pleasantry which now passes under the name of 'quizzing.'

[1] In the absence of any English words in common use which convey both the physical and the moral application of καλόν and αἰσχρόν, I have taken refuge in translating them by the somewhat poetical terms 'fair' and 'foul.' Dr Whewell renders them by 'handsome' and 'ugly.' The difficulty of translating them lies in this; that whilst sometimes the one sense and sometimes the other is uppermost in the originals, and this would lead us to choose different words to express them, yet the argument frequently obliges us to retain the same throughout, because it would be obscured or rendered unmeaning by

Pol. Wrong doing.

Soc. And so likewise worse, if fouler.

Pol No by no means.

Soc. Oh, I understand : you think fair and good and bad and foul are not the same things.

Pol. Certainly not.

Soc. But what of this? All fair things, as bodies and colours and figures and sounds and pursuits—is it with reference to no standard at all that you call them fair every time you use the word? for instance first, when you apply the term fair to fair bodies is it not either in respect of their use, with reference, that is, to the purpose which any of them may be made to serve ; or in respect of some kind of pleasure, when they give delight to those that look at them in the act of contemplation? Have you any account to give beyond this of beauty of body?

Pol. None.

Soc. And so with everything else in the same way, figures and colours, is it in virtue of some pleasure or advantage or both that you term them fair?

Pol. Yes it is.

Soc. And with sounds too and every thing in music, is it not just the same?

Pol. Yes.

Soc. And moreover in all that belongs to laws and habits of life, their beauty I presume is to be found nowhere beyond these limits, that is to say, either the utility or the pleasure that is in them, or both.

Pol. No, I think not.

Soc. And so again with the beauty of studies is it not **475** the same?

Pol. Yes no doubt; and this time, Socrates, I do really

changing them: and hence we are reduced to the alternative of either marring the argument or adopting some unfamiliar terms to represent two of the commonest words in the Greek language.

like your definition, when you define what is fair by pleasure and good.

Soc. And may I in the same way define what is foul by the opposites, pain and evil?

Pol. Of course you may.

Soc. So then when of two fair things one is fairer, it is so because it surpasses in one of these two things or both of them, either in pleasure or utility or both.

Pol. Certainly.

Soc. And when again of two foul things the one is fouler, it will be so by the excess either of pain or mischief. Is not that a necessary consequence?

Pol. Yes.

Soc. Come then, what was said just now about doing and suffering wrong? didn't you say that suffering wrong is worse, but doing it fouler?

Pol. I did.

Soc. Well then if doing wrong is fouler than suffering it, it is either more painful, and fouler by excess of pain, or of mischief or both? Does not this also necessarily follow?

Pol. Of course it does.

c. 31   *Soc.* First of all then let us consider whether doing wrong exceeds suffering it in pain, whether, that is, those that do wrong feel more pain than those that suffer it?

Pol. Oh no, Socrates, not *that*.

Soc. So then it is not in pain that it exceeds.

Pol. Certainly not.

Soc. And accordingly if not in pain, it cannot *now*[1] exceed in both.

Pol. It appears not.

Soc. It only remains then (that it exceed) in the other.

Pol. Yes.

Soc. In mischief.

---

[1] ἔτι, 'any longer, after this, as it might have done if this had *not* been the case.' Corresponding to ἤδη in *affirmative* sentences.

Pol. It seems so.

Soc. So it is because it exceeds in mischief that doing wrong is worse than suffering it.

Pol. Plainly so.

Soc. Is it not then admitted by the mass of mankind, as it was in fact by yourself a little while ago, that doing wrong is fouler than suffering it?

Pol. Yes.

Soc. And now it turns out to be worse.

Pol. It seems so.

Soc. Would *you* then prefer the greater evil and the greater deformity to that which is less? Don't hesitate to reply, Polus, it will do you no harm, but bravely submit yourself to the argument as to a physician, and answer yes or no to my question.

Pol. Well I should not prefer it, Socrates.

Soc. And would any one else in the world?

Pol. No I think not, as you put the case now.

Soc. Then I spoke the truth in saying that neither you nor I nor any one else in the world would prefer doing to suffering wrong; because it's worse.

Pol. So it appears.

Soc. You see then, Polus, that when the one mode of proof is brought into comparison with the other, there is no resemblance between them; but *you* have the assent of every one else except myself, whereas *I* am satisfied with your own assent and your own evidence single and alone, and I take 476 only your own vote and pay no sort of attention to the rest. And so let this be considered settled between us. And next let us examine the second question on which we differed; whether, namely, for a guilty man to be brought to justice is the greatest of all evils as you thought, or to escape it is a greater as was *my* opinion. Let us consider it thus. Do you call being brought to justice and being justly chastised for wrong doing the same thing?

Pol. Yes I do.

4

Soc. Can you deny that all just things are fair, in so far as they are just ? Now consider well before you speak.

Pol. Well I do think so, Socrates.

c. 32   *Soc.* Then look at this again. When any one does an act, is it necessary that there should be a something acted upon by this agent?

Pol. Yes I think so.

Soc. And does that something *suffer* exactly what the agent *does?* and receive an impression of the same kind as the action of the agent? To explain my meaning by an example—when any one strikes a blow, something must necessarily be struck ?

Pol. Just so.

Soc. And if the striker strikes hard or quick, the object struck is struck in the same way ?

Pol. Yes.

Soc. Consequently the effect is of the same kind in the object struck as is the action in the striking agent?

Pol. To be sure.

Soc. Or again, when a man burns, something must of necessity be burnt ?

Pol. Of course.

Soc. And if he burns severely or painfully, the object burnt must be burnt in the same way as the burning agent burns ?

Pol. Yes certainly.

Soc. And so when a man cuts, the same rule applies, that is to say something is cut ?

Pol. Yes.

Soc. And if the cut is large or deep or painful, the cut produced in the object cut is precisely of the same kind as the thing cutting cuts it ?

Pol. So it appears.

Soc. Well then in a word, see if you admit universally the rule I just stated : the effect in the patient is of exactly the same kind as the action in the agent.

Pol. Well I do.

Soc. This then being admitted, is to be punished to suffer something or to do it?

Pol. To suffer of course, Socrates.

Soc. And that too by the hands of some agent?

Pol. No doubt of it, by the hands of him that inflicts the punishment.

Soc. But he that punishes aright punishes justly.

Pol. Yes.

Soc. And in doing that does he do what is just?

Pol. What is just.

Soc. And again one that atones for his crime by punishment suffers what is just?

Pol. So it appears.

Soc. And what is just I believe we have admitted to be fair?

Pol. Yes certainly.

Soc. Consequently of these two the one does what is fair, and the other, the man who is punished, suffers it.

Pol. Yes.

Soc. And so if fair then good, for that is either pleasant or useful[1].   c. 33   477

Pol. Of course.

Soc. So then one who is punished for his sins suffers what is good?

Pol. It seems so.

Soc. Then he receives a benefit?

Pol. Yes.

Soc. Is it that kind of benefit which I suspect? namely that his soul is improved if he is justly punished.

Pol. Yes probably.

Soc. Then is one that is brought to justice relieved from vice of soul?

Pol. Yes.

---

[1] By the definition, c. 30, 474, D, E.

4—2

Soc. And is not that the greatest of all evils that he
is relieved from? Look at it in this way. In a man's
pecuniary condition do you discern any other evil than
poverty?

Pol. No, only poverty.

Soc. Or again in his bodily condition (constitution)?
would you not say the evil is weakness and disease and
ugliness and such like?

Pol. Yes I should.

Soc. And so in soul don't you believe that there is some
inherent vice?

Pol. No doubt of it.

Soc. And don't you call this injustice and ignorance and
cowardice and so forth?

Pol. To be sure.

Soc. So then in mind body and estate, these three, you
have pointed out three several vices, poverty disease injustice?

Pol. Yes.

Soc. Then which of these kinds of vice is the foulest?
Is it not injustice, or in a word the vice of the soul?

Pol. Yes by far.

Soc. And if foulest then likewise worst?

Pol. How mean you by that, Socrates?

Soc. This. It follows from our previous conclusions that
what is most foul is so always by reason of its bringing with
it either the greatest pain or bane or both.

Pol. Quite so.

Soc. And now we have just admitted injustice and in
general vice of soul to be what is foulest?

Pol. We have no doubt.

Soc. So then it is either most painful, or in other words
it is because it surpasses in painfulness that it is the foulest
of all of them (*i. e.* the beforementioned kinds of vice), or
banefulness or in both ways?

Pol. Necessarily.

Soc. Is then to be unjust and licentious and cowardly and ignorant more painful than poverty and sickness?

Pol. No I think not, Socrates, from what we have been saying.

Soc. Prodigious then must be the amount of banefulness and amazing the evil by which the soul's vice exceeds all the rest so as to make it the foulest of them all, since it is not by pain, according to your account.

Pol. So it appears.

Soc. But further, where the excess consists in the highest degree of banefulness that must I should think be the greatest of all evils.

Pol. Yes.

Soc. Injustice then and licentious indulgence and all the rest of the soul's vices are the greatest of all evils.

Pol. So it appears.

Soc. What is the art then that delivers us from poverty? c. 34 Is it not that of trading?

Pol. Yes.

Soc. And what from disease? Is it not the art of medicine?

Pol. Beyond all doubt.

Soc. And what from wickedness and injustice? If you 478 haven't an answer ready when the question is put in this way, look at it thus: Whither and to whom do we carry those whose bodies are diseased?

Pol. To the physicians, Socrates.

Soc. And whither do we send the evil-doers and licentious?

Pol. Before the judges do you mean?

Soc. To suffer for their crimes, isn't it?

Pol. Yes.

Soc. Is it not then by the application of a sort of justice that those chastise who chastise aright?

Pol. Plainly.

Soc. So then trading delivers us from poverty, medicine from disease, and justice from licentiousness and wickedness.

Pol. So it appears.

Soc. Which then is fairest of these?

Pol. What do you mean?

Soc. Trading, medicine, justice.

Pol. Justice, Socrates, is far superior.

Soc. So then, again, if it is fairest it produces either the greatest pleasure or profit or both? (recurring again to the definition).

Pol. Yes.

Soc. Well then, is medical treatment pleasant[1], and do those who submit themselves to such treatment like it?

Pol. No I should think not.

Soc. But it is beneficial, isn't it?

Pol. Yes.

Soc. Because the patient is rid of a great evil, and therefore it is well worth his while to undergo the pain and be well.

Pol. Of course it is.

Soc. Is this then the happiest condition for a man's body to be in, to be cured by medical treatment, or never to be ill at all?

Pol. Plainly never to be ill.

Soc. For, it seems, this is not what we said happiness consisted in, the deliverance from evil, but in never having had it at all.

Pol. It is so.

Soc. Again. Of two persons that have something wrong

---

[1] On the analogy here assumed (and so frequently repeated in this and other dialogues of Plato) between corrective justice and medicine, and the curative effect of the former upon the diseased human soul, Renouvier very justly remarks, *Manuel de Philosophie Ancienne*, II. 31: Quelquefois enfin Platon procède par simple comparaison et se laisse aller à une analogie douteuse: c'est ainsi qu'il compare celui qui *fait justice* au médecin, et que par suite il regarde le châtiment comme un bien pour le coupable, sans examiner si le châtiment améliore toujours, et si la peine est à l'injustice ce que la brûlure est à la plaie.

in body or soul which is the more miserable? The one who
puts himself into the physician's hands and so gets rid of
the mischief, or he who does not and retains it?

Pol. I should suppose the one who does not.

Soc. And didn't we say that to be punished for one's
faults is a deliverance from the greatest evil, that is wickedness?

Pol. We did.

Soc. Because I suppose justice brings us under control
and makes us juster, and so becomes the art by which wickedness is cured.

Pol. Yes.

Soc. Happiest of all then is he who is free from vice in
his soul, seeing that we proved this to be the greatest of all
evils.

Pol. Evidently.

Soc. And in the second degree, I should suppose, he
who gets rid of it.

Pol. It seems so.

Soc. And he as we said is one who is admonished and
rebuked and punished.

Pol. Yes.

Soc. Consequently one who retains injustice and is not
delivered from it leads the worst kind of life.

Pol. So it appears.

Soc. And is not he that man who in the commission of
the greatest crimes and the practice of the greatest iniquity 479
has managed to escape reproof and correction and punishment, as you say Archelaus has contrived to do, and the rest
of your tyrants and orators and potentates?

Pol. It seems so.

Soc. Because, I should think, my excellent friend, what c. 35
men of this sort have contrived to do for themselves is very
much the same as if a man afflicted with disease of the
worst kind were to contrive to escape giving satisfaction to
the physicians for the faults of his body, that is, undergoing

medical treatment, dreading like a child the pain inflicted by the cautery or the knife. Don't *you* think so yourself?

Pol. Yes I do.

Soc. In ignorance it would seem of the great advantage of health and soundness of body. For it appears from the conclusions at which we have just arrived that the conduct of those likewise who try to escape the penalty due to their transgressions is very much of this kind, Polus; they discern clearly enough its painfulness but are blind to its benefits, and are not aware how much more miserable than an unsound body[1] it is to be associated with a soul that is not sound but corrupt and unjust and unholy. And hence it is that they strain every nerve to escape punishment and deliverance from the direst evil, by providing themselves either with money or friends or the means of making themselves the most accomplished speakers. But if our conclusions are true, Polus, do you perceive what follows from our argument? or would you like us to reckon it all up together?

Pol. Yes if you don't object.

Soc. Is not one result then that injustice and wrong doing is the worst of evils?

Pol. So it appears.

Soc. And further it appeared that to suffer for one's faults is a deliverance from this evil?

Pol. It seems so.

Soc. And not to be punished for them is an abiding in us of the evil?

Pol. Yes.

Soc. Wrong doing then is second of evils in degree; but to do wrong and not suffer for it is the first and greatest of them all.

Pol. It seems so.

Soc. Well, my friend, was not this the point in dispute

---

[1] I have here intentionally preserved the false comparison of the original. Such blunders (exceptions we call them in the Classics) are as common in English as they are in Greek and Latin.

between us, that you pronounced Archelaus, the greatest
of all criminals, happy because he enjoyed a complete immunity from punishment for his crimes, whilst I thought on the
contrary that if any one, whether it be Archelaus or any one
else in the world, pay no penalty for the wrong that he does
he may justly be called preeminently miserable above all
other men; and universally, that he that does wrong is more
miserable than he that suffers it, and he that escapes the
penalty for his transgressions than he that submits to it? Is
not this what I said?

Pol. Yes.

Soc. Well then is it not now proved that what I said
was true?

Pol. It appears so.

Soc. Very good. If then this is true, Polus, what is the 480
great use of rhetoric? For, you know, it follows from our c. 36
present conclusions that a man should himself keep the
strictest watch over his own conduct to avoid all wrong,
seeing that thereby he will bring on himself great evil;
should he not?

Pol. Yes surely.

Soc. But if he do commit a wrong, either himself or any
one else he cares for, he must go of his own accord to the
place where he may most speedily be punished for it, to the
judge as to his physician, striving earnestly that the disease
of his iniquity may not become inveterate and so make the
ulcer of his soul deep-seated and incurable. Or if not, what
are we to say, Polus, supposing our former admissions are to
stand? *Can* the one be brought into harmony with the other
in any other way than this?

Pol. Why to be sure what else can we say, Socrates?

Soc. It follows then that for the purpose of a defence of
crime, whether the guilt be in oneself or one's parents or
friends or children or country, your rhetoric is of no use to us
at all, Polus, unless indeed one were to suppose the very
contrary, that it is a man's duty to accuse himself first of all,

and in the next degree his relations or any one else of his friends who may at any time be guilty of a wrong; and instead of concealing the wrong to bring it to light, that the offender may suffer the penalty and so be restored to health; and again to force oneself and others not to flinch out of cowardice, but submit bravely with closed eyes as it were to a physician to be cut or burned, in the pursuit of what is good and fair, not counting the pain; if his crimes have been worthy of stripes submitting to the rod, or if of bonds to imprisonment, or if of a fine to payment of the fine, or if of exile to banishment, or of death to die; himself the first to be his own accuser and of all his friends and relations as well, and to this end employing his rhetoric that they may all by the disclosure of their crimes be delivered from the greatest of all evils, which is unrighteousness. Is this to be our conclusion, or not, Polus?

Pol. A strange one, Socrates, it seems to me, but still perhaps you *do* find it (σοι) in agreement with what you said before.

Soc. Well then either the other must be disproved, or this is the inevitable result.

Pol. Yes, that is certainly so.

Soc. And conversely again; if on the contrary one were ever required to do a man a mischief, whether an enemy or any one else—provided only the wrong be not inflicted by the enemy on oneself, for that we must be very careful to avoid[1]—but supposing the wrong to be done by him to

---

[1] This simple and innocent observation has been so strangely misinterpreted by Stallbaum, that a word of explanation may not be out of place. His note is "quoniam scilicet isto pacto necesse fuerit ut alter in judicium vocetur (why? on the contrary, such a course would be inconsistent with the moral of the entire passage, which is, that if you want to punish an enemy you must let him alone and *not* bring him to justice), et justa pœna afficiatur, quod beneficii loco habendum fuerit." The plain meaning is that in punishing our enemies we must take care not to punish ourselves. If we desire to inflict real damage upon an enemy or offender, we must not send him before the tribunals of justice or subject him to any penalty personal or pecuniary—these are instru-

some one else, we should contrive by every means in our power both·by word and deed to secure him impunity and 481 prevent him from appearing before the judge, or if he do, we must devise means that the enemy may effect his escape and not suffer punishment; but if he have stolen large sums of gold we must contrive that he may not refund it, but keep and spend it, on him and his, lawlessly and godlessly; or if again he have committed crimes worthy of death, that he may not die; if possible never, but be immortal in his wickedness, or if not, that he may prolong his life to the utmost being such as he is. Such are the objects as it seems to me, Polus, for which rhetoric is serviceable, for to one who does not intend to do wrong the use of it does *not* seem to me particularly great—if indeed there be any use in it at all—for to be sure in our preceding discourse it no where came to light.

Cal. Tell me, Chærephon, is Socrates in earnest in all c. 37 this, or only joking?

Chær. I should say, Callicles, prodigiously in earnest. However there's nothing like asking him the question.

Cal. I'faith, that's just what I am curious to do. Tell me, Socrates, are we to suppose that you are serious now or in jest. For if you are serious and what you say is really true, the life of all of us must have been turned upside down, musn't it? and we are all doing the exact contrary it seems to what we ought to do.

Soc. Callicles, if we men had not certain feelings in common, though they do vary in different individuals[1], but

---

ments of correction and cure, they are no injury but a benefit. The true and real punishment of injustice and vice is to let them take their course, and to encourage and foster their growth as well as secure the impunity of the offender by every means in our power—only in so doing, he adds half in joke, we must take good care that the injustice which we encourage is not exercised at our own expense, which would rather spoil the fun for *us.*

[1] That is there are 'affections,' πάθη, παθήματα, feelings, sentiments, common to the whole human race, the same in kind, but varying in different individuals in the mode degree circumstances and objects of their exercise.

if one of us had feelings peculiar to himself and so differing
from the rest of mankind[1], it would not be easy for one of
us to exhibit to his neighbour any of his own impressions. I
make this remark in consequence of having observed that
you and I are just now in pretty much the same condition,
enamoured, that is, the pair of us, of two things apiece, I of
Alcibiades son of Clinias and philosophy, and you of the
Athenian Demus and the son of Pyrilampes[2]. Now I remark constantly that with all your cleverness however much
your favourite may talk and whatever opinion he may happen to pronounce about any thing, you can't contradict him,
but are constantly changing backwards and forwards. If it
be in the assembly that you are making a speech, and Demus
—the Athenian Demus I mean—doesn't agree with you,
you veer round at once and say any thing it pleases, or when
you are talking to that fair youth the son of Pyrilampes,
the very same thing happens to you; you can't resist any
thing that your minion resolves or says, and therefore if any
one were to express surprise at the oddity of what you are
constantly saying to oblige them, you would tell him I dare
482 say, if you chose to speak the truth, that unless your favourite can be prevented from talking in that way you too must
always go on saying the same. Imagine then that you
have to receive precisely the same answer from me, and don't
be surprised at my saying this, but (if you don't like it)
make my mistress Philosophy leave off talking in this way.
For, my dear friend, she always holds the same language
as you hear from me now, and is far less inconstant (capri-
ous) to me than any other mistress; for that son of Clinias
is at the mercy now of this now of that opinion, but Philosophy is ever constant to the same. Her assertions are what

---

[1] ῖδιον is followed here by the comparative ή, as ἄλλο, ἕτερον, ἀλλοῖον, διά-
φορον, ἐναντίον, even ἀνόμοιον, *Cratyl.* 435 Ε, and other words in which a comparison is implied. Peculiarity in an individual implies *a difference from* the
rest of the species, and in this the comparison is conveyed.

[2] His name was Demus; see Arist. *Vesp.* 97.

you are now so surprised at, though you were present yourself when they were made. So then either refute her, as I
said just now, by showing that wrong doing and impunity in
guilt is not the extremest of all evils; or if you leave this un-
refuted, by the dog, God of the Egyptians, Callicles, Callicles
won't agree with you, but there will be a discord between
you all your life long. And yet *I* should think that it were
better for me that my lyre should be out of tune and dis-
cordant, or any chorus that I had furnished, or that any
number of men should disagree with me and say the contrary,
than for my own single self to be out of harmony with and
contradict myself.

Cal. Socrates, you seem to be running riot (wantonly c. 38
extravagant) in your talk like a genuine popular orator; and
now you are declaiming in this way because Polus has fallen
into just the same error as he was accusing Gorgias of being
betrayed into in his argument with you. For he said if I
remember right, that when you asked Gorgias, supposing any
one came to him with the intention of studying rhetoric
without the knowledge of justice, whether he would teach
it him, he turned bashful and said he would, in compliance
with the popular prejudice, because people would be indignant if he said no; and so by reason of this admission he
was forced to contradict himself; which is exactly what you
are so fond of. And he was quite right in my opinion in
ridiculing you as he did then. But now this time he has met
with the very same disaster himself; and for my own part,
what I don't approve of in what Polus said is just this, that
he conceded to you that doing wrong is fouler than suffering
it; for it was in consequence of this admission that he himself in his turn got completely entangled by you in the argument and had his mouth stopped, because he was ashamed
to say what he thought. For, Socrates, you *do* really divert
the argument to such vulgar fallacies and popular claptrap,
whilst you pretend all the time to be in the pursuit of truth,
to what is 'fair' not by nature but merely by law or con-

vention: whereas in fact for the most part these are opposed
483 to one another, nature and convention: and so if a man
is timid and doesn't venture to say what he thinks, he
is forced to contradict himself. And this forsooth is your
ingenious device that you have discovered to take people in
with in your discussions; when a man asserts any thing as
according to law or convention you slyly substitute ' according to nature' in your questions, and when he is appealing
to natural principles you refer to convention. As for instance in the present case, of doing and suffering wrong,
when Polus was speaking of what is conventionally ' fouler,'
you followed up what he meant 'conventionally' by arguing
upon it in the 'natural' sense. For it is only by custom and
convention that doing wrong is fouler; by *nature* every thing
is fouler which is likewise worse, as suffering wrong. For
in fact the endurance of such a thing as wrong is not a man's
part at all, but a poor slave's, for whom death is better than
living—as it is indeed for any one who is unable to help himself when wronged and insulted or any one else for whom he
cares. However the law makers to be sure are the weaker
and more numerous part of mankind. It is with a view
therefore to themselves and their own interest that they
frame their laws and bestow their praises and their censures;
and by way of frightening the stronger sort of men who are
able to assert their superiority, in order that they mayn't
assert it over *them*, they tell them that self-seeking is foul
and unjust, and that this is what wrong doing consists in,
trying namely to get the advantage over one's neighbours;
for they are quite satisfied no doubt, being the inferiors
themselves, to be on an equality with the rest.

c. 39— Such then is the reason why seeking to get more than
the mass of mankind is conventionally styled unjust and foul,
and why they call it doing wrong: whereas the truth is, in
my opinion, that nature herself shows on the other hand[1]

---

[1] αὖ, Bekk. Edd. Tur.

that it is just that the better should have more than the
worse, and the abler than the less able. And it is plain
in many instances that this is so, not only in all the other
animals, but also in mankind in entire states and races[1], that
right I mean is decided to consist in this, that the stronger
should bear rule and have the advantage over the weaker.
For by what right did Xerxes invade Greece, or his father Scythia? or in any other of the ten thousand similar
cases of the kind that might be produced? No, no, these
men no doubt follow nature in acting thus, aye by my faith
and law too, the law of nature; not however I dare say that
which *we* frame by way of moulding the characters of the
best and strongest of us, whom we take from infancy, and
taming them like lions by spells and conjuring tricks reduce
them to abject slavery, telling them that they must be 484
content with their fair share and that this is the meaning of
fairness and justice. But I fancy when there arises a man of
ability he flings off all these restraints and bursts them
asunder and makes his escape; and trampling under foot all
our written enactments (formularies)[2] and juggleries and
spells and laws, clean against nature every one of them, our
would-be slave rises up against us and shows himself our
master, and *then* natural justice shines forth in its true light.
And it seems to me that Pindar too confirms what I say in
the ode in which he says "Law the Lord of all, mortals and

---

[1] *Lit.* in states and races as wholes, or collectively.

[2] γράμματα, non de psephismatis intelligenda sunt, quoa voluit Heindorfius,
sed omnino de formulis in quarum numero sunt psephismata, ut vere monuit
Schæferus ad Demosth. *Appar.* IV. 260. Stallb. The writings documents or
formularies expressed by γράμματα are of course the γεγραμμένος νόμος, the
human written laws, enacted by the several societies for their own purposes,
adapted to the habits customs and opinions prevailing in these societies, and
therefore varying according to time place and circumstance. To them are opposed the unwritten laws ἄγραφος νόμος, ἄγραπτα κἀσφαλῆ θεῶν νόμιμα, the
higher and immutable law, natural or divine, or rather natural *and* divine,
whose sanctions are always superior, and sometimes may be opposed, to human
institutions.

immortals :" He, you know, he continues, "inflicts, and justifies, the utmost violence with supreme hand[1]. I appeal in
proof to the deeds of Hercules, for unbought —" The words
are something like that, for I don't know the ode well. He
says however, that he neither purchased nor received as a
gift from Geryones the cows that he drove off, as though
this were natural right, that cows or any other property of
the inferior and weaker should all belong to the superior
and stronger.

c. 40   Such then is the truth in this matter, and you will be
convinced of it if at length you leave off your philosophy and
pass on to higher things. For to be sure, Socrates, philosophy
is a pretty thing enough, if only a man apply himself to it to
a moderate extent at the proper age; but if he go on spending
his time upon it too long, it's the ruin of a man. For if he
be ever so clever and yet carries these studies far on into life
he must needs turn out ignorant of every thing that one who
would be an accomplished and eminent citizen should be conversant with. For in fact people of this sort show themselves
ignorant of the laws of their own cities, and of all that a man
ought to say in his ordinary dealings with the world, public
or private, and of human pleasures and desires, and in short
quite unacquainted with the varieties of human character.
Accordingly when they come to undertake any private or
public business they make themselves ridiculous—just as no
doubt your public men do when *they* take part in your occupations and discussions. For the fact is, as Euripides says,

> Each shines in that, to that end presses forward,
> Devotes to that the better part o' the day,
> Wherein he chances to surpass himself:

485 Whereas everything in which a man is weak he shuns, and
calls it bad names; but the other he praises, out of regard
for himself, thinking in this way to praise himself at the same
time. But no doubt the best course is to take advantage of

---

[1] *i. e.* violence is justified by the same supreme authority which inflicts it.

both. Philosophy it is well to cultivate just so far as serves for education, and it is no disgrace for a lad to study it: but when a man already advanced in life still goes on with it, the thing, Socrates, becomes ridiculous; and for my own part the feeling which I have towards students of philosophy is very much the same as that with which I regard those that lisp in a childish way[1]. For whenever I see a little child to whom it is still natural to talk in this way with a childish lisp, I like it, and it strikes me as pretty and a sign of gentle breeding and suitable to the infant's age: but when I hear a little creature talk distinctly it gives me quite a disagreeable impression and offends my ears and seems to me vulgar and only fit for a slave. When on the other hand one hears *a man* lisp or sees him playing childish tricks it appears unmanly and one would like to give him a good flogging. Just the same is the feeling that I have towards philosophical studies. For when I observe attention to philosophy in a young lad I approve of it, and it strikes me as becoming, and I look upon it as a mark of gentle birth and breeding in him, and one who neglects it I account illiberal, and as one that will never deem himself capable of any fine or generous action: but then when I see one advanced in life still going on with his philosophy, and unable to lay it aside, such a man as *that* (ἤδη), Socrates, seems to me to want flogging. For as I said just now a man like that, clever as he may be, cannot fail to become unmanly by avoiding the centres (frequented places) of the city and the market-places which as the poet[2] said are the places where men acquire distinction; his fate is to skulk in a corner and pass the rest of his life whispering with three or four lads, and never give utterance to any free and noble and generous sentiment.

---

[1] Schleiermacher, note, p. 487, points out as singular and unPlatonic that παίζειν here has nothing opposed to it; σαφῶς διαλέγεσθαι alone standing in opposition to ψελλίζεσθαι and παίζειν. I have for this reason translated the two latter here and in the next sentence as a hendiadys.

[2] Homer, *Il.* IX. 441.

c. 41   Now, Socrates, I have a great regard for you; and accordingly I seem to be inspired now with the same feeling towards you as Zethus in Euripides, whom I just referred to, has towards Amphion. In fact it occurs to me to say very much the same to you as he says to his brother, that 'you neglect,' Socrates, 'what you ought to pay attention to, and a soul endowed by nature with her noblest gifts you
486 disfigure by a boyish disguise[1]; and neither amid the counsels of justice will you ever deliver an opinion aright, nor find aught probable and persuasive, nor devise any gallant resolution on another's behalf[2].' And yet, my dear Socrates— and now don't be angry with me, for all that I am about to say is out of regard for you—don't you think it a shame for a man to be in the condition which I consider you to be in, together with all those who are constantly going deeper and deeper into philosophy. For as it is, if a man were to arrest you or any one else of those like you and drag you off to prison charging you with some crime of which you were entirely innocent, you know very well that you wouldn't know what to do with yourself, but there you would stand with your head swimming and your mouth open not knowing what to say; and when you were brought up before the court, however contemptible and wretched your accuser might be, you would be condemned to die if he chose to lay the penalty at death. And yet how can this be a wise thing, Socrates, 'for an art to find a man highly gifted and make him worse,' unable either to help himself or to rescue

---

[1] See note A in the Appendix.

[2] The following verses may perhaps represent as much as *Plato* has here given us of what Euripides wrote:

> Thou shunn'st, Amphion, what thou should'st pursue;
> The nobly-gifted soul which nature gave thee
> Disgracing thus by womanish disguise.
> No voice hast thou where Justice holds her council,
> No words of weight persuasive canst thou find,
> Nor prompt in injured innocence' defence,
> The gallant counsel and the high resolve.

from the greatest dangers himself or any one else, and liable
to be stript by his enemies of all his substance, and to pass
his life in the city an absolute outlaw[1]. Why such an one,
though the expression is perhaps somewhat coarse, may be
slapped in the face with impunity. Come, come, my good
friend, 'take my advice, leave off' refuting, 'and cultivate
the accomplishment' of business, and cultivate what will gain
you the reputation of good sense; leave to others these over-
nice frivolities or nonsense or whatever else they should be
called, 'which will end in your dwelling in an empty and
desolate house' (i.e. end in poverty and isolation); and emu-
late, not men who waste their time in such trivial debates,
but those whose portion is wealth and fame and many other
good things.

Soc. If my soul had happened to be made of gold, Cal- c. 42
licles, don't you think I should have been delighted to find one
of those stones with which they test gold, the best of them,
which would enable me by the application of it—provided,
that is, it bore me witness that my soul had been duly cared
for—to be quite sure that I am in a satisfactory state, and
have no need of any other touchstone?

Cal. What is the meaning of this question, Socrates?

Soc. I'll tell you directly. It seems to me that in meeting you I have met with such a treasure.

Cal. Why so?

Soc. I am quite convinced that whenever you agree
with me in any of the opinions that my soul forms, *that must
needs* be the very truth. For I perceive that one who would

---

[1] ἄτιμος is usually understood to mean here 'in dishonour.' I think it
has rather the technical sense of 'one under ἀτιμία.' Callicles says that a man
who can't defend himself in a court of justice is in the same position as one who
has lost his civil rights, or is outlawed. The latter has lost the right of appearing
in court to defend himself, and the former by his ignorance and incompetency
is no better off, since he can make no good use of his privilege; he is equally at
the mercy of his enemies, and may like the other be wronged and insulted
with impunity. This interpretation is fully confirmed by the reference to this
passage at p. 508 D.

487 put a soul to a sufficient test as to whether she is leading a right life or the reverse, ought for that purpose (ἄρα, accordingly,) to be possessed of three things, all of which you have, knowledge and good-will and candour. For I meet with many people who are unable to test me because they are not wise, as you are; others again are wise enough, but don't choose to tell me the truth because they don't care for me, as you do; and our two foreign friends here, Gorgias and Polus, are no doubt wise and kindly disposed towards me, but they are somewhat deficient in frankness and are rather more shy and bashful than the occasion requires: surely it must be so, when they carried their modesty to such a pitch, that out of sheer *modesty* each of them *ventures* to contradict himself in the presence of a large company, and that on subjects of the highest importance. But you have all these qualifications which the others want. For you are sufficiently instructed as many of your countrymen will be ready to allow, and well disposed to me. What proof have I of that? I will tell you. I know, Callicles, that there are four of you that have set up a partnership for the pursuit of wisdom, yourself, and Tisander of Aphidnæ, and Andron son of Androtion, and Nausicydes of Cholarges. And I once heard you deliberating how far the cultivation of wisdom should be carried, and I remember that an opinion something like this was carried in your society; that the study of philosophy was not to be so eagerly pushed forward into all its minutiæ, but you recommended one another to be very careful not to make yourselves over wise for fear you should unconsciously get spoiled. So then when I hear you giving me the same advice as you did to your most intimate friends it is a satisfactory proof to me that you really have a kindness for me. And further that you are able to speak out your mind without any superfluous modesty, you not only say yourself, but the speech which you made us no long time ago fully bears out your assertion. Well then, this is plainly the state of the case at present; if there be any

point in which you agree with me in our argument *that must*
have been fully tested by both of us, and there will be no
further occasion to submit it to any other touchstone; for
it cannot have been either want of wisdom or excess of
modesty that induced you to make the concession, nor again
could it be for the purpose of deceiving me, because you
are my friend, as you tell me yourself: and so any argument
between you and me *must* in reality attain the very perfection of truth. And, Callicles, there can be no nobler subject
of inquiry than that on which you just now took me to task,
what a man's character ought to be, and what pursuits he
should engage in, and to what extent, early or late in life.
For of this you may be sure, that if there be any thing 488
in my own conduct in life that is wrong, the error on my
part is not intentional but is due solely to my ignorance.
Pray then don't desist from admonishing me as you did at
first, but point out to me clearly what it is that I ought
to pursue, and how I may best attain it. And if you find
me assenting to you now, and afterwards not acting in conformity with what I agreed to, set me down for an absolute dunce and never give me any advice again as an
irreclaimable reprobate. And now pray repeat to me all
over again what you and Pindar understand natural justice
to consist in. Is it that the superior should carry off by
force the property of the inferior, and the better rule the
worse, and the nobler have more than the meaner? Is
justice any thing else according to you, or does my memory
serve me right?

Cal. No, I said that before, and I say so now.　　　c. 43

Soc. And do you mean the same thing in calling a man
better and superior? For to tell you the truth I was just as
unable before as now to make out your precise meaning. Is
it the stronger that you call superior, and are the weaker
bound to listen to the stronger— as for example I believe you
showed us before that it is in pursuance of their natural
right that the great states attack the little ones, because they

are superior and stronger, on the assumption that what is superior and better and stronger is all the same—or is it possible to be better and at the same time inferior and weaker, and to be superior and yet worse? or is the definition of the better and superior the same? This is precisely the thing that I want you distinctly to determine for me, whether what is superior and what is better and what is stronger are the same thing or different.

Cal. Well I tell you distinctly that it is all the same.

Soc. Well but are not the many superior by nature to the one? those you know that make the laws to control the one, as you said yourself just now.

Cal. Of course.

Soc. Consequently the institutions of the many are those of the superior.

Cal. No doubt.

Soc. And so of the better? for the superior are far better according to your account.

Cal. Yes.

Soc. And so their institutions are naturally 'fair,' since they are superior?

Cal. I allow it.

Soc. Is not this then the opinion of the many, as you said just now yourself, that justice consists in having an equal share, and that it is 'fouler' to do wrong than to suffer it? Is
489 that so or not? And mind *you* don't allow yourself this time to be caught in a fit of modesty. Is it, or is it not, the opinion of the many that to have one's fair share, and not a larger share, is just, and that there is more disgrace in doing than in suffering wrong? Don't grudge me an answer to my question, Callicles; in order that, supposing you agree with me, I may *then* fairly assure myself of the truth of it as coming from you, when I find it admitted by a man so competent to decide.

Cal. Well to be sure the generality of men do think so.

Soc. Then it is not by law (convention) alone that doing wrong is more disgraceful than suffering it, and that justice

consists in having one's fair share, but by nature too. And
so you seem to be mistaken in what you said before and to
find fault with me unjustly in saying that law and nature are
opposite to one another, and that I, you know, am perfectly
aware of all that, and take an unfair advantage of it in
arguing; when a thing is asserted 'according to nature'
recurring to law, and when 'according to law' is meant, to
nature.

Cal. Here's a fellow that can *not* forbear trifling. Tell c 44
me, Socrates, are you not ashamed to be word-catching at
your age, and if a man happen to trip in an expression to
take that for a wonderful piece of luck? For do you suppose
I mean anything else by being superior than being better?
Haven't I been telling you ever so long that I maintain what
is better and superior to be the same thing? Or do you suppose I mean that if a rabble of slaves and all sorts of fellows
good for nothing except perhaps in mere bodily strength
get together, and they pronounce anything, that this and
nothing else is law.

Soc. Very good, most sagacious Callicles: *that's* your
opinion, is it?

Cal. To be sure it is.

Soc. Well, my dear sir, I have been surmising myself
ever so long that you meant something of that sort by
superior, and I now repeat my questions from a real curiosity
to know what your meaning is. For I presume you *don't*
think that two are better than one or that your slaves are
better than yourself because they are stronger than you are.
Come now tell me all over again, what you really mean by
'the better,' since it is not the stronger. Only, my good
friend, do pray be a little milder in your lessons that I may
not be obliged to run away from your school.

Cal. You are sarcastic, Socrates.

Soc. No by Zethus, Callicles, whose character you assumed just now to indulge in a good deal of sarcasm against
me; but come, do tell us who you mean by the better.

Cal. I mean the more worthy.

Soc. There now, you see you are word-catching your-self and explaining nothing. Won't you say whether you mean by the better and superior the wiser or any others?

Cal. Why to be sure of course I mean these, most em-phatically.

490   *Soc.* Then according to your account one man of sense is often superior to ten thousand fools, and he ought to be master and the others submit to his authority, and the governor ought to have more than the governed. That is what your words seem to me to imply—and I am not word-catching—if the one is superior to the ten thousand.

Cal. Well that *is* what I mean. For my opinion is that this is what natural justice consists in, and that one that is better and wiser should have power and other advantages over the meaner and inferior.

c. 45   *Soc.* Stop there now. What is it that you say again this time? Supposing that there are a number of us together, as now, in the same place, and we have in a common stock a quantity of eatables and drinkables, and are people of all sorts, some strong others weak; and one of us, a physician say, be wiser than the rest in such matters, and be as is likely stronger than some of us and weaker than others, will not he as being wiser than we are be better and superior in these things?

Cal. No doubt of it.

Soc. Is he then to have a larger share than the rest of us in these provisions because he is better? or ought he in virtue of his authority to have the distribution of them all, but in respect of spending and consuming them upon his own person to have no advantage at all, but only have more than some and less than others? or if he chance to be the weakest of us all, ought he not, Callicles, though the best to have the smallest share of all? Is it not so, my good friend?

Cal. You are talking about things to eat and drink and physicians and a parcel of stuff; but that's not what I mean.

Soc. Well then, do you call one that is wiser better? say yes or no.

Cal. Yes I do.

Soc. But don't you allow that the better ought to have the larger share ?

Cal. Yes, but not of things to eat and drink.

Soc. I understand. Well, of clothes perhaps, and the most skilful weaver ought to have the largest coat and go about dressed in the most extensive assortment of the finest clothes.

Cal. Clothes indeed ! Nonsense.

Soc. Well in shoes then; plainly the wisest in them and the best ought to have the advantage. The shoemaker I dare say ought to walk about in the biggest shoes and the largest stock of them.

Cal. Shoes ? Stuff. What nonsense you keep talking.

Soc. Well if you don't mean that sort of thing, perhaps it is something of this kind : a farmer for instance of knowledge and skill in the cultivation of land; *he* perhaps ought . to have an advantage in seed, and use the largest allowance of seed upon his own land.

Cal. How fond you are of perpetually repeating the same things, Socrates.

Soc. Yes, and not only that, Callicles, but on the same subjects too[1].

Cal. Yes by heaven, you absolutely never leave off 491 talking about cobblers and fullers and cooks and physicians, just as if our argument had any thing to do with them.

Soc. Well then will you tell me what the things are

---

[1] This repartee was really made by Socrates to the omniscient and all accomplished Hippias, Xen. *Memor.* IV. 4. 6, to whom it is applied with much greater force and propriety than to Callicles here—and I think also, in spite of the a priori improbability of the supposition, expressed by the dry matter-of-fact Xenophon with more point and pungency than by Plato in the text.

With the next sentence compare Xen. *Memor.* I. 2. 37 ; IV. 4. 5 ; Grote, *Hist. of Greece,* Vol. VIII. p. 597, ed. 2.

in which the superior and the wiser man has a right to a larger share? or will you neither tolerate any suggestion of mine nor offer one yourself?

Cal. Why I *have* been telling you ever so long. First of all by 'the superior' I don't mean shoemakers nor cooks, but those who have skill and ability in the administration of the affairs of state, and not only skill but energy and vigour too, able to execute any designs they have conceived and not men to flinch from feebleness of spirit.

c. 46 　　*Soc.* Do you observe, most worthy Callicles, that you don't find the same fault with me that I do with you? For you say that I am constantly repeating the same things and reproach me for it, whereas I charge you on the contrary with never saying the same thing on the same subject; but first you defined the better and superior to be the stronger, and next the wiser, and now here you are again with something different; you tell us that superiority and merit consists in a certain manliness and energy. Nay, my good friend, do tell us and have done with it who you really do mean by the better and superior and in what.

Cal. Why I *have* told you already, men of ability and energy in affairs of state. These are the men that ought to be masters in their cities, and justice means this, that these should have more than the rest, the governors than the governed.

Soc. How's that? Than themselves, my friend[1]?

---

[1] I have followed here, as usual, the text of the Zurich Editors, who with Bekker from one MS. omit the words ἢ τί ἄρχοντας ἢ ἀρχομένους, as an explanatory gloss on αὐτῶν. Heindorf retains them without alteration, and it cannot be denied that they make perfectly good sense in that position. Otherwise they may be made to follow Callicles' πῶς λέγεις; and then Socrates' answer ἕνα ἕκαστον κ.τ.λ. will be a direct reply to them. Stallbaum extracts from Olympiodorus' commentary an entirely different reading, which makes excellent sense, but is not as it seems to me a very Platonic bit of dialogue. The object of the question is, as Olympiodorus notes, to introduce the subject of σωφροσύνη, self-government or self-control. What do you say, asks Socrates, to the case of a man governing himself? must he have a larger share than—

Cal. What do you mean?

Soc. I mean that every man is his own governor. Or is this governing one's self not required, but only governing others?

Cal. What do you mean by governing one's self?

Soc. Nothing that need puzzle you, but just what people in general mean; one that is temperate and has the control over himself, master of all the pleasures and desires in himself.

Cal. What a charming person you are! you mean those simpletons 'the temperate.'

Soc. How should I? every one knows that I don't mean that[1].

Cal. No indeed I should think not, Socrates. For how can a man be happy if he is a slave to any one whatever? But this is what is fair and just according to nature, as I tell you now quite frankly, that[2] a man who would lead a right life is bound to let all his desires grow to their full extent and not to repress them, and to be competent to minister to them when they are as great as they can be by his manly energy and wisdom and to satisfy every desire that he may chance to conceive. But this I dare say is for the many impossible. And this is why they find fault with such characters, out of shame, to disguise their own weakness, and

himself ! It is of course only half in earnest. I should myself have preferred τί δὲ αὐτῶν, ὦ ἑταῖρε; without the interrogation at τί δέ. 'What say you to— themselves, my friend?' There are other conjectures besides those mentioned, which may be found in Stallbaum's note.

[1] Here again there is a difference of reading. The MSS. have πῶς γὰρ οὐ; and οὐ τοῦτο. One of the two negatives must be rejected. The Zurich Editors, after Hermann, have omitted the first. Stallbaum retains this, and alters οὐ τοῦτο into οὕτω in this sense; 'Of course I do, *i. e.* mean those that *you* call simpletons: every one must know that this *is* my meaning.' Then πάνυ γε σφό- δρα in Callicles' reply will signify, yes indeed those *are* what you mean; *i. e.* they really *are* simpletons that you call temperate.

[2] ὅτι δεῖ κ.τ.λ. *may* be the epexegesis of τοῦτο, but I think rather that there is a slight change of construction, and that ὅτι δεῖ is accommodated to the λέγω immediately preceding.

say forsooth that unrestrained indulgence is disgraceful, enslaving as I said before the more highly gifted of mankind; and, unable themselves to procure the gratification of their appetites, they commend self-control and justice by reason of their own want of manhood. For to such men as have had the advantage of being either kings' sons or of having abilities of their own adequate to procure for themselves any kind of power or tyranny or despotic authority[1] what in very truth were baser and worse than self-control? if, when they are at liberty to have the enjoyment of all good things and nothing stands in their way, they were of their own accord to invite to be masters over them the laws and notions and censures of the vulgar herd of men? Or how could they fail to have been made miserable by the 'fairness' as you call it of justice and self-control, if they have no more to bestow upon their own friends than their enemies, and that too when they are rulers in their native cities? Nay, in good truth, Socrates, which you profess to seek after, the case stands thus: luxury and self-indulgence and liberty to do as you please, provided they have power to back them, *these* are virtue and happiness: and all the rest of these fine-sounding phrases, your conventions in violation of nature, are nothing but people's nonsense and utterly contemptible.

c. 47   *Soc.* Upon my word, Callicles, there is really something quite noble in the candour with which you follow out your

---

[1] δυναστεία. Thucyd. III. 62. ἡμῖν μὲν γὰρ ἡ πόλις τότε ἐτύγχανεν οὔτε κατ' ὀλιγαρχίαν ἰσόνομον πολιτεύουσα, οὔτε κατὰ δημοκρατίαν· ὅπερ δέ ἐστι νόμοις μὲν καὶ τῷ σωφρονεστάτῳ ἐναντιώτατον, ἐγγυτάτω δὲ τυράννου, δυναστεία ὀλίγων ἀνδρῶν εἶχε τὰ πράγματα. Arist. Pol. IV. 5 (Bekk.), τέταρτον δ' (ὀλιγαρχίας εἶδος) ὅταν ὑπάρχῃ τό τε νῦν λεχθὲν καὶ ἀρχῇ μὴ ὁ νόμος ἀλλ' οἱ ἄρχοντες. καὶ ἔστιν ἀντίστροφος αὕτη ἐν ταῖς ὀλιγαρχίαις ὥσπερ ἡ τυραννὶς ἐν ταῖς μοναρχίαις......καὶ καλοῦσι δὴ τὴν τοιαύτην ὀλιγαρχίαν δυναστείαν. So that δυναστεία is despotic power shared amongst several rulers: tyranny is confined to one. That the meaning of this word however and of δυνάστης is not confined to this special sense will appear from p. 525 E, compared with 526 B, where δυνάσται is equivalent to οἱ δυνάμενοι, and the Lexicons. I have therefore usually rendered it 'potentates.'

theory: you are indeed stating now distinctly what the rest
of the world thinks no doubt, but doesn't choose to express.
I beg you therefore by no means to relax your efforts, that it
may be made really plain how one ought to live. And now
tell me; you say, do you, that the desires are not to be re-
pressed if a man would be what he ought to be, but that he
is to let them grow to their fullest extent and procure from
some source or other satisfaction for them, and that this is
virtue?

Cal. Yes, that's what I say.

Soc. Then it isn't true as people say that those that
want nothing are happy.

Cal. Why at that rate stones and corpses would be
happy.

Soc. Well to be sure, as you say, our life is indeed a
strange one. For to say the truth I shouldn't be surprised if
Euripides is right when he says,

> Who knoweth if to live is to be dead,
> And to be dead to live?

and we are all really dead—as indeed I once heard from one 493
of our sages, that in our present state we are dead, and the
body is our tomb, and that part of the soul in which the
desires reside is of a nature liable to be over persuaded and
to be swayed continually to and fro. And so some smart
clever fellow, a Sicilian I dare say or Italian, turned this into
a fable or allegory, and, playing with the word, from its sus-
ceptibility to all impressions and capacity for holding belief
gave it the name of a jar, and the foolish he called uninitiated: in these uninitiated, that part of the soul where the
desires lie, the licentious and non-retentive portion of it, he
compared to a jar full of holes, because there was no possibility of filling or satisfying it. So then he you see, Callicles, takes the opposite view to you, showing that of all those
in Hades—meaning you·know the invisible—those who are
uninitiated will be the most miserable, and have to carry
water into their leaky jar in a sieve perforated just like the

other.   And then[1] by the sieve, as my informant told me, he
means the soul: and the soul of the foolish he likened to a
sieve because it is full of holes, as incapable of holding anything by reason of its incredulity and forgetfulness (i. e. its
inaptitude for receiving and retaining knowledge).   Now all
this to be sure is pretty tolerably whimsical; still it repre-
sents clearly what I want to prove to you, if I can manage it
any how, in order to persuade you to change your mind; to
choose, that is, in preference to a life of insatiable self-indulgence one that is orderly and regular and ever content and
satisfied with what it has for the time being.   But now am I
making any impression upon you, and are you coming round
to my opinion that the regular livers are happier than those
who indulge themselves without restraint? or none at all?
and will no amount of such fables incline you a bit the more
to change your mind?

  Cal.   The latter is nearer the truth, Socrates.

c. 48   *Soc.*   Well then, let me give you another comparison
from the same school[2] as the preceding.   See if you allow
something of this sort to be a representation of each of the
two lives, the life of self-control and of self-indulgence, as it
might be if of two men each had several jars, and those of
the one were sound and full, one of wine and another of
honey and a third of milk and a number of others full of
various things, and of these there were streams scanty and
hard to get at and procurable only by many severe toils.
Well, the one when he has filled himself draws no more and
troubles himself no more about the matter, but as far as this
is concerned remains quite at his ease: but the other finds,
like the former, the streams possible though difficult to come
at, and his vessels leaky and decayed, and is forced to be
494 constantly filling them all day and all night on pain of suf-

---

  [1] *ἄρα* may be here either the mere mark of a quotation, or, as I have
translated it, indicate the consequence or connection of one part of the allegory
with the preceding—how the one thing *follows* the other.
  [2] See note B, Appendix.

fering the extremity of misery. If such be the nature of
each of these two lives do you maintain that that of the
self-indulgent man is happier than that of the regular and
orderly? Have I moved you at all by what I have said to
admit that the life of order is better than that of self-indulgence, or have I not?

Cal. You have not, Socrates. For the one who has
filled himself has no more pleasure remaining, but that is
just what I called awhile ago living like a stone after a man
is full[1], no more sensible to pleasure or pain. But the real
pleasure of life consists in this, in the influx of as much as
possible.

Soc. Well but if the amount of the influx be great must
not that of what runs away be great too? and must not the
holes for these discharges be of large size?

Cal. No doubt.

Soc. Then it's a plover's life[2] that you are describing this
time, and not that of a corpse or a stone. And now tell me,
do you mean (by a life of pleasure) something of this kind,
as for instance to be constantly eating when you are hungry?

Cal. Yes I do.

Soc. And to be thirsty, and always drinking when you
are thirsty?

---

[1] πληρώσῃ, the reading of MSS., requires us to understand τοὺς πίθους, or
something similar; but this ellipse is so awkward and seems so unlikely, that
I think the true reading must be πληρωθῇ, a conjecture which Stallbaum has
also hit upon. And so I have translated it.

[2] χαραδριός. The habit of this bird which determines Socrates' selection of
it for his illustration may be found in the Scholiast and in Ruhnken's note on
Timæus, p. 273, but cannot be further discussed here. We gather from the
derivation of its name (χαράδρα) that it haunted the narrow rocky ravines
which formed the beds of mountain-torrents; from Arist. *Av.* 2¼6, that it had
a shrill cry; from the same play, v. 1141, that it was a river-bird; and again
from Aristotle, *Hist. Anim.* VIII. 3. 593, b. 15, that it lived by the water—it is
classed by him with the white cormorant, λαρὸς λευκός, the κέπφος and αἴθυια,
all *sea*-birds—and said to live upon the fish and other waifs and strays that were
thrown on shore. I have used the word plover merely as the customary rendering; the real species is I believe unknown.

Cal. That is what I mean, and to have all the other de-sires, and to be able by the enjoyment one feels in the satis-faction of them to lead a life of happiness.

c. 49·· *Soc.* Bravo, most worthy Callicles; only go on as you have begun, and mind you don't let your modesty balk you. And it seems that *I* mustn't be deterred by any shyness either. So tell me first of all if a man in a constant state of itching and irritation, provided he have abundant oppor-tunity of scratching himself, may pass his life happily in continual scratching¹?

Cal. What a strange creature you are, Socrates; and a thoroughpaced declaimer² (platform orator).

Soc. Just so, Callicles, and that's how I came to startle Polus and Gorgias before and put them out of countenance; but you never will be either startled or disconcerted, you are such a brave fellow. Come now, just answer my question.

Cal. Well then I allow that a man may pass a pleasant life in scratching himself.

Soc. And if a pleasant one a happy one too?

Cal. Yes certainly.

Soc. Is that so if the itching be confined to his head? or what more must I ask you? See, Callicles, what answer you will make if you be asked all that is naturally connected with (logically follows from) this theory of yours one after another. And the climax of all things of this sort, the life of those who addict themselves to the indulgence of unnatural appe-tites, is not that scandalous and shameful and miserable? or will you venture to say that these are happy, provided they are abundantly supplied with what they want?

Cal. Are you not ashamed, Socrates, to introduce such abominations into the conversation?

---

¹ See Bacon, *de Augmentis*, Bk. vii. c. 2, Vol. i. p. 725, Ellis and Spedding's Edition. Compare Phileb. 47 B.

² The sense in which the word δημήγορος 'declaimer or popular orator' is here applied to Socrates, is that from what he had just said it appears that he would have recourse to any kind of vulgar claptrap, any rhetorical or dialectical trick—in short that he was ready to say anything in order to gain his point.

Soc. What? is it *I* that introduce them, my fine fellow, or the man that pronounces so recklessly that all that feel pleasure, whatever that pleasure may be, are happy; and 495 makes no distinction between the good and bad sorts of it? But come now, tell me once more whether you say that pleasure and good are the same thing, or that there is some kind of pleasure which is not good?

Cal. Well then in order to avoid the inconsistency of pronouncing them to be different, I say they are the same.

Soc. You are spoiling all the professions[1] you made at the outset, Callicles, and you can no longer go along with me satisfactorily in the investigation of the truth, if you say what is contrary to your real opinion.

Cal. Why so do you, Socrates.

Soc. Well then I am quite in the wrong if I do, and so are you. But now, my dear fellow, look whether good be not something entirely different to what you say, that is to pleasure from whatever source derived: for not only those that I have just now hinted at, but a number of other shameful consequences manifestly follow, if this is really so.

Cal. Yes in your opinion, Socrates.

Soc. And do you really mean to maintain this, Callicles?

Cal. Yes I do.

Soc. Then are we to suppose you to be serious and so c. 50 enter upon the discussion of the question?

Cal. Oh yes by all means.

Soc. Well then since that is your opinion explain me this distinctly. There is some thing I presume to which you give the name of knowledge?

Cal. To be sure there is.

Soc. And didn't you say just now that there is such a thing as courage also as well as knowledge?

Cal. I did no doubt.

---

[1] Professions of dealing frankly and openly in stating his convictions. *Schol.*

Soc. And you meant, didn't you, to speak of them as two things, because the one is distinct from the other?

Cal. Yes quite.

Soc. Again; pleasure and knowledge, are they the same thing or different?

Cal. Different to be sure, you mighty genius.

Soc. And courage again, is that distinct from pleasure?

Cal. Of course it is.

Soc. Come now, mind we don't forget this, that Callicles of Acharnæ pronounced pleasure and good to be the same thing, and knowledge and courage to be different from one another and from the good.

Cal. And Socrates of Alopece we can't get (ἡμῖν) to admit it. He doesn't, does he?

Soc. He does not; and I think not Callicles either, when he has duly examined himself. For tell me this, don't you think that those that are well off are in the opposite condition to those that are ill off?

Cal. Yes I do.

Soc. If then these two states are opposite to one another, must not the case be the same with them as with health and disease? For to be sure a man is never well and ill at once, nor is he delivered from health and disease at one and the same time.

Cal. How do you mean?

496 . *Soc.* Take for instance any part of the body you please separately and look at it. A man we may suppose has that complaint in his eyes which is called ophthalmia?

Cal. Of course we may.

Soc. Then, it is to be presumed, he can't be sound in those same eyes also at the same time?

Cal. By no manner of means.

Soc. And again, when he gets rid of his ophthalmia, does he at that same time get rid of the health of his eyes too, and so at last get rid of them both together?

Cal. Quite impossible.

Soc. Because such a result would be marvellous and unreasonable, wouldn't it?

Cal. Very much so.

Soc. On the contrary, I should suppose, he acquires and loses either of them alternately.

Cal. I agree.

Soc. And so with strength and weakness in the same way?

Cal. Yes.

Soc. And speed and slowness?

Cal. Certainly.

Soc. And likewise good things and happiness, and their opposites, bad things and misery, does a man acquire each of *them* in turn, and in turn lose it?

Cal. Most assuredly.

Soc. Then if we find any things which a man loses and retains simultaneously, it is plain that these cannot be what is good and what is bad. Do we admit this? Now consider very carefully before you answer.

Cal. Oh, I admit it to the most unlimited (prodigious, supernatural) extent.

Soc. Then let us pass on to our former admissions. Did c. 51 you say that hunger is pleasant or painful? hunger I mean in itself.

Cal. Painful to be sure; though at the same time eating when one is hungry is pleasant.

Soc. I understand: however at all events hunger in itself is painful, is it not?

Cal. I allow it.

Soc. And so with thirst likewise?

Cal. Quite so.

Soc. Must I then ask you any more questions, or do you admit that every kind of want and desire is painful?

Cal. I admit it, dont ask me any more.

Soc. Very good. But drinking when one is thirsty, you admit, don't you, to be pleasant?

Cal. Certainly I do.

Soc. And in this phrase of yours the words 'when one is thirsty' imply pain I presume.

Cal. Yes.

Soc. But 'drinking' is the supplying of a want, and a pleasure?

Cal. Yes.

Soc. So then in the act of drinking you say a man feels pleasure?

Cal. Certainly.

Soc. When he is thirsty?

Cal. To be sure.

Soc. That is with pain?

Cal. Yes.

Soc. Do you perceive then what follows, that you allow that pleasure and pain are felt at once when you say that a man drinks when he is thirsty? Or does this not take place at once at the same time and place, in the soul or the body, whichever you prefer to call it: for I fancy it makes no difference. Is this so, or not?

Cal. It is.

Soc. But moreover you said it was impossible to fare well and ill at the same time.

Cal. And so I do.

497　　*Soc.* But to feel pleasure in feeling pain you have admitted to be possible.

Cal. So it appears.

Soc. Consequently to feel pleasure is not to fare well, nor pain ill, so that it follows that what is pleasant is different from what is good.

Cal. I don't know what all this quibbling of yours means, Socrates.

Soc. Oh yes you do, but you affect ignorance, Callicles. Pray now go on yet a little further[1], in order that you may

---

[1] I have followed the Zurich Editors and Heindorf in omitting the words ὅτι ἔχων ληρεῖς which are not only inconsistent with Socrates' scrupulous and

learn what a clever fellow *you* are that take me to task. Do
not in each one of us the thirst and the pleasure conveyed by
drinking cease simultaneously?

Cal. I don't know what you are talking about.

Gorgias. Don't do that Callicles, but answer him, if it
be only for our sakes, that the argument may be fairly
brought to a conclusion.

Cal. Oh but Socrates is always like this, Gorgias; he
goes on asking over and over again a number of trifling and
unimportant questions and so refutes one.

Gor. Well but what does that matter to you? Any how
the penalty does not fall upon you, Callicles: come, come,
submit yourself to Socrates to refute as he pleases.

Cal. Well then go on with your paltry trumpery questions, since Gorgias wishes it.

Soc. You are a lucky fellow, Callicles, in having got ini- c. 52
tiated into the greater mysteries before the lesser; I thought
that wasn't allowed. So then let us begin at the point where
you left off, and let us know whether each of us doesn't cease
to feel thirst and pleasure simultaneously.

Cal. I allow it.

Soc. And the same with hunger; and in all other cases,
doesn't he cease to feel the desires and the pleasures together?

Cal. It is so.

Soc. So then the pains likewise and the pleasures he
ceases to feel together?

Cal. Yes.

Soc. But the cessation of what is good and bad is not
simultaneous in him, as you admitted before—and won't you
do so now?

Cal. Yes I will; and what then?

---

unfailing politeness, but also interrupt the natural run of the sentence. I take
ὅ τι ἔχων ληρεῖς to be a gloss on σοφίζει. Heindorf would transfer them to Callicles' next reply and read οὐκ οἶδα ὅ τι ἔχων ληρεῖς. Stallbaum's defence and
interpretation of them seem to me unsatisfactory.

Soc. Only that it turns out, my friend, that the good is
not the same as the pleasant nor the bad as the painful; for
the one pair ceases in a man simultaneously and the other
does not, because they *are* distinct[1]. How then can what is
pleasant be the same as what is good or what is painful as
what is bad? Or if you please, consider it again in this way;
for I dare say even yet you don't admit it. However look at
it. In those that you call good, is not that name due to the
presence of goodness, just as it is in the handsome to the
presence of beauty?

Cal. To be sure.

Soc. Well; do you give the name of good men to fools
and cowards? You didn't just now at any rate, but to the
brave and wise. These *are* the sort of people that you call
good, are they not?

Cal. Certainly.

Soc. Well; have you ever seen a silly child pleased?

Cal. Yes I have.

Soc. And have you never seen a silly man pleased before
now?

Cal. I should think so; but what has that to do with it?

Soc. Oh nothing; only answer the question.

Cal. I have.

498   *Soc.* And again, a man of sense under the influence of
pain or pleasure?

Cal. Yes.

Soc. And which of the two are more susceptible of pleasure and pain, wise men or fools?

Cal. I should suppose there isn't much difference.

Soc. Well even that's enough. And have you ever seen
a coward in time of war?

Cal. Of course I have.

Soc. Well then, upon the enemy's retreat, which of the

---

[1] ὡς ἑτέρων ὄντων may be translated either as in the text, as a repetition of
ὅτι οὐ ταὐτὰ γίγνεται, which is Stallbaum's view: or 'which shows that they
are distinct' as Schleiermacher understands it.

two seemed to you to feel more pleasure, the cowards or the brave?

Cal. Both of them, I thought: or if not more, pretty nearly equal.

Soc. That'll do just as well. However, the cowards *do* feel pleasure?

Cal. Oh yes, keenly.

Soc. And the fools, it seems.

Cal. Yes.

Soc. And upon their approach, do the cowards alone feel pain, or the brave as well?

Cal. Both.

Soc. In an equal degree?

Cal. More perhaps the cowards.

Soc. And on their retreat don't they feel more pleasure?

Cal. Very likely.

Soc. So then according to you the fools and the wise men, and the cowards and the brave feel pain and pleasure in pretty nearly the same degree, or the cowards more than the brave?

Cal. That is my opinion.

Soc. But further, are the wise and brave good, and the cowards and fools bad?

Cal. Yes.

Soc. Then the good and the bad are susceptible of pain and pleasure pretty nearly in the same degree?

Cal. True.

Soc. Are then the good and the bad good and bad in pretty nearly the same degree? or the bad even in a higher degree good and bad?

Cal. Upon my word I don't know what you mean.   c. 53

Soc. Don't you know that you affirm that it is by the presence of good things that the good are good, and of evil things (that men) are bad? and that the good things are the pleasures, and the pains evil things?

Cal. Yes I do.

Soc. Accordingly in those that feel pleasure, good, that is pleasure, is present whenever they are pleased?

Cal. Doubtless.

Soc. And so, since good is present in them, those that feel pleasure are good?

Cal. Yes.

Soc. Again, in those that feel pain is not evil present, that is pain?

Cal. It is.

Soc. And it is by the presence of evil you say that the bad are bad. Or are you no longer of the same mind?

Cal. Oh yes, I am.

Soc. It follows then that all that feel pleasure are good, and all that feel pain bad?

Cal. Certainly.

Soc. And are they better the more they feel it, and worse the less, and if in the same degree about the same?

Cal. Yes.

Soc. Well and you admit don't you that the wise and the fools, the cowards and the brave, are about equally accessible to pleasure and pain, or the cowards even more so?

Cal. Yes I do.

Soc. Aid me then in reckoning up the results we obtain from our conclusions. For, to be sure, as the saying is, 499 'twice yea thrice is it good to repeat fair things[1]' and reconsider them. We say that the wise and brave man is good, don't we ?

Cal. Yes.

Soc. And the fool and coward bad ?

Cal. No doubt.

Soc. And again one that feels pleasure good ?

---

[1] A proverb derived, as the Scholiast informs us, from a verse of Empedocles, καὶ δὶς γὰρ ὃ δεῖ καλόν ἐστιν ἐνισπεῖν, a fragment which does not appear in Karsten's collection. The same proverb is referred to *Phileb.* 59 E, and *Legg.* VI. 754 B; XII. 956 E. It seems probable from three of these references that the verse ran, δὶς καὶ τρὶς γὰρ κ. τ. λ.

Cal. Yes.

Soc. And one that feels pain bad ?

Cal. Necessarily.

Soc. And that the good and bad are susceptible of pleasure and·pain in the like degree, or perhaps the bad even more ?

Cal. Yes.

Soc. So then is the bad man made good or bad in the same degree as the good one, or even good in a greater degree ? Does not this follow as well as what we said before from the assertion that pleasure is identical with good ? *Is* not this necessarily the consequence, Callicles ?

Cal. To tell you the truth, Socrates, all this while that c. 54 I have been listening to you and assenting to all you say, I have been thinking, if one makes you any concession even in joke, how delighted you are with it, and hold it tight like a child. Just as if you suppose that I or any one else in the whole world does not believe that some pleasures are better and others worse.

Soc. Ho ho! Callicles, what a sly rogue you are[1]. You do indeed use me like a child, sometimes telling me that things are one way sometimes another, trying to mislead me. Why I thought you were my friend, and never would mislead me intentionally: but now I see I was mistaken, and it seems I must needs, as the old saying has it, make the best of what I can get, and accept anything you are pleased to offer me.— Well then what you say now, it seems, is that there are certain pleasures, some good and some bad. Isn't it ?

---

[1] I have translated *ἰοὺ ἰοὺ* as an exclamation 'mirantis et exultantis' after Heindorf Stallbaum and Suidas. Perhaps however from the tone of what follows, in which Socrates is affecting the manner of a child, to which Callicles had compared him, in a pet, the interjection is rather *σχετλιαστικόν*—another of its senses—and the words should be interpreted, 'Oh for shame, Callicles, what a sly fellow you are, you are indeed treating me like a baby.' Upon the whole however I think the other is to be preferred.

Cal. Yes.

Soc. Are then those that are beneficial good, and the injurious bad?

Cal. Certainly.

Soc. And are those beneficial which effect something that is good, and injurious something that is bad?

Cal. I believe so.

Soc. Are then these the sort you mean? To take for instance the bodily pleasures of eating and drinking that we were speaking of a moment ago, if some of them produce in the body health or strength or any other bodily excellence are those good, and those whose effects are contrary bad?

Cal. No doubt.

Soc. And so with pains in like manner, are some of them good and some bad?

Cal. Of course.

Soc. Accordingly the good pleasures and pains we are to choose and try to bring about?

Cal. To be sure.

Soc. And the bad ones not?

Cal. Evidently.

Soc. Because if you remember, Polus and I decided that all our actions should be done for the sake of what is good. Do you too agree in this view, that good is the end and aim 500 of all our actions and that for the sake of that everything else is to be done, not that for the sake of the rest? Do you vote on our side as well, and make a third?

Cal. Yes I do.

Soc. Then it is for the sake of what is good that everything else including what is pleasant is to be done, not the good for the sake of what is pleasant.

Cal. No doubt.

Soc. Is it then in everybody's power to make the selection amongst things pleasant what are good and what bad, or is professional knowledge required for each case?

Cal. Professional knowledge.

Soc. Then let us recall to mind what I was saying to c. 55
Polus and Gorgias. I said, if you recollect, that there were
contrivances some extending only to pleasure, effecting
merely that and no more, and ignorant of the distinction
between better and worse, and others which distinguish what
is good and bad : and I placed amongst those which deal
with pleasure, the empirical skill, not art, of the cook, and
amongst those which have good for their object the art of
medicine. And now, by the God of friendship, Callicles,
don't be so ill natured as either to jest with me yourself,
or answer at random contrary to your real opinion, or again
to take what I say as if *I* were joking. For you see that
this subject on which we are talking is of a nature to engage
the most serious attention of every man of the smallest
sense, I mean what course of life one ought to follow ;
whether it be that to which you invite me, taking part in
those manly duties you wot of (δή), speaking in the public
assemblies and cultivating rhetoric and engaging in public
business as you do now a days, or this life of philosophical
study; and what it is in which the one differs from the other.
Perhaps then it is the best way to distinguish them first, as
I attempted to do before, and when we have done that and
come to an agreement between ourselves as to whether these
two lives really are distinguishable[1], to consider next what is
the difference between them and which of the two ought to

---

[1] εἰ ἔστι τούτω διττὼ τὼ βίω. Compare Arist. *Vesp.* 58, ἡμῖν γὰρ οὐκ ἔστ'
οὔτε κάρυ' ἐκ φορμίδος δούλω παραρρικτοῦντε τοῖς θεωμένοις. The explanation
of this union of singular verb with dual substantive is that the notion presents
itself first collectively as a single whole or pair to the writer's mind and is
afterwards separated into its parts by the introduction of the dual. Hence it
is that in this construction the verb precedes the substantive, as it *usually* does
likewise in the analogous case of the Schema Pindaricum or Bœoticum (ἐνῆν
δ' ὑφαντal γράμμασιν τοιaῖδ' ὑφal. Eur. *Ion*, 1146, &c. See for examples, Mat-
thiæ, *Gr. Gr.* § 303, Jelf, *Gr. Gr.* § 386). Similar considerations explain the
combination of plural substantive and dual verb. In this case the persons
or things spoken of in the plural are tacitly divided by the writer into two
separate groups or classes so as to form a pair or two pairs. See the examples and authorities quoted by Jelf, *Gr. Gr.* § 388. 1.

be adopted. Perhaps now you don't yet quite understand my meaning.

Cal. No indeed I don't.

Soc. Well I will explain it more clearly.   Now that you and I have agreed that there is such a thing as good and also such a thing as pleasant, and the pleasant different from the good, and that there is a particular mode of pursuit and contrivance for the acquisition of either of them, the one the quest of pleasure, the other of good—but first of all let me know whether you assent to as much as this or not : do you ?

Cal. I do.

c. 56   *Soc.* Well then to proceed, let us come to an understanding about what I was saying to our friends here, and see whether you think that what I then said was true.   What I said was if I remember right, that cookery seems to me to be no art at all but a mere empirical habit ; medicine an

501 art ; meaning that the one, that is medicine, has inquired into the nature of that which it treats and the causes of what it does, and can give an account of each of them ; but the other enters upon the pursuit of the pleasure which is the object of all her care and attention quite unscientifically, without having bestowed any consideration upon either the nature or the cause of pleasure, and proceeds in a manner absolutely irrational, as one may say, without the smallest calculation, a mere knack and routine, simply retaining the recollection of what usually happens, by which you know in fact she provides all her pleasures[1].   Now consider first of all whether you think that this account is so far satisfactory, and that there are in like manner certain other occupations of the same sort which deal with the soul, some of them scientific, exercising some forethought for the soul's best interests ; and others that pay no regard to this, but again as in the former case, study merely the soul's pleasure, how, that

---

[1] Compare Aristotle's account of ἐμπειρία in the first chapter of his *Metaphysics*.   It is possible that his description of it there may be one of his countless obligations to his master.

is, it may be procured for her, neither inquiring which of the
pleasures is better or worse, nor concerning themselves with
any thing else but mere gratification, whether that be better or
worse. For to me Callicles, it seems that there are, and this
sort of thing I call flattery whether it be applied to body or
soul or anything else, when the pleasure alone is studied
without any regard to the better and the worse. And you
now, do you coincide with us in opinion upon this matter or
dissent?

Cal. Not I, I assent—in order that you may get through
your argument, and I oblige my friend Gorgias here.

Soc. And is this true of only one soul, and not of two or
many?

Cal. Not so, it is true of two and of many.

Soc. Then is it possible to gratify them in a mass all at
once without taking any thought for what is best?

Cal. Yes I suppose so.

Soc. Can you tell me then which are the practices that c. 57
do this? Or rather, if you please, as I ask you, when any of
them seems to you to belong to this class say yes, and when
not say no. And first of all let us examine the case of flute
playing. Don't you think it is one of that sort, Callicles? that
it aims only at our gratification and cares for nothing else?

Cal. Yes I do.

Soc. And so with all others of the same kind, for example harp playing, as it is practised in the musical contests?

Cal. Yes.

Soc. And again the Choral exhibitions and dithyrambic
compositions, don't they appear to you to belong to the same
class? Or do you suppose that Cinesias[1] son of Meles ever

---

[1] Cinesias was one of the principal living representatives of the modern or
florid school of dithyrambic composers, who in the opinion of severe judges had
corrupted and debased this species of poetry and its musical accompaniment by
the relaxation of the gravity, sobriety, and antistrophic arrangement of its
earlier form. Melanippides, contemporary with Cinesias, was the earliest of
these innovators. Aristophanes likewise ridicules the wild rambling flights and
affected far-fetched phraseology of the modern dithyrambic in the person of

5C2 troubles himself in the least about the improvement of the audience by anything he says, or merely thinks of saying what will please the mob of spectators?

Cal. There is no doubt about that, Socrates, in Cinesias' case at least.

Soc. And his father Meles again—Did you ever suppose that he looked to what is best in his harp playing? Or rather, *his* aim perhaps was not what is most agreeable either; for he used to annoy the audience by his performance. But just consider; don't you think that all harp music and dithyrambic composition has been invented for the sake of pleasure?

Cal. Yes certainly.

Soc. But what say you now to the object of all the efforts of that stately and wonderful Tragic poetry? Are all her efforts and her pains, think you, bestowed merely upon the gratification of the spectators? or does she strive to the uttermost, if there be anything that is pleasant and agreeable but bad for them, not to say *that*, but if there be aught unpleasant but profitable, *that* to say and to sing whether they like it or not? Which of these two, think you, is the fashion that Tragic poetry assumes?

Cal. There can't be any doubt, Socrates, that she is more bent upon pleasure and the gratification of the spectators.

Soc. Well but this kind of proceeding, Callicles, we said just now is flattery.

Cal. Certainly we did.

Soc. Again, if any kind of poetry be stript of its melody and rhythm and metre, is not the residue plain prose?

Cal. No doubt of it.

Soc. And this prose is addressed to great crowds of people.

Cal. It is.

Cinesias. *Av.* 1373 foll. Compare *Nub.* 332, *Pax.* 817 foll. See on the entire subject, Müller, *Hist. Gr. Lit.* ch. XXX, and on the earlier form of the dithyramb, ch. XIV.

Soc. Consequently poetry is a kind of public speaking.

Cal. So it appears.

Soc. And so it will be a *rhetorical* address to the public. You *do* think, don't you, that the poets in the theatres practise rhetoric?

Cal. Yes I do.

Soc. So then *now* we have found a kind of rhetoric addressed to such a popular audience as consists of a mixture of women and children with men, and slaves as well as free, which we don't altogether approve of, because we say it is of the nature of flattery.

Cal. Quite so.

Soc. Very good. But again, as to the rhetoric that is c. 58 addressed to the Athenian people or to any other popular assemblies of freemen established in the various cities, what are we to say to *that?* Think you that the orators always speak with a view to what is best, with the sole aim of improving the citizens as far as possible by their speeches? Or do they too, bent upon gratifying their fellow-citizens, and sacrificing the public weal to their own private interest, deal with these assemblies as with children, trying only to humour them? and whether they will be better or worse in consequence trouble themselves not at all?

Cal. Your present question is not a simple one like the 503 preceding; for there are some who show a real regard for their fellow-citizens in saying what they say; others there are again such as you describe.

Soc. That's enough. For if this also is two-fold, the one branch of it is, it may be presumed, a trick of flattery and a base kind of popular declamation; the other noble—the attempt, that is, to improve to the utmost the souls of the citizens, and the earnest striving to say what is best, whether that will prove more or less agreeable to the audience. But such rhetoric as this you never yet saw; or if you have any one of this sort to point out amongst the orators, let me know at once who he is.

Cal. No, by my faith, I can't name you any one, at any rate of the orators of the present day.

Soc. Well then, can you name any one of those of bygone days to whom the Athenians are indebted for any improvement, dating from the commencement of his harangues, from the worse condition in which they were previously? For for my own part *I* don't know who it is.

Cal. What? Haven't you heard of the virtues of Themistocles and Cimon and Miltiades and the famous Pericles who is lately dead[1], whom you have heard speak yourself?

Soc. Yes, Callicles, if that *is* true virtue which you spoke of just now, the satisfaction namely of one's own and other people's desires (this may be all very well); but if this is *not* so, but the truth is what we were forced to admit in the argument that followed, that those desires only which improve a man's character by their gratification should be fulfilled, and those which deteriorate it not, and that there is an art by which this may be effected—can you affirm that any one of these men *has* shown himself such an artist as that?

Cal. I really don't know what to say.

c. 59   *Soc.* Nay if you search well you will find out. So then let us just consider this matter quietly and see whether any of these men has shown himself such— To begin; a good man and one who looks to what is best in everything that he says will not speak at random, will he, but always with some definite object in view? He will proceed in fact just like all other workmen, each with his own proper work in view, selecting anything that he happens to apply towards the forwarding of his work not at random, but for the purpose of giving some particular form to the work that he is engaged upon. Look at the painter for instance, if you please, or the builder or the shipwright, and all other trades and professions, any one

---

[1] The scene of the dialogue being laid in the year 405 B.C., the word νεωστί here is either an oversight on Plato's part—perhaps the more probable supposition—or it must be interpreted with great latitude of a period of twenty-four years. Pericles died in 429 B.C.

of them you please, how each of these disposes everything in 504
a fixed order, and forces the one part into conformity and
harmony with the other, until he has constructed a regular
and well ordered whole; and the same may be said you know
of all other artists; and so with those that we were speaking of just now that deal with the body, trainers and physicians, they likewise it would seem introduce order and system
into the body. Do we admit that this is so or not?

Cal. Let it be as you say.

Soc. So then a house in which order and harmony appear
will be a good one, and where there is disorder a bad one?

Cal. I allow that.

Soc. And a vessel again in like manner?

Cal. Yes.

Soc. And further in our own bodies do we admit the
same principle?

Cal. Yes certainly.

Soc. And how about the soul? Is it by disorder that it
will be made good, or by some kind of order and harmony?

Cal. In accordance with our previous conclusions we
must needs admit this too.

Soc. What name then do we give to that which arises
in the body from order and harmony?

Cal. Health and strength I dare say you·mean.

Soc. I do. And what again to that which is engen-
dered in the soul from the same? Try to find the name of
it, and tell it me as in the other case.

Cal. And why don't you name it yourself, Socrates?

Soc. Well if you prefer it I will. And you, if you think
what I say is right, say so; or if not, refute it and don't let
it pass. For my opinion is that order in the body of every
kind bears the name of 'healthy,' whence it is that health
is produced in it and every other bodily excellence. Is it so
or not?

Cal. It is.

Soc. And the name of all the orders and harmonies of

7

the soul is lawfulness and law, by which also men are made observant of law and orderly; and these are justice and self-control. Do you allow this or not?

Cal. Be it so.

c. 60   *Soc.* So then it is to this that that genuine orator, the man of science and virtue, will have regard in applying to men's souls whatsoever words he addresses to them, and will conform all his actions; and if he give any gift he will give it, or if he take aught away he will take it, with his mind always fixed upon this, how to implant justice in the souls of his citizens and eradicate injustice, to engender self-control and extirpate self-indulgence, to engender all other virtue and remove all vice. Do you agree or not?

Cal. I agree.

Soc. To be sure, Callicles, for what can be the advantage of offering to a sick and diseased body a quantity of the nicest things to eat and drink or anything else, when, fairly considered, they will do it no more good sometimes than the contrary, nay less[1]? Is this so?

505   *Cal.* So be it.

Soc. Because I presume it is no advantage to a man to live with his body in a vicious state, since in that case his life also must needs be a vicious[2] one. It is so, isn't it?

Cal. Yes.

---

[1] I have followed Stallbaum in the interpretation of this passage, who agrees with Heindorf in understanding ἢ τοὐναντίον to mean, 'than not giving it any at all,' *i. e.* entire abstinence. Heindorf, after Cornarius, would prefer to read, τοὐναντίον, ἢ κατά, "the contrary, or fairly considered even less than that contrary," but this has no MSS. authority. Schleiermacher renders it; 'was ihm bisweilen um nichts mehr dient, oder im gegentheil recht gesprochen, wohl noch weniger,' apparently understanding ὀνήσει ἔλαττον in the sense of 'doing harm;' but this is very doubtful Greek.

[2] μοχθηρός 'vicious,' that is, here, 'miserable,' belongs to a large family of words which transfer the signification of physical distress to moral depravity or *vice versâ.* Everything which is vicious or depraved is in an unhealthy abnormal condition, diseased and therefore not what it ought to be, or bad. But a life, for example, may be bad or diseased in two different senses, according to the standard which you have in view. Referred to an exclusively moral

Soc. And so again when a man is in health, the physicians for the most part allow him to gratify his appetite, as for instance to eat as much as he pleases when he is hungry or drink when he is thirsty, but a sick man they never so to speak allow to indulge his appetites to the full. Do *you* agree to this too?

Cal. Yes I do.

Soc. And with the soul, my excellent friend, is it not the same? as long as it is in a bad condition, senseless and self-indulgent and unjust and unholy, we must prevent it indulging its appetites, and not suffer it to do anything but what will make it better? Do you assent, or not?

Cal. I assent.

Soc. For so I presume it is better for the soul itself?

Cal. No doubt of it.

Soc. And is not restraining a man from what he desires correcting him?

Cal. Yes.

Soc. Then correction or restraint is better for the soul than *unrestrained* self-indulgence, as you thought just now.

Cal. I don't know what you are talking about, Socrates? do pray put your questions to some one else.

Soc. Here's a man that can't bear to have a service done him, and to submit to that himself which is the very subject of our conversation, to be corrected.

Cal. Well and I *don't* care a straw for anything that *you* say, and I only answered you thus far to oblige Gorgias.

Soc. Very good. Then what shall we do? Are we to break off our argument in the middle?

standard it is an immoral life, but measured by the popular notions of happiness and good it is a life of calamity and wretchedness.

In Greek, the words πονηρός, κακός and κακότης, δειλός, δύστηνος, μέλεος, σχέτλιος, ταλαίπωρος, τλήμων, are all employed, by the poets principally, in this double sense. In Latin we have miser and tristis (te triste lignum, Hor. *Od.* II. 13. 11); in French misérable; in Italian tristo (see Trench, *Proverbs,* p. 37); and in English wretch and wretched, and sad, as a sad fellow, a sad dog.

Cal. You must decide that yourself (*I* don't care).

Soc. Well they say that we have no right to leave off even one of our stories in the middle, in fact not till we have put a head upon it, that it mayn't wander about like a headless monster. So pray finish your answers, that *our* argument may have a head too.

c. 61   *Cal.* What a tyrant you are, Socrates; if you will take my advice, you will let this argument drop, or else carry on the conversation with some one else.

Soc. Who else *will* then? Surely we ought not to leave off the argument before it is finished.

Cal. Can't you go through with it by yourself, either continuously in your own person, or (by way of dialogue) answering your own questions?

Soc. And so as Epicharmus has it, that 'what *two* men said before' I may show myself equal to single-handed. Well it seems it must absolutely be so. Still if we are to do this, my own opinion is that we ought all of us to vie with one another in trying to discover what is true and what is false in this matter that we are discussing, for it is a common benefit to all that it be made plain. Well then I

506 will carry on the discussion of this question as seems to me to be right; but if any of the admissions that I make to myself appear to any one of you to be untrue, it is his duty to lay hold of it and confute me. For to tell you the truth neither do I myself say what I say as having any certain knowledge, I am only engaged with you all in a search; and therefore if any one that disputes my assertions appear to have right on his side, I will be the first to admit it. This however I say on the supposition that you think the argument ought to be finished: but if you don't like that, let us drop it and go home.

Gor. Well *my* opinion is, Socrates, that we ought not to go away yet, but that you should finish your argument: and I believe the rest of the company agree with me. For in fact I am myself desirous of hearing you go through the remainder by yourself.

Soc. Well to be sure, Gorgias, I should have been very glad on my own account to have continued the conversation with Callicles here until I had paid him Amphion's speech in return for his Zethus. But since you, Callicles, refuse to join me in bringing the argument to an end, at any rate check me as you listen whenever you think me wrong. And if you refute me I won't be angry with you as you were with me, on the contrary you shall be recorded in my memory as my greatest benefactor.

Cal. Go on, my good sir, by yourself, and make an end of it.

Soc. Then listen to me whilst I resume the argument c. 62 from the beginning. Are pleasure and good the **same thing**? Not the same, as Callicles and I agreed. Is pleasure to be pursued for the sake of the good, or good for the sake of pleasure? **Pleasure for the sake of the good.** And is that pleasant which brings pleasure by its presence, and that good which by its presence makes us good? Just so. But further, we ourselves, as well as every thing else that is good, have that character by the acquisition of some virtue or other? In *my* opinion, Callicles, that is necessarily so. But to be sure the virtue of every thing, whether it be implement or body, or again soul or any living creature whatsoever, cannot be acquired best by accident; it must be due to that particular order and rightness and art which is assigned severally to each of them. Is that so? That is certainly my opinion. So then the virtue of everything implies order and harmonious arrangement? *I* should say so. In everything then it is by the introduction of some kind of order, that viz. which is proper to each, that this is in every case made good? I think so. Consequently a soul also when it has its own proper order and harmony is better than one which is devoid of order? Necessarily. But further one which is endowed with order is orderly? Of course it is. And the orderly 507 soul is 'temperate'? Beyond all doubt. Consequently the temperate soul is good. *I have nothing to say to the contrary, my dear Callicles:* but if you have, pray inform us.

Cal. Go on, my good sir.

Soc. I proceed then to say, that if the temperate soul is good, that which has the properties contrary to temperance or soundness of mind[1] is bad: and that was one that is devoid of sense and self-control? No doubt. And further the man of sound mind will do what is right towards gods and men? for no man could be sound in mind if he did the contrary? This must needs be so. And again when he does what is right and proper towards men, his actions will be just, and towards the gods pious; but a man who does what is just and pious must needs be a just and pious man? It is so. And to be sure he must be brave too: for certainly temperance or self-control consists not in pursuing or avoiding what one ought not, but in pursuing and avoiding what one ought, whether things or men, or pleasures or pains, and in stedfast endurance at the call of duty. So that we may be fully convinced, Callicles, that the 'temperate' man, as our argument has shown, being just and brave and pious has attained the perfection of goodness, and that the good man does well and fairly all that he does, and that he that *does well* is blessed and happy, and the bad man and evil doer wretched. And this must be the man who is in the opposite condition (of mind) to the temperate, the licentious namely, whom you were applauding.

c. 63   Such then is the view that I take of these matters, and this I assert to be the truth; and if it be true, that every one, as it appears, who desires to be happy must seek after and practise self-control, and flee from licentiousness, every one

---

[1] The virtue σωφροσύνη here appears in a new aspect, that of soundmindedness or sanity, the mens sana in corpore sano (its proper meaning in accordance with the derivation), as opposed to ἀφροσύνη. We have seen it hitherto contrasted with ἀκολασία, the absence of κόλασις, correction or restraint, unrestrained self-indulgence; in which view it is properly rendered by self-control.

of us as fast as his feet will carry him, and contrive if possible to stand in no need of correction ; but if he do require
it, either himself or any of those connected with him, be it
individual or state, then justice must be applied and correction, if he is to have any chance of happiness. Such
seems to me to be the aim which a man should keep in view
through life, and so act as to concentrate all his own efforts
as well as those of the state upon this one object, that justice
and temperance may be essential to the attainment of happiness, not letting his desires grow without restraint, and so
in the attempt to satisfy them, a never-ending torment,
leading the life of a robber. For neither to any man else[1]
can such an one be dear, nor to God ; for he is incapable of
fellowship, but with one in whom there is no fellowship
friendship is impossible. And, Callicles, the heaven and
the earth and gods and men, as the wise tell us, are kept 508
together by fellowship and friendship and orderliness and
temperance and justice, and this is why, my friend, they give
the name of ' order ' to yonder universe and not of disorder
or licence (unrestraint). But you it seems have not paid
attention to this, clever as you are, but have overlooked the
mighty power of geometrical equality[2] in heaven as well as
earth. *You* suppose that a spirit of inequality, the desire of
obtaining more than one's fair share, is what ought to be cultivated ; because you don't care for geometry. Well. Either
then we must refute this argument that it is by the possession of justice and self-control that the happy are happy,
and by that of vice that the wretched are wretched ; or if
this be true, we must consider what are its consequences.
All those former results follow, Callicles, about which you
asked me if I was in earnest, when I said that a man should
accuse himself or his son or friend if he do wrong, and that
this is what rhetoric should be used for. And what you sup-

---

[1]   "Of all men *else* I have avoided thee." *Macbeth.*

[2] That is, proportion : which assigns to every man what is his due in accordance with his deserts, and to every thing its due rank and place in a given system.

posed Polus to concede out of mere shame was true after all,
that to do wrong is worse than to suffer it in the same proportion as it is baser: and that any one who means to be a
rhetorician in any true sense of the word must after all be
a just man, and fully acquainted with the principles of
justice, which again Polus said that Gorgias was forced by
shame to admit.

c. 64   This being the case, let us consider what amount of truth
there really is in all that you taunt me with; that I am unable to help myself or any of my friends or connections, or
to rescue them from the greatest dangers; and that, like the
outlaws who are at every one's mercy, I am in the power of
any one that chooses to slap me in the face, according to your
truly spirited expression, or rob me of my property, or expel
me from the city, or, worst of all, put me to death: and to be
in such a condition is according to your account the very worst
of all infamies.   But my view you know—and though it has
been already repeatedly stated, yet there is no reason why it
should not be repeated once more—(is this): I deny, Callicles,
that to be slapt on the cheek wrongfully is the worst of all
disgrace, or to have my purse cut or my person; but I say
that to strike or wound me or mine wrongfully is more disgraceful and worse: aye and stealing besides and kidnapping
and housebreaking, and in a word any wrong whatsoever
done to me or mine, is worse and more disgraceful to the
doer of the wrong than to me who suffer it.   All this, which
has already been brought before us in an earlier part of our
509 discourse in the way that now I state it, is bound down and
fastened—though the expression may appear somewhat too
strong[1]—with arguments of iron and adamant, as it would

---

[1] ἀγροικότερον is literally 'too rude or coarse, ill-bred or ill-mannered.'
This coarseness and want of good breeding may be shown in the expression,
either by the absence of refinement and delicacy, in which case the word
means, too broad, not sufficiently guarded or reserved, or 'too strong' as I
have rendered it; or by a want of modesty, an undue arrogance or presumption, as Stallbaum understands it—which in fact does not materially differ
from the other.   Schleiermacher has 'derb' 'harsh.'

seem at any rate on the face of it; which you, or some still
more gallant and enterprising spirit than yourself, must answer, or else you will find it impossible to speak aright upon
the subject in any other language than that which I now use.
For I for my part always say the same, that I am ignorant of
the true nature and bearings of these things, and yet of all
that I have ever encountered as now none has ever been able to
maintain any other views without making himself ridiculous.
Well then I assume again that it is as I say. But if it be so,
and injustice is the greatest of all evils to the wrong doer,
and still greater than this greatest, if that be possible, to do
wrong with impunity, what sort of help is that which a man
must be able to render to himself on pain of being really
ridiculous? is it not that which will avert from us the greatest
mischief? Nay surely *this* must needs be the kind of help
which it is most disgraceful[1] not to be able to render to one's
self or one's friends or connections, and second to it the inability to avert the second degree of evil, and the third the
third, and so forth; in proportion to the magnitude of each
kind of evil, so likewise is the glory of being able to find help
against each sort, and the disgrace of failure. Is it so, Callicles, or otherwise?

Cal. Not otherwise.

Soc. Then of the two, doing and suffering wrong, we pro- c. 65
nounce doing wrong to be the greater, and suffering it the
lesser evil. What provision then must a man make for helping himself in order to secure both of these advantages, those
namely which arise from not doing and not suffering wrong?
Is it power or will? What I mean is this. Will a man escape
suffering wrong by merely wishing not to suffer it, or will he
escape it by procuring power to avert it?

---

[1] Plato has here fallen into a not uncommon error in expressing himself—
attraction Stallbaum calls it—by coupling αἰσχίστην with βοήθειαν, so that he
makes Socrates say ‘the most shameful help to be unable to render,’ whereas
it is the inability or failure that is shameful and not the help. This blunder
I have, with some misgivings, corrected in the translation.

Cal. Oh *that's* plain enough, by power.

Soc. But what say you to doing wrong? Is the mere wish to avoid injustice sufficient for a man, because in that case he wont do it? or again to effect this must some kind of power or art be provided, because if he do not learn and practise it he will do wrong? This is a point on which I particularly want your answer, Callicles, so tell me at once whether you think there was any real necessity or not for Polus and me to admit as we did in the foregoing argument that no one desires to do wrong, but all that do wrong do it against their will.

510   *Cal.* Let it be as you please, Socrates, that you may get your argument finished.

Soc. Then for this purpose again, it seems, we must provide ourselves with some kind of power or art, to avoid *doing wrong.*

Cal. Yes by all means.

Soc. Then what may be the art that supplies the means of suffering no wrong at all or as little as possible? See if you agree with me as to what it is. For in my opinion it is this: one must either be a ruler—or indeed a tyrant—in one's state, or else a friend of the existing government.

Cal. I hope you observe, Socrates, how ready I am to praise you when you say anything that deserves it. This seems to me to be extremely well said.

c. 66   *Soc.* Then see if you think this well said too. It seems to me that the strongest bond of friendship between man and man is that which the wise men of old tell us of; 'like to like.' Don't you agree with me?

Cal. Yes I do.

Soc. And so where a savage and illiterate ruler is lord and master, if there were any one in the city far better than he, the tyrant it may be presumed would be afraid of him and never could possibly become his friend with his whole heart?

Cal. It is so.

Soc. Nor again the friend of one who was far inferior to himself, any more than the other; for the tyrant would despise him, and never treat him with the attention due to a friend.

Cal. That is true too.

Soc. So then the only friend worth speaking of that is left for such an one is the man who resembling him in character, blaming and praising the same things, chooses to submit to his authority, and to be *subject* to him as his ruler. He it is that will have power in such a state, him none will wrong with impunity. Is it not so?

Cal. Yes.

Soc. Accordingly if in such a city as this one of the young men were to reflect within himself—how can I acquire great power and no one do me wrong?—he has the same path it seems to follow, to accustom himself from his very earliest years to feel delight and displeasure in the same things as his master, and to make himself as nearly as possible like the other: hasn't he?

Cal. Yes.

Soc. And so he will establish for himself a lasting[1] immunity from suffering wrong, and to use your own language, great power in the city.

Cal. No doubt of it.

Soc. And from doing wrong too? or quite the contrary, if he is to resemble the wicked governor and acquire great influence with him? Nay *I* should think that his efforts will be directed to the exact opposite, to the acquisition that is of the power of doing as much wrong as possible, and escaping the penalty for all the wrong that he does. Wont they?

Cal. It seems so.

Soc. So then the greatest of all evils will befal him, to 511 have his soul depraved and deformed by the imitation of his master and the power that he has acquired.

---

[1] διαπερδἔεται, Matth. *Gr. Gr.* § 498.

Cal. You have the oddest way, Socrates, of twisting arguments every now and then and turning them upside down. Don't you know that this imitator, as you call him, will put to death any one that does *not* imitate him if he pleases, or strip him of all he possesses?

Soc. Indeed I do, my worthy Callicles, if I am not deaf, so often have I heard it from you and Polus of late, and indeed from nearly every body else in the city. But now do you in your turn hear what I have to say, that he may kill me if he pleases, but it will be a villain killing an honest man.

Cal. Well and isn't this the very thing that arouses one's indignation?

Soc. Not in a man of sense, as our argument indicates. You don't think, do you, that the object of all a man's efforts should be to live as long as possible, and to study those arts which preserve us from dangers; like that for instance which you bid me study, the art of rhetoric, which ensures us safety in courts of justice?

Cal. Yes indeed I do, and very good advice it is.

c. 67   *Soc.* Well but, my excellent friend, do you think the art of swimming a very dignified one?

Cal. No faith not I.

Soc. And yet that too saves men from death when any accident happens to them in which the knowledge of the art is required. But if this appears to you of too trivial a character, I'll mention to you another of more importance than this, the art of navigation, which not only saves men's lives, but their bodies too and goods from the extremest perils, just like rhetoric. And yet this is modest and sober, and does not give itself airs, and throw itself into attitudes, as if it were performing some very extraordinary feat: but for a service at least equal to that of the art forensic, for conveying one safe home, it may be from Ægina, it asks a fee I dare say of a couple of obols; or if it be from Egypt or the Pontus, at the utmost in return for this important service, for carrying

safe as I said just now self and children and goods and
women (i. e. female slaves and their mistress), when it has
landed them all in the harbour its fare is a couple of drach-
mas: and the possessor of the art himself after he has done
all this gets out and takes his walk by the shore alongside of
his vessel with a perfectly unassuming demeanour. For he
knows I dare say how to take into account that it is quite
uncertain which of his passengers he has done a service to
by saving them from drowning, and which of them he has
injured, fully aware that he has landed them not a bit better
than they were when they went on board in body or soul. 512
He reflects accordingly that it cannot be that a man who has
escaped drowning whilst he labours under the affliction of
great and incurable *bodily* diseases is miserable in that he
has been preserved from death, and has received no benefit
from him at all—and yet that one who is laden with many
incurable diseases in that which is so much more precious
than the body—in the soul—that *he*, I say, should be allowed
to live on, and that he did *him* service in rescuing him
whether it be from the sea or a lawcourt or anywhere else
you please—No, he knows that it is better for man in a
vicious state *not* to live, for he must needs live ill.

This is why it is not the fashion for the pilot to give him- c. 68
self airs, though he *does* save our lives. No nor the (military)
engineer either, my worthy friend, though he *has* sometimes
the power of saving lives just as much as a general—to say
nothing of a pilot—or any one else. For sometimes he saves
whole cities. Think you he is to be compared with the
lawyer? And yet if he chose to talk and magnify his business as you do, Callicles, he might overwhelm you with his
words, arguing and urging upon you the duty of making
yourselves engineers, for there is nothing else like it : for
he would have plenty to say for himself. Still you none the
less look down upon him and his art, and as a term of reproach would nickname him 'the machine maker,' and you
wouldn't consent to bestow your daughter upon his son,

nor to take his yourself for your own. And yet on the
principles upon which you extol your own pursuits, what
fair excuse have you for despising the engineer and all the
rest that I just now mentioned? I know you would say that
you are a better man and better born. But if 'better' does
not mean what I say it does; if virtue means this and
nothing more, to save one's self and what belongs to one,
whatever one's character may chance to be, your contempt
for the engineer and the physician and all the other arts
which have been invented with the object of saving men's
lives becomes ridiculous. Nay, my dear fellow, see to it,
whether the noble and the good be not something quite
different from saving and being saved.

Consider whether the true man ought not to disregard
this, I mean any particular length of life[1], and to renounce all
love of mere life; ought not rather to leave all this to the will
of heaven, and, believing what the women say that no one
can escape his destiny, consider hereupon how he may best
513 pass his allotted portion of life ; whether it be in assimilating
himself to any form of government under which he may happen to live, and so now accordingly, whether *you* are bound
to make yourself as like as possible to the Athenian people,
if you mean to gain its affections and acquire great power in
the city. Consider whether this is really beneficial to you and
me, that we mayn't meet with the fate of the Thessalian
women who draw down the moon from heaven[2]: upon the

---

[1] I have here, for once, abandoned the Zurich text which is adopted by
Stallbaum, and followed the old reading retained by Heindorf, Buttmann,
and Ast, μὴ γὰρ τοῦτο μὲν, τὸ ζῆν ὁπόσον δὴ χρόνον κ.τ.λ. The negative is
implied in μὴ ἐατέον, as it so often is in interrogative sentences beginning with
οὐκοῦν, and in other cases. It seems to me that in the reading of the Zurich
Editors, which is taken from the Vatican MS., there is no proper and reasonable opposition between τοῦτο μὲν τὸ ζῆν and ὁπόσον δὲ χρόνον, and that the
construction of the whole is intolerably awkward. The validity of Stallbaum's
explanation rests mainly upon his interpretation of δέ by 'immo;' but he would
have found it difficult to produce another example of the particle used with
a similar emphasis.

[2] εἴρηται ἡ παροιμία ἐπὶ τῶν ἑαυτοῖς κακὰ ἐπισπωμένων. Suid.

choice of this power in the state our dearest interests will be staked. But if you suppose that any one in the world can impart to you such an art as will raise you to great power in the state without being like the government either for the better or worse, it seems to me, Callicles, that you are very ill advised : for you must be not a mere imitator but radically like them, if you mean to effect any thing genuine in the way of friendship with Demus the Athenian people, aye faith and with Demus the son of Pyrilampes to boot. Whoever therefore shall produce in you the nearest possible resemblance to them, he it is that will make you a statesman, in the sense in which you desire to be a statesman, and a rhetorician : for with words accommodated to their own character every body is pleased, but such as are adapted to a foreign one they dislike—unless you have any thing to say to the contrary, my darling. Have we (*insinuatingly*) anything to say[1] against all this, Callicles?

Cal. Some how or other, Socrates, there seems to me to be truth in what you say. But I feel as most people do, I don't quite believe you. c. 69

Soc. That's because the love of Demus has planted itself in your soul and resists me, Callicles; but if perhaps we were to examine these same questions often over again and better, you'd be convinced. Remember however that we said that there are two processes which may be adopted in training anything, whether body or soul, one to make its pleasure the object of all our dealings with it; the other what is best for it, not humouring it, but striving against it to the uttermost. This is the distinction that we drew before, is it not?

Cal. Yes, certainly.

Soc. Well then, the one, that which is directed to pleasure, is ignoble and nothing but flattery, is it not?

Cal. Be it so, if you please.

Soc. And of the other the object is to make that which

---

[1] Read λέγομεν with v. l. and Stallbaum. The Zur. Edd. give λέγωμεν.

we have charge of, whether it be body or soul, as good as possible?

Cal. Yes, no doubt.

Soc. Ought not then our object to be in undertaking the care of our city and its citizens to make them as good as possible? For without this, you know, as we found in our preceding argument, there is no use in offering any other 514 kind of service, unless, that is, the thoughts and intentions of those who are to acquire either wealth or authority over others or any other kind of power be honest and virtuous. Are we to assume this?

Cal. Yes, by all means, if you prefer it.

Soc. Supposing then that you and I, Callicles, in the ordinary course of public business[1], were inviting one another to undertake the building department, the most important structures it may be of walls or docks or temples, would it have been our duty to consider and examine ourselves, first of all whether we are acquainted or not with the art of building, and from whom we learnt it? would it, or not?

Cal. Yes no doubt.

Soc. And again, in the second place, whether we have ever erected any building for private use, either for one of our friends or ourselves, and whether this building is handsome or ugly? And if we found upon consideration that we had had good and well-reputed masters, and that many handsome buildings had been erected by us under our masters' direction, and many by ourselves of our own, after we had parted from our masters; under such circumstances men of sense might be permitted to undertake public works; but if we had no master of ourselves to produce, and of buildings either none at all, or ever so many and all worthless, surely

---

[1] The *aorist* participle πράξαντες denotes, as Stallbaum observes, quod quis jam facere instituit. It would be more fully rendered by the addition of the words 'in which we had engaged' or something equivalent; but as this is rather too long for the translation of a single participle, I have endeavoured to express the notion by the words 'ordinary course.'

in this case it would be the height of folly to attempt public works, and invite one another to undertake them. May we pronounce this to be correct, or not?

Cal. Yes, certainly.

Soc. And similarly with the rest; supposing for in- c. 70 stance[1] we had undertaken the office of state-physicians, and were inviting one another to it as thoroughly well qualified for the task, our first step would be, I presume, to examine one another's qualifications, you mine and I yours. Marry now, let us see, how stands the case with Socrates in regard of the health of his own body? or has any one else, slave or free man, ever yet been cured of a disease by means of Socrates? And I again, I dare say, should have made exactly similar inquiries about you. And if we found that we had never been the means of making any one better in his bodily health, citizen or stranger, man or woman, in heaven's name, Callicles, would it not be truly absurd that human beings should ever be brought to such a pitch of folly as to begin with the wine-jar in learning the potter's art, as the saying is, you know, and before they had in their private practice, often failing it may be, and often succeeding, exercised themselves sufficiently in the art, undertake to serve publicly as physicians themselves and invite others like them to do the same? Don't you think it would be folly to act so?

Cal. Yes I do.

Soc. And now, my excellent friend, as you yourself are 515 just beginning to enter into public life, and are urging me to do the same, and reproaching me for not doing it, shall we not examine one another, as thus, Let us see, has Callicles ever yet made any of the citizens better than he was before? Is there any one of them who was before wicked, unjust and licentious and foolish, and by Callicles' means has been made an honest man, stranger or citizen, bond or free? Tell me, Callicles, if any one examines you thus, what will you say?

---

[1] τά τε ἄλλα, καί...

What human creature will you claim to have improved by his intercourse with you? Do you hesitate to answer, if you *have* anything to show which you have done in your private capacity as a preliminary to engaging in public business?

Cal. You are captious, Socrates.

Soc. Nay it is not out of captiousness that I put the question but from a real wish to know what you think your duty as a public man is in our city, whether, that is to say, we shall find you (ἡμῖν) concerning yourself about anything else in your administration but making us citizens as good as possible. We have already several times admitted, haven't we, that this is the statesman's proper business? Have we admitted it or not? Answer me. We have; I will answer for you. If then this is what a good man is bound to effect for his native city, now call to mind those men whom you mentioned just now, Pericles, and Cimon, and Miltiades, and Themistocles, and tell me if you still think that they approved themselves good citizens.

Cal. Yes I do.

Soc. Well then if they were good, it is plain that every one of them made the citizens better than they were before. Did they do so, or not?

Cal. They did.

Soc. Accordingly when Pericles began to speak before the People the Athenians were worse than when he made his last speeches?

Cal. Perhaps.

Soc. Not *perhaps* at all, my very good sir: it follows *necessarily* from our admissions, if at least he was a good statesman.

Cal. Well what then?

Soc. Oh nothing. Only just tell me this as well, whether the Athenians are commonly said to have owed any improvement to Pericles, or just the contrary, to have been corrupted by him. For what *I* hear is this, that Pericles has made the

Athenians lazy and cowardly and talkative and greedy, by establishing first the system of fees.

Cal. You hear all that from those broken-nosed[1] gentry, Socrates.

Soc. Aye but *this* I don't hear merely, but know full well, and so do you, that first of all Pericles was popular with the Athenians, who never passed a sentence upon him involving any disgrace as long as they were 'worse;' but as soon as they had been made by him thoroughly honest and good men, at the end of Pericles' life they found him guilty of peculation, and nearly condemned him to death—plainly because they thought him a rogue.   516

Cal. What then? did *that* make Pericles a bad man?   c. 72

Soc. At all events a herdsman of that sort who had the care of asses or horses or oxen would be thought a bad one, if the animals which he took under his charge free from all propensity to kick or butt or bite turned out under his management given to all these tricks out of mere wildness. You would call, wouldn't you, any keeper of any animal whatsoever a bad one who makes those which he has received under his charge tame and gentle wilder than they were when he took them? Would you do so or not?

Cal. Oh yes, by all means, to oblige you.

Soc. Then oblige me still further by answering this one question whether man too is one of the animal creation or no?

Cal. Of course he is.

Soc. And had not Pericles the charge of man?

Cal. Yes.

Soc. Well then, ought they not, as we agreed just now,

---

[1] I have here taken a liberty with the Greek text by substituting the *nose,* the aim of modern boxers, and the mark of addiction to such exercises, for the *ears* which told the same tale to the Athenian public. The unpatriotic 'Laconisers,' the admirers of Spartan habits institutions and policy, are here indicated. Explanatory references are given in Stallbaum's note.

to have been improved by him in justice if they really were under the care of a good statesman.

Cal. Yes certainly.

Soc. Well and the just are tame and gentle, as Homer said[1]. But what say you? Is it not so?

Cal. Yes.

Soc. But yet he made them wilder and more savage than they were when he took them in hand, and that against himself, the very case in which he would least have desired it.

Cal. Do you want me to agree with you?

Soc. Yes if you think I speak the truth.

Cal. Then let it be as you say.

Soc. And accordingly if wilder, more unjust and worse.

Cal. Be it so.

Soc. So then it follows from what we have said that Pericles was *not* a good statesman.

Cal. So *you* say.

Soc. Faith and so must *you* say too, after the admissions you just made. And now again about Cimon, tell me; did not those whom he tended ostracise him in order that they mightn't hear the sound of his voice for ten years? And didn't they treat Themistocles in the very same way, and punish him with exile to boot? and Miltiades the hero of Marathon they sentenced to be thrown into the pit, and had it not been for the president into it he would have been thrown. And yet these men had they been good in the way that you describe them, would never have been treated thus. At all events good drivers don't keep their seat in the chariot at the commencement of their career, and *then* get thrown out after they have trained their horses and improved themselves in driving. This is not the case either in charioteering or in any other business whatsoever. You don't think so, do you?

Cal. No, not I.

517　　*Soc.* So then what we said before was true, that we know

---

[1] *Odyss. ἱ'. 120.*

no one who has approved himself a good statesman in this city of ours. You admitted this of the men of the present day, but (urged that) some of those of former times (were entitled to be so regarded), and to these men you gave the preference. But these now turn out to be on a par with the men of the present day; and therefore if these were orators, they employed neither the genuine art of rhetoric, else they would not have lost the popular favour, nor the flattering sort of it.

Cal. But surely, Socrates, none of the present generation c. 73 has ever done anything like such deeds as one of those others, any one of them you please.

Soc. My dear sir, neither do I find any fault with them, at least as ministers in the state's service, on the contrary I think they have shown themselves more dexterous ministers than the men of our time, and better able to provide the city with all that she desired. However in changing the direction of the citizens' desires instead of giving way to them, leading them by persuasion or compulsion to that which would improve their character, in all this so to speak these were in no respect superior to the others: and yet this is the only business of a good statesman. But as to providing ships and walls and docks and a variety of other such-like things, I grant you myself that these men were cleverer than the others. So it seems you and I are doing an absurd thing in this argument of ours. For during the whole time that our conversation has lasted we have never ceased coming round constantly to the same point and misunderstanding one another's meaning. I at all events believe that you have admitted ever so many times and decided that this business of dealing with either body or soul is two-fold, and that the one of these is ministerial; whereby meat may be provided for our bodies when they are hungry, and drink when they are thirsty, and when cold clothing, bedding, shoes, or anything else that bodies are led to desire. And I purposely use the same images in my illustration that you may the more easily understand me. For as to being capable of supplying such

things, either as a shopkeeper or merchant, or maker of any
of the things themselves, baker or cook or weaver or shoe-
maker or tanner—it is no wonder, I say, that a man being
such should fancy himself and be considered by others as one
who takes care of the body; by every one, that is, who is not
aware that there is besides all these an art of medicine and
gymnastics which really is a training of the body; which has
in fact a natural claim to authority over all the arts, and a
right to make use of their works, because it knows what is good
and bad in meat and drink for promoting a perfect condition
518 of body, of which all those others are ignorant; and so it is
that all these are servile and ministerial and illiberal in their
treatment of the body, I mean all the rest, and medicine and .
gymnastics have a fair claim to be their mistresses. That I
maintain the very same to be the case with the soul you
seem to me at one time to understand, and admit it as though
you knew what I meant; and then by and by you come and
tell me that men in our city have shown themselves citizens
of sterling worth, and when I ask you who, you seem to me
to put forward men of exactly the same sort in statecraft, as
if when I asked you who are or ever have been good trainers
of the body in gymnastics you told me quite seriously, The-
arion the baker, and Mithæcus the author of the treatise on
Sicilian cookery, and Sarambus the vintner, *these* are they
that have shown marvellous skill in training men's bodies by
supplying the one admirable loaves, the second entrées, and
c. 74 the third wine. Now perhaps you would have been offended
if I had said to you, My friend, you know nothing at all
about gymnastics: you tell me of a parcel of fellows, ministers
and caterers to men's appetites, with no sound and true
knowledge of them whatever, who, very likely, will first stuff
and fatten men's bodies—applauded by them for it all the
while—and *then* make them lose even the flesh they had of
old. *They* in their turn from ignorance will not throw the
blame of their diseases and the loss of their old flesh upon
those who thus indulge them; but whoever happen to be

near them at the time or to offer them any advice, just at the moment when the original stuffing and pampering, carried on as it was without the least regard to what is wholesome, has at length, it may be ever so long after, brought disease upon them, *them* they will accuse and find fault with and do them a mischief if they can, whilst they will applaud those earlier advisers, the real authors of the disaster. And you, Callicles, are now doing something precisely similar: you are applauding men who have indulged those charges of theirs with all the good things that they desired. And people say that they have made the city great: but that it is mere swelling[1] and internal ulceration that has been brought about by these famous statesmen of old, they do *not* perceive. For disregarding temperance and justice they 519 have stuffed the city with harbours and docks and walls and tribute and suchlike nonsense: and so whenever the fit of sickness we spoke of actually comes, they will lay the blame upon their then present advisers, and applaud Themistocles and Cimon and Pericles, the authors of all the mischief: and when besides their subsequent acquisitions they have lost all that they originally had into the bargain, they will probably lay hold of you, if you don't take good care, and my friend Alcibiades, who though not the immediate authors of all the mischief are yet perhaps partly to blame for it. There is however one senseless thing which I see happening now, and hear of the men of the past generation. Whenever, that is, the city takes one of these public men in hand as a wrong-doer, I hear them venting their indignation with loud outcries against such shameful treatment: 'so then after all their long and valuable services to the city the return she makes is injustice and ruin,' according to their story. But all this is entirely false. For there is no single instance in which the ruler of a city could ever be unjustly brought to ruin by the

---

[1] " Where great additions swell 's and virtue none,
  It is a dropsical honour."
          All's Well that ends Well, II. 3. 124.

very city over which he bears rule. For the case appears to
be precisely the same with those that pretend to the name of
-statesmen as with those who profess the sophistical art. The
sophists in fact with all their cleverness in everything else in
this one point are guilty of an egregious absurdity: for
~~claiming to be teachers of virtue they often charge their~~
~~pupils with wronging them by cheating~~ them of their fees
~~and in other respects showing them no gratitude for all~~
~~the service they have done them.~~ Now what can be more
unreasonable than such language? That men after they have
been made good and just, after all their injustice has been
eradicated by their teacher and justice planted in its stead,
should commit injustice by means of that which they have
not. *Does* not this seem to you absurd, my friend? You
have really forced me to make quite a speech, Callicles, by
refusing to answer.

c. 75   *Cal.* So *you* then pretend that you can't speak unless
some one answer you?

Soc. It seems I can. This time at any rate I have gone
on talking a good while, because you wont answer me. Come
now, my good fellow, tell me in the name of the god of
friendship, don't you think it *is* unreasonable for a man to
profess to have made another good, and then, after he has
been made by him and still is good, to find fault with him
for being bad?

Cal. Yes, I do think so.

Soc. Well and you hear, don't you, those that profess to
train men in virtue say such things?

520   *Cal.* Yes I do. But what is to be said [what's the use of
talking] of such a worthless set of fellows?

Soc. And what is to be said of those who, pretending to
control the state and to take care that it be made as good
as possible, turn round upon her when the occasion arises, and
accuse her of being as bad as she can be? Think you there
is any difference between these and the others? ~~The sophist~~
~~and the orator my good fellow are the same thing~~

nearly as possible alike, as I said to Polus. But you for want
of knowledge think the one, rhetoric, a very fine thing, and
the other you despise. Whereas in truth sophistic is a finer
thing than rhetoric, in proportion as legislation is superior
to the administration of justice, and gymnastics to medicine.
In fact for my own part I always thought that public speakers
and sophists were the only class of people who have no right
to find fault with the thing that they have themselves trained
for behaving ill to them; or else they must at the same time
by these very same words charge themselves as well with
having done no good to those that they pretend to benefit.
Is it not so?

Cal. Yes, quite so.

Soc. Aye, and they alone might be expected according
to all probability to have the power of bestowing their services freely without fee or reward, if what they say were
true. For a man when he has received any other benefit, as
for instance if he has been taught to run fast by a trainer,
might perhaps cheat him of his reward, supposing the trainer
gave him his services for nothing, and made no agreement
with him for a fee which was to be paid as nearly as possible
at the very moment of imparting to him the speed in question: for it is not by slowness of foot I conceive that men
do wrong, but by injustice; isn't it?

Cal. Yes.

Soc. And so if any one removes from others this particular vice, that is injustice, he need never be afraid of
being unjustly treated; but this benefit alone can be bestowed for nothing with security—supposing that is, that any
one really has the power of making men good. Is it not so?

Cal. I allow it.

Soc. This then, it appears, is the reason why there is no c. 76
disgrace in taking money for giving advice of any other kind,
as about building or the rest of the arts.

Cal. So it seems.

Soc. But about this particular process of making a man

as good as possible, and enabling him to manage to the best
advantage his own household or a state, it *is* reckoned disgraceful to refuse to give advice without receiving money
for it. Isn't it?

Cal. Yes.

Soc. The reason plainly being this, that this is the only
kind of service that makes the recipient desire to requite the
benefit; and therefore the symptom seems a favourable one
[of something having been really taught], when any one after
having performed this particular service is repaid for it; and
if not, the contrary [an unfavourable one]. Is this as I say?

521   *Cal.* It is.

Soc. Then tell me definitely which of those two modes
of serving the state it is that you invite me to? that of
carrying on a constant struggle with the Athenians, like a
physician, to make them as good as possible, or (of behaving)
as one that would minister to all their humours and deal
with them solely with a view to their gratification? Tell me
the truth, Callicles: for you are bound, as you began by
speaking your mind so freely to me, to go on now and tell
me all that you think. So now pray speak out fairly and
frankly.

Cal. I say then, as one that would minister to them.

Soc. Then, my very ingenuous friend, you invite me to
play the flatterer.

Cal. (*angrily*). You may call yourself a Mysian[1], if you
like it better, Socrates; for if you don't do as I say—

___

[1] The proverb Μυσῶν λεία is plainly *not* alluded to here, except so far as it
shows the low estimation in which the Mysians were held by the Greeks. The
proverb is explained by Aristotle, *Rhet.* I. 12. 20, to mean ' an easy prey,' and
is applied to τοὺς ὑπὸ πολλῶν ἀδικηθέντας καὶ μὴ ἐπεξελθόντας; whence it appears that the Mysians were regarded as pusillanimous and feeble, unable to
protect themselves from injury or resent it when inflicted; and the national
designation of Mysian, like that of Carian, passed into a by-word and a term
of reproach. Socrates had implied in his last observation that if he took
Callicles' advice he should render himself liable to be called a flatterer; to this
Callicles angrily replies; you may call yourself something worse if you please,

Soc. Don't repeat what you have said so often, that I
am at the mercy of any one that chooses to put me to death,
that I may not be obliged to repeat in my turn, that it will
be the case of a rogue putting to death an honest man: nor
that any one can strip me of all that I have, that I may not
be obliged to say in my turn, Well, but after he has done so,
he wont know how to use what he has got, but as he robbed
me wrongfully so in like manner he will employ wrongfully
what he has taken; and if wrongfully then basely; and if
basely then ill (mischievously, to his own detriment).

Cal. It seems to me, Socrates, that you don't believe in c. 77
the possibility of your meeting with any one of these calamities, as though you were dwelling far out of harm's way, and
never could be dragged into a court of justice by some perhaps utterly wretched[1] and contemptible fellow.

Soc. Then I must indeed be a fool, Callicles, if I think
that in this city of ours any one whatsoever is exempt from
the risk of any possible form of calamity. Of this however I
am quite sure, that if I ever am brought before a court of
justice and incur any of those risks you speak of, it will be
some villain that brings me there: for no honest man would
ever prefer a criminal charge against an innocent person. Aye
and it were no marvel if I were condemned to death. Would
you have me tell you why I expect this?

Cal. Yes, by all means.

Soc. I think that I am one of very few, not to say the
only man in all Athens, that attempts the true art of Politics,
and that I am the only man of the present day that performs
his public duties at all. Seeing then that the gratification of
my hearers is never the object of the discussions that I am
in the habit of taking part in, that they aim at what is best,
not what is most agreeable, and because I don't choose to do
those fine clever things that you recommend, I shall have not

a poor-spirited contemptible wretch, unable to protect or avenge yourself, like
a Mysian.

[1] See note 2, p. 98.

a word to say before the tribunal. And the same case may now be applied to me as I was describing to Polus: for I shall be like a physician tried before a jury of children on a charge brought by a cook. Only consider what defence a man like this would make in such a predicament, if the prosecutor were to open his case thus: My dears, here's a man that has done you all (καὶ αὐτοὺς) a vast deal of mischief, and even the very youngest of you he maims for life by 522 cutting and burning, and drives you to your wits' end by starving and choking you, administering the bitterest draughts and forcing you to abstain from eating and drinking; not like me, who used to feast you with every variety of nice things in abundance. What think you that a physician reduced to such a strait would find to say for himself? Or supposing he were to say the truth, All this I did, my boys, for your health—how great think you would be the outcry that such judges would set up? a loud one, wouldn't it?

Cal. I dare say: one would think so.

Soc. Don't you suppose then that he would be utterly at a loss what to say?

Cal. Certainly he would.

c. 78   *Soc.* Such however I well know would be my own fate if I were brought before a court of justice. For I shall have no pleasure to describe that I have provided for them ; which *they* account as benefits and services—whereas I envy neither those that procure them nor those for whom they are procured—and if any one charges me either with corrupting the juniors by perplexing their minds with doubts, or with reviling the seniors with bitter words either in private or in public, I shall not be able to tell them either the truth, 'all this that I say is right, and it is your interest, alone, o my judges, that I am serving in acting thus,' or indeed anything else. And therefore very likely there is no saying what my fate may be.

Cal. Do you think then, Socrates, that a man in such a

condition and unable to help himself cuts a good figure in a city?

Soc. Yes, Callicles, he would if he had that advantage which you have so often admitted; if he had 'helped himself' by never having said or done any wrong either to men or gods. For this we have repeatedly allowed to be the best of all possible kinds of self-help. Now were I to be convicted of incapacity for rendering help of this kind to myself or another, of *such* conviction I should be ashamed whether it took place before many or few or by myself alone; and if my death were due to *this* kind of incapacity I should indeed be vexed. But if it were for want of your 'flattering' rhetoric that I died, I am very sure you would see *me* meet my death with calmness and composure. For death itself no man fears, unless he be an absolute fool or coward; it is doing wrong that a man fears: for to arrive at the world below with the soul laden with many offences is the uttermost of all evils. And now, if you please, I'll tell you a tale to show you that this is really so.

Cal. Well as you have done all the rest, you may as well finish this too.

Soc. 'Listen then,' as they (the story-tellers) say, 'to a c. 79 very pretty story;' which you, I dare say, will take for a fable, 523 but I regard as a true story : for all that I am about to say I wish to be regarded as true.

Zeus Poseidon and Pluto, as Homer[1] tells us, divided amongst themselves the empire which they derived from their father. Now in the days of Cronus there was a law concerning mankind, which still at the present day as ever prevails in heaven, that every man who has lived a just and holy life departs after death to the Islands of the Blest, and there dwells in perfect happiness beyond the reach of ill; but whosoever has led a life of injustice and impiety is consigned to the dungeon of vengeance and punishment, which, you know, they call Tartarus. Of these

---

[1] *Il.* xv. 187 foll.

there were in the days of Cronus, and still are in more
recent times under the empire of Zeus, living judges of
living men, who were appointed to sit in judgment upon
every man on the very day on which he was to die. And so
the cases were (often) decided amiss. So Pluto and the
guardians from the Isles of the Blest came and reported to
Zeus how that men undeserving were constantly coming
to them as well as to the other place. So spake Zeus: Nay,
said he, I will put an end to this. For true it is that now
the cases are ill judged. And this is because they that are
brought to trial are tried with their clothes on, seeing that
they are tried alive. Now many, said he, whose souls are
wicked are clothed with fair bodies and nobility and wealth,
and at the judgment many witnesses appear to testify on
their behalf that their lives have been passed in justice. So
the judges are confounded not only by their evidence, but at
the same time because they themselves sit in judgment
wrapt in clothes, with the veil of eyes and ears and indeed of
the entire body interposed before their own soul. All this
therefore stands in their way, their own wrappings as well as
those of them that stand before their bar. First of all then,
he continued, we must put an end to their foreknowledge of
their own death, for now they have this foreknowledge. This
however Prometheus has already received my orders to put a
stop to. Next they must be stript of all these clothes before
they are brought to trial; for they must be tried after death.
The Judge too must be naked, dead, with very soul scruti-
nising the very soul of each the moment after his death, each
man bereft of the aid of all his friends and relations and with
all that ornamental furniture left behind him upon earth that
the judgment may be just. Knowing all this before yourselves, I have already appointed judges sons of my own,
524 two from Asia, Minos and Rhadamanthus, and one from
Europe, Æacus: These three after their death shall sit in
judgment in the Meadow at the Cross Roads, whence the
two lead, one to the Isles of the Blest, the other to Tartarus.

And the souls from Asia Rhadamanthus shall try, and those
from Europe Æacus : and upon Minos I will confer the privilege of deciding in the last resort (or, reviewing their sentence) in case of doubt on the part of the other two, that the
judgment upon man's final journey may be perfectly just.

This, Callicles, is what I have heard and believe to be true, c. 80
and I reckon that from these tales may be drawn some such
moral as this. Death, as it seems to me, is nothing but the
dissolution, the parting from one another, of two things, the
soul and the body. And accordingly after their separation,
each of them retains its own state and condition pretty
nearly the same as it had when the man was alive, the body
retaining its own nature with the results of its training and
its accidental affections, all quite visible. For instance, if any
one's body was of great size either naturally or by feeding or
both, whilst he was alive, his corpse will be of great size too
after he is dead : and if he was fat, it will be just as fat after
his death ; and so on for the rest. Or if again he adopted
the fashion of wearing his hair long, his dead body in like
manner will have long hair. Again if any one had been flog-
ged and bore traces of the stripes in the shape of scars on his
body, whether these were left by the scourge or by wounds
of any other kind, in life, his body visibly retains the marks
of them when the man is dead. And if the limbs of any one
were broken or distorted in life the very same will be visible
in death. And in a word, whatever characteristics a man's
body presented in life, the same likewise are visible in it
after his death, all or most of them, for a certain time. And
so, Callicles, it seems to me, the very same is the case with
the soul also ; when a man's soul is stript of its bodily covering,
all its natural properties, as well as those accidental ones
which the man's soul contracted from his various habits and
pursuits, are visible in it. So as soon as they are arrived at
the place of judgment, they of Asia before Rhadamanthus,
them Rhadamanthus sets before him, and examines each man's
soul, not knowing whose it is ; nay often when he has laid

hold upon the Great King himself, or any other prince or potentate, he detects at once the utter unsoundness of his soul, deeply marked by the scourge and covered with wounds inflicted by perjury and iniquity, of which its own acts have
525 left the print on each individual soul; full of distortion arising from falsehood and imposture, and all crooked by reason of its having been reared without truth: or from power and pride and insolence and incontinence finds the soul laden with disproportion and ugliness. When he has found such an one he sends it away in disgrace straight to the place of ward, where on its arrival it is doomed to endure all the sufferings that are its due.

c. 81   Every one who undergoes punishment, if that punishment be rightly inflicted by another, ought either to be made better thereby and derive benefit from it, or serve as an example to the rest of mankind, that others seeing the sufferings that he endures may be brought by terror to amendment of life. Now those who derive benefit from the punishment which they receive at the hands of Gods and men are they that have been guilty of remediable offences: yet still the benefit both here and in the world below is conveyed to them through the medium of pain and suffering; for in no other way can the release from iniquity be effected. But all those that have done extreme wrong and by reason of such crimes have become incurable, these are they of whom the examples are made: and these are no longer capable of receiving any benefit themselves, seeing that they are incurable, but others are benefited who behold them for their transgressions enduring the severest most painful and most fearful sufferings in that prison house in the world below, time without end; hung up as signal examples there, a spectacle and a warning to the wicked as they continually arrive. Of whom I say Archelaus too will be one, if what Polus tells us is true, and every other tyrant that resembles him. And I believe that the majority of these examples is derived from tyrants and kings and potentates and ministers of the affairs of states: for they by reason of the licence that they enjoy are usually guilty of the greatest and most impious transgressions. Homer too is a witness to the truth of this; for he has introduced kings and lords, Tantalus and Sisyphus and Tityus, as those who are suffering everlasting punishment in the lower world. But Thersites or any other private person that was wicked no poet has described as incurable and therefore subjected to any heavy punishment; because no doubt he wanted the power, and therefore was so far happier than those that had it. However, Callicles, be that as it may, it is to the class of the powerful that the men who are distinguished for wickedness actually belong. Still there is nothing to prevent good men being found even 526 amongst these, and eminently worthy of admiration are those that prove themselves such: for it is hard, Callicles, and highly praiseworthy for a man to lead a just life when he has full liberty of doing wrong. But small indeed is the number of such: for true it is that here and elsewhere there *have* been, and I don't doubt there will be hereafter, men thoroughly accomplished in this virtue, the virtue of administering justly all that has been confided to their care. And one there has been very celebrated indeed, whose fame is spread all over Greece, Aristides son of Lysimachus. But most powerful men, my good friend, turn out bad.

So as I was saying, whenever such an one appears before c. 82 that Rhadamanthus we spoke of, he knows nothing else about him whatsoever, neither who he is nor whence derived, except that he is a bad man: and as soon as he discovers this he sends him away at once to Tartarus, with a mark set upon him to show whether he is curable or incurable; and upon his arrival there he is submitted to the sufferings appropriate to his case. And sometimes, when he sets his eyes upon another soul that has lived a holy life in the society of truth, a private man's or any other's, especially as I should say, Callicles, that of a philosopher who has attended to his own business, and not meddled in the affairs of (public) life, he is struck with admiration and sends it off to the Isles of the Blest. Precisely the same is the practice of Æacus. And each of these two sits in judgment with a rod in his hand. But Minos sits alone overlooking the proceedings holding a golden sceptre, as Ulysses in Homer says that he saw him,

'Wielding a sceptre of gold, and judging amongst the Departed.'

Now for my part, Callicles, I am convinced by these stories, and I consider how I may appear before my judge with my soul in its healthiest condition. So renouncing the honours which are the aim of the mass of mankind I shall endeavour in the search after truth really to the utmost of my power to lead a life of virtue and so to meet death when it comes. And all other men I invite likewise to the best of my ability, and you especially I invite in return to this course of life and this conflict, which I say is worth all other conflicts here on earth put together; and I retort your reproach, that *you* will be unable to help yourself when that trial and that judgment comes upon you of which I was even now speaking; 527 but when you appear before your judge, the son of Ægina, and he lays hold on you to drag you to his bar, *you* will stand with open mouth and dizzy brain, you there no less than I here, and some one perchance will smite you, yea shamefully slap you in the face, and treat you with every variety of insult.

All this however may perhaps seem to you a mere fable, like an old wife's tale, and you look upon it with contempt. And there would have been no wonder in our despising it, if we could have found by any amount of search anything better and truer. But as it is, you see that you three, three of the wisest of the Greeks of our time, you and Polus and Gorgias, are unable to prove that we should lead any other life than this, which appears to be of advantage to us for the other world as well as this; but amidst the multitude of questions that we have been arguing, whilst all the rest were refuted this doctrine alone stands unshaken, that doing wrong is to be more carefully avoided than suffering it; that before all things a man should study not to *seem* but to *be* good in his private and public life; that if a man become bad in any respect, he is to be corrected; and that this is good in the second degree, next to *being* just to *become* so, and to be corrected by punishment: and that all kinds of 'flattery,' whether of oneself or others, of few or of many, are to be avoided: and that rhetoric, as well as every other kind of action, is to be employed ever for the maintenance of the right, and for that alone (οὕτως).

So take my advice and follow me to that bourn, where c. 83 when you have attained it, you will be happy in life and after death, as our argument promises, and let any one look down upon you as a fool and insult you if he pleases—aye, by heaven, and cheerfully submit to endure from him even that blow of infamy: for it will do you no harm if you be really an honest and true man, practising virtue. And hereafter when we have so practised it together, then and not till then will we set about politics, if it seem right to do so, or consult then about any other plans we think proper, better prepared for deliberation than we are now. For it is a shame for men in the condition in which we now manifestly are to assume airs of consequence, though we are never of the same mind for two moments together upon the same subjects, and those of the deepest moment; such is the undisciplined state of our minds. Let us then take as a guide the views that have even now declared themselves to us, which point out that this course of life is best, in the practice of justice and of every other virtue to live and to die. These then let us follow and invite all others thereto; not those you put faith in and invite me to: for they are nothing worth, Callicles.

'Unhappy,' is another English word which "unites the meanings of wicked and miserable"; as Trench notes in his Select Glossary, p. 220, illustrating the former by quotations from our earlier writers. 'Unlucky' has the same double meaning. And similarly 'poor rogue, poor devil,' are often employed, without intending thereby to impute to the persons so designated any other crimes but those of misfortune or misery.

Another remarkable example of this association or confusion of physical and moral good and evil appears in the modern application of the English villain, and the French vilain, which have transferred to the signification of moral depravity in the former case, and of all that is mean and contemptible including even personal ugliness in the latter, a term which originally marked the low servile condition of the adscripti glebæ under the Feudal system. The moral application of the word 'base' seems to be similarly derived. The exact converse of this is shown in the identification of high social rank and position with moral worth in the names ἀγαθοί, ἄριστοι, ἀριστῆες, in the earlier Greek authors, and καλοί, κἀγαθοί, ἐπιεικεῖς in the later; of optimates, boni, optimi, by the Latins; and Gute Männer, Herrn von Rechte, and similar terms by the old Germans; which are bestowed upon the nobility, the men of rank and wealth, of the highest social and political importance in the state.

See more on this latter subject in Donaldson's New Cratylus, §§ 321—327, and Welcker, Theognis, Introd. p. xxi foll to which Dr Donaldson refers.

The explanation however of this association or transfer which he gives seems hardly correct. The 'virtue' which is ascribed to the higher classes in the early and half-civilized times in which these terms originated is of a different kind to that more comprehensive sort which is afterwards understood under the same name. This is apparently overlooked by Dr Donaldson when he says, Art. 327, "it was because the better classes, having no temptations like their poorer brethren, abstained from those vices which common opinion reprobated, that their regular name became an epithet descriptive of good moral conduct."

This no doubt would help to fix such a designation upon them: but the ἀρετή, or virtus, which was ascribed to them was above all others the martial prowess in which their wealth and consequent superiority in arms and armour over the less favoured classes, and the leisure for the cultivation of military habits and exercises which it allowed, enabled them actually to excel: whilst the same circumstances would admit and encourage the exercise of generosity, liberality, courtesy, affability, and those other shining qualities by which especially in rude and simple times the popular imagination is most captivated.

APPENDIX.

Note A.

CALLICLES' bad memory has here deprived us of the true reading of an interesting fragment of Euripides. The interpretation and restoration of this much vexed passage are alike doubtful. As to the former, Stallbaum construes διαπρέπεις in a neuter sense, indolem animi adeo generosam puerili conspicuus es decore; but I think such a construction is far too awkward to be found in a writer celebrated for the neatness of his style like Euripides; and that we ought certainly to give the verb a transitive sense, 'make conspicuous.' Next, it appears from the general tenor of the passage, and from the adverb αἰσχρῶς, which is attached to διαπρέπεις by Philostratus in a reference to be cited below, that the word has an unfavourable sense, and implies a disgraceful notoriety; αἰσχρῶς διαπρέπεις being, turpiter insignem reddis: whence it may be translated 'disfigure' or 'disgrace.'

Valckenaer actually proposes διαστρέφεις, and Heindorf, who thinks διαπρέπεις corrupt, hesitates whether to accept this inexcusable false quantity or Grotius' vox nihili, διατρέπεις.

As regards the restoration of the verses, we are told by Olympiodorus in his commentary that the word μειρακιώδει is substituted by Plato for γυναικώδει in the original. The more probable reading γυναικομίμῳ is supplied by a quotation in Philostratus' life of Apollonius of Tyana, IV. 21, p. 160, referred to by Grotius, γυναικομίμῳ μορφώματι κατὰ τὸν Εὐριπίδην αἰσχρῶς διαπρέπειν. It would seem from this latter passage that αἰσχρῶς likewise stood in Euripides' text—a word which may be thought almost necessary to qualify the favourable sense which is elsewhere attached to διαπρέπειν. Valckenaer's restoration, which Stallbaum unsuspicious of the violation of metre reproduces without remark in his note, as Heindorf had done before him, is as follows;

Ἀμφίον ἀμελεῖς ὧν ἐπιμελεῖσθαί σε δεῖ·
αἰσχρῶς τε, ψυχῆς ὧδε γενναία φύσις,
γυναικομίμῳ διαπρέπεις μορφώματι.

in which, besides the metrical objection, the phrase ψυχῆς...φύσις
as an apposition to σύ the suppressed nominative to διαπρέπεις,
seems to me quite un-Euripidean. I had thought of the following:

αἰσχρῶς τε τῆς σῆς ὧδε γενναίαν φύσιν
ψυχῆς γυναικῶν διαπρέπεις μορφώματι.

To this reading of course the words of Philostratus are opposed,
supposing them to be a direct and literal quotation. Yet such a
supposition is by no means necessary, for they do not run in verse;
or again the author may have been quoting from memory, in
which case the compound γυναικομίμος, which occurs in all three
tragedians, might very naturally suggest itself as the more poetical
representative of γυναικῶν.

Nauck, *Trag. Græc. Fragm.* p. 329, substitutes ὧν σε φροντίζειν
ἐχρῆν for ὧν ἐπιμελεῖσθαί σε δεῖ, apparently because he thinks it is
more poetical. If that be his reason, he might have remembered
that the language of Euripides is often so familiar as nearly to
approach that of every-day life; and also that the poet employs
the word himself in *Phœn.* 559. Besides this, the apparently intentional opposition between ἀμελεῖν and ἐπιμελεῖσθαι seems to
vindicate the claim of the latter to a place in the text of Euripides.
Of Nauck's reading of the second line, ψυχῆς ἔχων γὰρ ὧδε γενναίαν
φύσιν, I need say nothing τοῖς συνετοῖσιν.

Valckenaer's restoration of the next line runs thus;

οὔτ᾽ ἐν δίκης βουλαῖσιν ὀρθῶς ἂν λόγον
προθεῖο πιθανὸν, οὔτ᾽ ἂν ἀσπίδος ποτὲ
κύτει γ᾽ ὁμιλήσειας, οὔτ᾽ ἄλλων ὑπὲρ
νεανικὸν βούλευμα βουλεύσαιό τι.

The words οὔτ᾽ ἂν ἀσπίδος—ὁμιλήσειας are adapted from another
hint of Olympiodorus.

This likewise is open to the objection that it omits the word
λάβοις, which certainly would not have been chosen here by Plato,
and therefore probably belongs to Euripides. It would be easy
to express the whole of this clause in a verse such as

οὔτ᾽ εἰκὸς οὖν (or ἂν) καὶ πιθανὸν οὐδὲν ἂν λάβοις,

but much more difficult to accommodate the verse when made to
the structure of the entire passage.

The remainder of the verses are I think satisfactorily recon-
structed by Valckenaer. Except that for παῦσαι δ' ἀοιδῶν it seems
to me that the *participle* substituted by Callicles, παῦσαι δ' ἐλέγ-
χων, leads us rather to the reading ἀείδων. Nauck, from Aristoph.
Av. 1382, and another passage, writes μελωδῶν, but I cannot see
how the fact of Aristophanes having once used the phrase παῦσαι
μελωδῶν can have any bearing upon the present passage: all that
can fairly be inferred from it is that Euripides might have so
written in conformity with the laws of the Greek language,
which no one even without this evidence would probably be
disposed to deny.

It has not been observed that the injunction τοιαῦτ' ἄειδε comes
in rather oddly after the very decided recommendation ῥίψον
λύραν, in one of the previous lines, however it may be qualified
by the reference of τοιαῦτα to πολεμίων, 'feats of war, martial
achievements,' exclusively. Perhaps the word is corrupt; and
the mistake *may* have arisen from a confusion with ἀείδων in the
line before.

See Valckenaer's *Diatribe on the Fragments of Euripides*, and
Wagner's and Nauck's *Collections of the Tragic Fragments*.

Note B.

This 'school' is, I have little doubt, the Pythagorean. First,
that the doctrine or fancy that the soul is buried in the body as
in a grave, or place of ward or punishment, was held by the
Orphic mystics, is distinctly shown by the passage of the *Cratylus*,
400 B. Compare *Phæd.* 62 B, where it is referred to as an ἀπόρ-
ρητος λόγος by Cebes, *who had been intimate with Philolaus* in
Thebes his native city. p. 61 D. See also Brandis, *Handb.* I. p. 87
and the reff. Now with the Orphics the Pythagoreans were
closely connected in doctrine and discipline. Herod. II. 81. See
Lobeck, *Aglaoph.* p. 795 foll. Prof. Thompson's note on Butler's
Lectures on the Hist. of Phil. I. 343. On the Orphics, their
traditions, poems, doctrines, and ceremonies, Müller, *Hist. Gk. Lit.*

c. XVI. And this very same opinion on the condition of the
soul in this life was held likewise and expressed in the same
words by the Pythagoreans. Brandis, *Handbuch*, I. 495, notes
h and *i*; and Böckh, *Philolaus*, pp. 178—180 and foll. See especially the extracts from Clemens Alexandrinus, Theodoret and
Athenæus cited by both writers. Brandis refers to the whole of
this passage of the Gorgias as Pythagorean. And Böckh *u. s.*
pp. 186, 7 adds some other considerations, especially the fondness
of the Pythagoreans for etymologizing, tracing verbal resemblances,
or 'playing with words;' of which there are no less than four
examples here in Plato—σῶμα and σῆμα, πιθανὸς and πίθος, ἀνόητος
and ἀμύητος, and ἀειδὴς and Ἄιδης (the last of which occurs likewise, *Phæd.* 50 D and 81 C); all which coupled with the direct
authorities cited by him is to my mind almost conclusive in favour
of ascribing these opinions to that sect together with the Orphics.

Karsten however, *Comm. in Empedoclem*, pp. 301—303, and
Stallbaum in his note on this passage, differ from Böckh and Brandis, and agree in attributing them to Heraclitus and Empedocles.
Heraclitus' claims may be despatched in a very few words. He is
neither a *Sicilian* nor an *Italian*, but an Ephesian: and though he
said no doubt in his symbolical mysterious way that life is death
(or what is equivalent to it), and that our souls are buried in our
bodies, there is no *verbal* correspondence as there is in the other
case. The authorities on which they both rely are Olympiodorus
and the Scholiast, who agree in calling Empedocles a *Pythagorean*,
and are therefore at least half in favour of the other supposition.
Karsten's remaining arguments are almost too trifling to deserve
notice. The first is derived from the words Σικελὸς ἢ Ἰταλικός,
which he says suit no one so well as Empedocles on account of
his Sicilian birthplace. But at all events he was not born *in
both;* and Philolaus and the Pythagoreans were all natives of
Italy, and therefore seem to have at least as good a claim to be
represented by Plato's alternative as the other. Next he says
that the paronomasiæ are rhetoricæ argutiæ Empedocli non
alienæ—but Böckh gives a much better reason, Philolaus' actual
practice, for ascribing them to the latter. The last two are
that Empedocles was Gorgias' master; and that in a passage of
the Sophist, 242 D, Heraclitus and Empedocles are coupled toge-

ther in a similar phrase, Ἰάδες δὲ καὶ Σικελικαὶ Μοῦσαι; both true, but apparently not very much to the purpose.

In illustration of the hidden meaning of the allegory I cannot do better than quote the words of Steinhart in his *Introduction to Hieron.* Müller's translation of this dialogue, p. 378. Denn das dichterische Gewand lässt die grossen Gedanken durchschimmern, dass die Herrschaft der Lust nicht das wahre Leben, sondern der Tod des Geistes sei, dass sie die Seele zur Aufnahme reinerer und höherer Ideen unfähig mache, und zu einem eitlen nichtigen unseligen Leben führe. The same writer goes on to ascribe a serious meaning, and an argumentative intention to both of these fables; a view which is likewise adopted by Susemihl, another recent writer on the Platonic Philosophy. On this Bonitz, *Platonische Studien* (in *Sitzungs berichte der Kais. Akad. der Wissenschaften*, Vol. XXVI. p. 255) justly observes, that the expressions used by Plato on the subject, 493 D, 494 A (and he might have added the introductory phrases, 493 E, οὐ γὰρ θαυμάζοιμ' ἄν κ.τ.λ.) are entirely opposed to the notion that he designed to lay any stress whatever upon them as a proof: vielmehr bezeichnen die angeführten Worte des Sokrates in aller Deutlichkeit, dass Platon in solchen Bildern nicht eine beweisende Kraft anerkennt, sondern nur den bildlich anschaulichen Ausdruck für eine Überzeugung, welche bereits auf anderem Wege sicher gestellt sein muss. The same may be said of the Myths; with the exception that in their case no other kind of confirmation is possible; in them poetical imaginations and popular convictions and traditions take the place of the unattainable truth. Schleiermacher in his note on the passage, p. 489, had already guarded his readers against the error of attributing a serious purpose to these allegories and an intention on the author's part of employing them in establishing his conclusions: he says that Plato is speaking half in derision of such pompous trifling, and means to imply that the argument can make no real progress until it returns to his own simple and natural method.

Note C.

The late Dr Donaldson, in his little book on Classical Scholarship and Classical Learning, Appendix, p. 253, writes thus : "Now it is well known to all really good Scholars that οὐ πάνυ does not mean, as it is so often rendered by those who are imperfectly trained, whether Germans or Englishmen, 'not altogether,' which admits that the thing may be so partially, but 'altogether not,' which contradicts the supposition that it can be so at all," quoting Soph. Œd. Col. 142 οὐ πάνυ μοίρας εὐδαιμονίσαι πρώτης as necessarily meaning "not at all of an enviable condition," though Hermann had rendered it non primæ profecto sortis hominem. οὐ πάνυ therefore is always omnino non, never non omnino.

To the same effect Buttmann, Index to Plato's four Dialogues, p. 223, says, οὐ voces non solum negat, sed in contrarium vertit (cf. φάναι) : sic imprimis οὐ πάνυ non vertendum est 'non omnino' sed *omnino non, prorsus non*, [I presume he means invariably, as he adds no qualification or exception] ut apparet ex locis quales sunt Men. 77 D, Crit. 48 A : sic *igitur* intelligenda sunt etiam Men. 71 C, Alc. I. 128 B. This inference I altogether deny.

To these authorities I have nothing to oppose but reason and facts. First it is unreasonable and improbable to suppose that two words which express by the very order in which they are placed a qualified negative should *invariably* be applied to convey an unqualified negation. The emphatic negation is of course naturally and properly expressed by the words in the reversed order πάνυ οὐ, as in Thucydides, I. 8, ἀλλὰ τὰ μὲν πρὸ Ἕλληνος τοῦ Δευκαλίωνος καὶ πάνυ οὐδὲ εἶναι ἡ ἐπίκλησις αὕτη ; though it is true that by some caprice of language usage *has* attached the same signification to them in the other collocation, and this sense has become perhaps the more common of the two ; all that I argue for is that this is not the only, nor the original, sense of οὐ πάνυ in this their usual order. This stronger sense, when it occurs, may arise out of the other by giving an ironical tone to the words ; 'not quite' may convey by the tone and manner of utterance iden-

tically the same meaning as 'absolutely not,' and so may pass by
usage into that signification when no irony at all is intended ; and
this is probably the actual origin of the unqualified meaning ; at
least I can see no other way of accounting for it.   This view is
further confirmed by the parallel case of οὐχ ἥκιστα, which by the
same μείωσις, softening of the language, expressing a decided
meaning in mild terms, (and this is a sort of irony), has acquired
by usage the sense of μάλιστα.

As to the question of fact, the difficulty in deciding the point
lies in this, that in the great majority of instances *either* sense is
sufficiently applicable, and many of them may be quoted in support
of either interpretation.   Thus in the passage above quoted from
the Œdipus Coloneus it seems to me that it is by the ironical emphasis that the words are made to convey the unqualified negative,
and that they do really mean there 'not altogether ;' which I have
always regarded as at once more poetical[1] and more forcible than

[1] That this is no mere fancy of mine, but is actually warranted by the
facts of the case, will appear from the following considerations.   Bp Thirlwall,
in his famous paper on the Irony of Sophocles, *Phil. Mus.* II. 483, thus defines
verbal irony.   "This most familiar species of irony may be described as a
figure which enables the speaker to convey his meaning with greater force by
means of a contrast between his thought and his expression, or, to speak more
accurately, between the thought which he evidently designs to express, and
that which his words properly signify."

But there is a melancholy as well as a sportive irony; and, "where irony
is not merely jocular, it is not simply serious, but earnest."   It is this kind of
irony which here gives character to the expression; and I need hardly point
out how much more appropriate such a subdued tone of melancholy is to the
old, blind, desolate Œdipus, in whose mouth the words are put, and how much
more in conformity with the spirit which, as Dr Thirlwall shows in detail, pervades and characterises the dramas of Sophocles, that deep feeling of the contrast between the reality and the outward appearance which constitutes the
very essence of Tragic pathos, than the sharp, flippant, querulous, "not at all
of an enviable condition," which is the rendering of Dr Donaldson.   In fact
when we look at the interpretation of the passage of Sophocles from this point
of view, it may I think be safely asserted that here at all events the ironical
or qualified sense of the negative is the only one that good taste will tolerate.

It is singular that this of the Œdipus Coloneus is the only instance of the
use of this phrase that is to be found in the extant plays of Sophocles—this
may be stated with confidence on the authority of Ellendt's elaborate Lexicon
to this author.   In Æschylus it never occurs at all: nor does it appear in the

the naked statement of the fact. Still, examples may be produced which establish incontrovertibly that the words are susceptible of the milder interpretation; some of these I will now proceed to cite. In Xen. Œcon. VII. 1, we have: τί, ὧ 'Ισχόμαχε, οὐ μάλα εἰωθὼς σχολάζειν κάθησαι; ἐπεὶ τάγε πλεῖστα ἢ πράττοντά τι ὁρῶ σε ἢ οὐ πάνυ σχολάζοντα ἐν τῇ ἀγορᾷ. Here plainly the opposition is between being 'actively engaged' and 'not entirely idle:' were οὐ πάνυ to be understood in the sense of omnino non, 'not at all idle, quite busy,' there would be no distinction or opposition at all. In Cyrop. II. 4. 13, αἱ μὲν οἰκήσεις οὐ πάνυ ἐν ἐχυροῖς...ὄρη μέντοι ἐστὶ κ.τ.λ. though the instance is not decisive, the probability is, as the country spoken of is Armenia, and from the ὄρη μέντοι that follows, that the meaning intended is 'not very strong positions,' rather than, 'not at all strong.' The same may be said of VIII. 2. 24, οὐ πάνυ ἐπιμελουμένους. II. 4. 27. ἐὰν μὴ πάνυ πολὺ ἐλάττων ἡ ὁδὸς ᾖ, is a more certain example; as is also Anab. I. 8. 14, ὁ Κῦρος παρελαύνων οὐ πάνυ πρὸς αὐτῷ τῷ στρατεύματι¹, and Hellen. VI. 4. 14, ἦν μέντοι οὐ πάνυ ἐν ἐπιπέδῳ, ἀλλὰ πρὸς ὀρθίῳ μᾶλλόν τι τὸ στρατόπεδον. These examples, with the exception of the first, I have taken from Sturz's Lexicon: his list however is by no means complete.

Lexicons to Homer, Pindar, Herodotus, or Euripides. It seems that it did not become common till Plato's time: and the fact that it *is* more common in him than in any other writer, is as far as it goes an additional argument in favour of the ironical interpretation. In all earlier writers, so far as my memory (and Indices) serve me, it is comparatively rare. In Caravella's very complete Index to Aristophanes I find no instance of οὐ πάνυ. οὐδὲν πάνυ "nothing at all," occurs *Nub.* 733, and οὐδὲ πάνυ "no such thing at all as..." *Ib.* 902. μηδὲ πάνυ in the same sense, *Pac.* 121, and οὐδὲ πάνυ, *Lysistr.* 588. In Thucydides it appears from Bétant's Lexicon that there are only two examples, VIII. 38. 3 and 56. 2, both of them indeterminate. It first becomes tolerably frequent in Xenophon.

I had not seen until this Appendix was written the following explanation in Rost and Palm's Lexicon, Art. πάνυ. οὐ πάνυ, 'nicht sehr, nicht eben,' mit ironischer wendung bisweilen so viel wie 'durchaus nicht.'

¹ Krüger's note on this passage is, non adeo prope ab exercitu suo, s. satis longinquo a suis intervallo. Weisk. He refers also to v. 9. 26 as a similar instance.

In Demosthenes the phrase is seldom found. Adv. Neær. 1347.
14, is the only example given in Reiske's Index. Here, ἡ μὲν γὰρ
οὐσία οὐδὲ τριῶν ταλάντων πάνυ τι ἦν seems plainly to mean, "did
not altogether amount to," though Schäfer thinks differently. In
Olynth. γ΄. 34. 18, μιμοῦνται δ᾽ οὐ πάνυ, on the other hand, I agree
with Schäfer, Appar. Crit. ι. 297, in interpreting it, omnino non,
haudquaquam. Again, οὐ πάνυ δεῖ...ἰσχυρίζεσθαι, Χερρ. p. 90. 18,
may be rendered either 'there is no occasion at all,' or, 'there
is no great need, no particular occasion to...;' the qualified sense
however seems to me to agree rather better with the preceding
context. In the Philippics, Olynthiacs with the one exception
quoted, de Pace, de Symmoriis, de Rhod. Libertate, Pro Megalop.,
de Coronâ, no example occurs. In de F. L. § 189, οὐ πάνυ καλὸν
οὐδ᾽ ἀσφαλές, there is nothing to fix the meaning either way.
In Contra Lept. 480. 1, οὔτε πάνυ ῥᾴδιον, the adverb seems to belong to ῥᾴδιον rather than to the negative. In Contra Aristocr.
§ 104, ἵνα δὲ μὴ πάνυ θαυμάζητε is interpreted by the last Editor
Weber in the milder or qualified sense, as seems reasonable;
though Schäfer, App. Crit., renders it as usual by μηδαμῶς. Weber says, "Quippe hæ dicendi formæ ad eas pertinent quibus ali-
quid lenius exprimitur quam intelligi debet, sed quomodo id intelligi debeat in loquendo sono vocis indicatur;" thus plainly taking
the same view that I have done of the mode in which the
emphatic denial is conveyed. He seems however to go too far, if
he means to reject altogether the sense omnino non, when he adds,
"Quare non in negatione ea vis est, ut cum Buttmanno Gr. p. 135.
n. 2, Passovio Lexic. s. v. οὐ, et Hartungio de Part. ιι. Gr. ιι. p.
87, contendamus, eam quia coalescat cum πάνυ hujus notionem non
solum negare, sed plane in contrarium convertere. Id quam fal-
sum sit, jam inde apparet, quod negatio non ubique cum πάνυ con-
juncta est, ut Xenoph. Cyrop. ι. 6. 21, οὔτε ζημίαις πάνυ τί θέλουσιν
εἴκειν, &c." The last observation however deserves attention:
where πάνυ belongs to the adjective and is to be construed with it,
the transposition of the negative and the interpretation 'not at
all' are alike inadmissible.

On Isæus, de Nicostr. Hered. § 12, περὶ μὲν γὰρ τῶν ἄλλων συμ-
βολαίων οὐ πάνυ χαλεπὸν τοὺς τὰ ψευδῆ μαρτυροῦντας ἐλέγχειν, Schömann writes thus : non tollit negatio vim adverbii, sed adverbium

negationem intendit, quasi dicas, πάνυ οὐ χαλεπόν, h. e. πάνυ ῥᾴδιον, οὐδαμῶς χαλεπόν. There is nothing in this sentence to determine the meaning of the two words except the general scope and intention of this passage; and it is certainly truer, and at least equally probable that Isæus intended to say, that in the case of all other contracts (except wills) false evidence is *not very* difficult to detect, rather than that the detection of it is *not at all* difficult. But as all orators are prone to exaggerate, this must be classed with the doubtful instances.

Schömann refers to οὐ μάλα[1], οὐ πρὸ πολλοῦ, οὐ μετὰ πολύ, οὐχ ὡς δεῖ (to which may be added οὐ προσποιεῖσθαι for προσποιεῖσθαι μή, οὔ φημι, οὐκ οἶμαι, οὐχ ἡγοῦμαι, οὐκ ἐᾶν, οὐ βουλοίμην ἄν, Dem. Phil. β΄. p. 73. 24, οὐ προσίεσθαι, Dem. de F. L. § 365, and other similar phrases) as parallel examples of the transposition of the negative, explaining the signification 'omnino non' by this transposition. This however cannot I think be the true explanation of the usage; for, if it were, it would seem that the phrase ought always to have the same meaning, which is certainly not the case. In Aristotle, Eth. Nic. I. 8. 16 (c. 9 Bekk.), οὐ πάνυ γὰρ εὐδαιμονικὸς ὁ τὴν ἰδέαν παναίσχης ἢ δυσγενὴς ἢ μονώτης καὶ ἄτεκνος, ἔτι δὲ ἴσως ἧττον εἴ τῳ κ.τ.λ., it is quite clear that if the first class of persons mentioned 'are incapable of any happiness at all,' the second class must have less than none, which is absurd, and therefore οὐ πάνυ must here signify non omnino.

In the same treatise VIII. 3 in speaking of φιλία διὰ τὸ χρήσιμον he says that this kind of friendship is generally contracted by men advanced in life; and that it is only men of a selfish disposition who form intimacies from such motives in youth or middle life. He then continues οὐ πάνυ δ᾽ οἱ τοιοῦτοι οὐδὲ συζῶσι μετ᾽ ἀλλήλων· ἐνίοτε γὰρ οὐδ᾽ εἰσὶν ἡδεῖς. Here again it is equally plain that if he had meant to say that such men never live together at all he would not have added ἐνίοτε γάρ. The fact that they are *sometimes* disagreeable is given as a reason for their *not being very fond of* intimate association, for their *not often* entering into it. In the same book, c. 7, ἀλλ᾽ οἱ τοιοῦτοι εὔνοι μέν εἰσιν ἀλλήλοις...

---

[1] ἄρχεσθαι δ᾽ ὑπὸ ἄλλων οὐ μάλα ἐθέλειν ἐλέγετο, Xen. *Anab.* II. 6. 15, and οὐ μάλα ἀφαμαρτάνειν, *Hellen.* VI. 1. 4, are examples of this use of οὐ μάλα.

φίλοι δ' οὐ πάνυ... clearly means that such persons are kindly disposed to one another, but that their friendliness does *not quite* amount to friendship. Towards the end of the same chapter the phrase occurs three times, and in each case denotes the rarity of the union of agreeable and useful qualities in the same person. Aristotle cannot mean to affirm (1) that men in high station can *never* find friends who are at once useful and agreeable, however rare such a combination may be ; nor (2) that easy good manners and conversational powers are *never* united in the same individual with skill and dexterity in the conduct of business ; in the third instance he *may* mean to say that 'such persons are *never* to be found.' Similarly in c. 15 of the same book : οὐ πάνυ δ' οὐδ' ἐν τοῖς δι' ἡδονήν. He had begun by saying that complaints and accusations arise between friends in that form of friendship which is founded on interest, ἡ μόνη ἡ μάλιστα εὐλόγως, the latter alternative therefore implies the possibility of their arising in the two other kinds also. Then after explaining why they are not likely to take place in the friendship which is founded on virtue, he adds the words which I have already quoted. So that not only would it be altogether unreasonable to deny the *possibility* of their occurrence in this third kind of friendship, but that supposition is already excluded by the above-mentioned alternative ἡ μάλιστα εὐλόγως. In other words οὐ πάνυ here necessarily means 'not often, rarely' and not 'never.'

The next example from Categ. c. 8. p. 9. a. 6, is equally decisive. The author is explaining the difference between ἕξις and διάθεσις : φανερὸν δὲ ὅτι ταῦτα βούλονται ἕξεις λέγειν, ἅ ἐστι πολυχρονιώτερα καὶ δυσκινητότερα· τοὺς γὰρ τῶν ἐπιστημῶν μὴ πάνυ κατέχοντας...οὔ φασιν ἕξιν ἔχειν, καίτοι διάκεινταί πως κατὰ τὴν ἐπιστήμην ἡ χεῖρον ἡ βέλτιον. He cannot mean that these have no power of retaining knowledge at all ; because they *have* sufficient to constitute a transient διάθεσις though not a permanent ἕξις.

Waitz in his brief note on Categ. 6. a. 32 says, οὐ πάνυ, non omnino, non proprie ; and cites 5. a. 32 and 500. a. 21 in illustration.

Lucian, Ver. Hist. II. 43, has οὐ πάνυ πόρρωθεν, and again Quomodo Hist. sit conscr. § 5, οὐ πάνυ πολλούς.

Hermogenes περὶ ἰδεῶν, β'. (II. 424, ed. Spengel), οὐ πάνυ τι, μᾶλλον δὲ οὐδ᾽ ὅλως, a passage which, if it stood alone, is quite sufficient to decide the point in question.

Of the multitude of examples which occur in Plato's writings, most are somewhat doubtful and can be interpreted either way without prejudice to the sense. There can however be no doubt about the meaning of the following. Symp. 178 A, πάντων μὲν οὖν ἃ ἔκαστος εἶπεν, οὔτε πάνυ ὁ Ἀριστόδημος ἐμέμνητο οὔτ᾽ αὖ ἐγὼ ἃ ἐκεῖνος ἔλεγε πάντα· ἃ δὲ μάλιστα κ.τ.λ. and by the light of this I should be disposed to interpret ὧν οὐ πάνυ διεμνημόνευεν, which follows at p. 180 C. Also, Lys. 204 D, δεινὰ ὄντα οὐ πάνυ τι δεινά ἐστιν is an unquestionable example of the milder or qualified negation. οὐ πάνυ ἐνεθυμήθην Cratyl. 411 C, I should certainly understand to mean 'I have paid no particular attention to it;' though of course it may signify 'I have never considered it at all.' So οὐ πάνυ τι σοφός, applied to Epimetheus, Protag. 321 B, should in my opinion be rendered 'not being particularly wise,' which with the help of the Platonic irony amounts to much the same thing as the 'absolutely silly person' which Dr Donaldson, op. cit. p. 254, tells us is the only admissible rendering, and much more conformable to Plato's usual style. The same may be said of the rendering of the same phrase in Theæt. 150 C, where Socrates' modesty in disclaiming all pretension to wisdom is quite sufficiently expressed, and more in his own style, by the milder form of abnegation : and I have equally little doubt that οὐ πάνυ εἰμὶ μνήμων, Meno, 71 C, is to be interpreted, "I have not a very good memory," rather than "I am altogether without it, or, I have no memory at all," though Buttmann (see above p. 139) takes the other view. In Rep. IV. 432 D, καί μοι δοκεῖ οὐ πάνυ τι ἐκφευξεῖσθαι ἡμᾶς seems to me to mean 'not very likely to escape us,' rather than 'there is no chance of its escaping us,' 'it is certain not to escape us' for the same reason, viz. that Socrates is not in the habit of expressing himself strongly, or assuming the certainty of any given result.

Philebus, 38 C, ἰδόντι τινὶ πόρρωθεν μὴ πάνυ σαφῶς is more naturally understood in the sense of seeing 'not quite distinctly,' than 'quite indistinctly;' though the latter is certainly admissible. But the constant and scrupulous politeness of Socrates will not allow of any other rendering of οὐ πάνυ ἔτυχες οὗ λέγω, Rep. VII. 523 B, than "you did not quite catch my meaning." Again, οὐ

10

πάνυ ἔγωγε θαρρῶ περὶ τῶν γονέων τοῦ τοιούτου Rep. ιχ. 574 Β, certainly means 'I have no great confidence as to the fate of the parents of such a man,' and in Rep. ιχ. 582 Α, οὐ πάνυ ἔγωγε ἔχω εἰπεῖν seems to express a qualified rather than an unqualified ignorance. These examples might be multiplied almost indefinitely, but I have already cited sufficient for my purpose. In the Gorgias the phrase occurs in five places, in all of which I have rendered it by not quite, not exactly, not altogether, or something equivalent. 448 D, 457 E, 472 C, 502 D, 513 C. In none of them is the meaning *absolutely* certain, but in the second and last of them the general sense is decidedly in favour of the milder form of interpretation.

As I have already said, a very large number of the instances of this formula in Plato are of doubtful interpretation, in which the sense will admit of either rendering indifferently ; but in most of these doubtful cases, as I have shown that we *have* the choice, considerations such as I have already referred to, the Socratic irony, the modest and ill-assured tone which the hero and chief speaker of these dialogues is so fond of affecting, will, at all events when the phrase is put into *his* mouth, usually incline us to reject the decided and peremptory, in favour of the milder and qualified form of denial.

CAMBRIDGE: PRINTED AT THE UNIVERSITY PRESS.

9 783742 864857